WASHINGTON AND HAMILTON

THE ALLIANCE THAT FORGED AMERICA

STEPHEN F. KNOTT AND TONY WILLIAMS

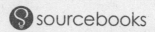

Published by Sourcebooks, Inc.
P.O. Box 4410, Naperville, Illinois 60567-4410
(630) 961-3900
Fax: (630) 961-2168
www.sourcebooks.com

Library of Congress Cataloging-in-Publication Data

Knott, Stephen F.
  Washington and Hamilton : the alliance that forged America / Stephen F. Knott
and Tony Williams.
     pages cm
  Includes bibliographical references and index.
  (hard cover : alk. paper) 1. Washington, George, 1732–1799—Friends and
associates. 2. Hamilton, Alexander, 1757–1804—Friends and associates. 3. United States—Politics and government—1789–1809. 4. United States—Politics and
government—1783–1789. I. Williams, Tony, 1970– II. Title.
  E312.17.K57 2015
  973.4'10922—dc23
                              2015008435

Printed and bound in the United States of America.

WOZ 10 9 8 7 6 5 4 3 2 1

For J. David Gowdy,
patriot and friend

And for Brianna Doherty
"Ask, and it shall be given you: seek, and you shall find..."

CONTENTS

INTRODUCTION

AMERICANS HAVE PERENNIALLY BEEN fascinated with our Founding Fathers. For example, the amicable relationship between Thomas Jefferson and James Madison, or the volatile relationship of Jefferson and John Adams, has captured the American imagination for almost two hundred years. Many excellent books about these partnerships have been written in addition to individual biographies of each and practically every Founding Father himself.

But one of the more important founding collaborations has been overlooked by readers: the unlikely partnership of George Washington and Alexander Hamilton. This extraordinary alliance between a wealthy Virginia planter and a brash immigrant from the Caribbean helped to win the Revolutionary War and establish a "new order for the ages." These men fought together for the better part of twenty-five years to win independence and forge a new nation. Indeed, no other founding collaboration was as important to achieving victory and nationhood as Washington and Hamilton's.

Theirs was an unlikely alliance, for George Washington and Alexander Hamilton could not have been more different. Washington was a gentleman farmer from the patrician colony of Virginia and the owner of a great estate enriched by the labor of African slavery. As a rising member of the Virginia gentry, he satisfied the expectations of his station by entering into public service. Hamilton, on the other hand, was an illegitimate child—the "bastard brat of a Scotch peddler," as John Adams brusquely put it once—and an immigrant from the West Indies. A self-made man, he made his way to America on his own and earned his positions in the army and the government. Despite their differences, Washington and Hamilton shared a lot of common ground. They collaboratively pursued their vision of a continental republic throughout the Revolutionary War and through the founding of the nation. They both embraced the revolutionary ideals of the era, though with Hamilton usually playing a subordinate role to Washington, who was seen as essential to the successful creation of America.

If George Washington was the "indispensable man" of the American founding, then Washington and Hamilton's collaboration was the "indispensable alliance" that determined the outcome of the fight for (and founding of) the United States. This is not to diminish the other important relationships that reveal much about the American founding: John Adams and Thomas Jefferson crafted the Declaration of Independence, suffered a partisan rupture, and wrote a famous exchange of letters discussing the nature of the Revolution. Hamilton and Jefferson feuded heatedly for years over how best to preserve republican principles and offered contrasting visions of American institutions. Fellow Virginians James Madison and Jefferson struggled for liberty in Virginia and then bolstered each other as they fought what they perceived to be dark forces that threatened the republican principles of the new nation.

What makes Washington and Hamilton unique from these other founding collaborations was that their bond was forged in the crucible of the Revolutionary War. Unlike their great contemporaries, Washington and Hamilton saw war up close and personal; they were brothers in arms in a sense, and as any combat veteran will attest, battle is a bonding experience like no other. Their mutual experiences helped them form the core cadre of leadership in the struggle for independence from Great Britain and win the war against overwhelming odds. They drove the nationalist forces that would culminate in a more perfect union formed at the Constitutional Convention and ratified in 1788. They breathed life into the institutions of the early republic while setting important precedents as president and secretary of the treasury. Thus, their joint efforts can be seen as the "indispensable alliance" of the founding. Their story has all the elements of a Shakespearean drama—war, the quest for fame, scandal, the birth of a new nation. Additionally, Washington and Hamilton's story bolsters the somewhat unfashionable notion that the actions of great individuals can influence the course of history.

The months in which they first met remain shrouded in mystery, and little of what they wrote, especially in the early years of their relationship, reveals anything beyond a professional collaboration. How then can we describe their relationship? The word "friendship" does not seem to apply. Indeed, one wonders whether Washington can accurately be described as having any friends. He was purposefully distant and aloof as he jealously guarded his reputation, rarely letting his guard down, even with those who were considered intimates. He constantly warned others about the dangers of familiarity and scrupulously kept his relations formal. Hamilton, for his part, had some very close friends, such as John Laurens, and often gushed with emotions characteristic of eighteenth-century romanticism. But he never expressed himself in that way with Washington.

Washington and Hamilton may not have been best friends for the entire time they knew each other, but they shared a strong and lasting admiration, trust, and even affection for each other that had a significant impact upon the country. Some have described the childless Washington as playing the role of a surrogate father to the illegitimate Hamilton. Richard Brookhiser, in his excellent study of George

Washington and fatherhood, notes the "group of surrogate children was his staff during the Revolutionary War, which he called 'his family.'" This view probably comes closest to the mark, since Hamilton and the other staff members deferred to their "father" with respect and admiration for his virtue, though at times engaging in youthful rebellion. Many interpretations related to Washington's surrogate fatherhood for Hamilton border on the Freudian and offer little insight; for instance, Pulitzer Prize–winning author Ron Chernow argued that Hamilton had "suppressed Oedipal rage" toward Washington. Hamilton may have been driven incessantly by the desire for honor and glory, and this may have impeded his relationship with Washington, but Hamilton (unlike John Adams and others) was not competitive with Washington.

Perhaps it would be best to leave the term describing Washington and Hamilton's collaboration inexact. We might revel in the mystery. In the end, the story of their collaboration is what matters: it is not only interesting and dramatic, it is also essential to understanding how America came to be the great nation it is today. Their characters were animated by different qualities, they often reached conflicting conclusions, and they lent different abilities in the service of the republic. Nevertheless, they were both guided by a sense of American nationalism, working closely together to create an enduring republic that guaranteed liberty to its citizens. Thus, as we explore their special collaboration here, we will use the terms "friendship" and "partnership" interchangeably throughout the book, while recognizing the limitations of both terms in providing a precise understanding of their relationship. In the end, it is clear there was a genuine bond between the pair, and together they defeated the superpower of their day and founded a nation that became the superpower of our time.

"I HEARD BULLETS WHISTLE"
YOUNG GEORGE WASHINGTON

GEORGE WASHINGTON AND ALEXANDER Hamilton could not have had more different childhoods. Washington was born to a moderately successful planter who aspired to join the upper ranks of Virginia gentry. He grew up in a world where planters like his father voraciously acquired land, raised tobacco, and owned slaves. Hamilton, on the other hand, was raised in the Caribbean by his mother and then orphaned. He worked in mercantile houses involved in the international trade in sugar and slaves before America finally offered him an opportunity to find a stage large enough for his talents.

However, Washington and Hamilton shared certain characteristics. Both lost their fathers at an early age and depended upon the patronage of important men to climb the ranks of society. They both received educations in the libraries of their patrons, where they studied the classics. The patrons provided much advice about civility and gave the young men opportunities to make their way in their respective milieus. Although their early lives were bereft of much formal education, they learned more practical subjects such as mathematics, whether for surveying land on the Virginia frontier or running a Caribbean import-export business. Each young man sought to perform heroic military deeds that would bring him lasting glory—by the time they were in their twenties, this dream would be realized, although in different wars. Washington and Hamilton were both men on the make with a burning ambition to rise in prominence militarily and politically. These characteristics would propel them to the forefront of the revolutionary opposition to British tyranny and the creation of the American republic.

George Washington's father, Augustine Washington, was a rising planter in Virginia's hierarchical society. He had the means to send his two sons from his first marriage, Lawrence and Augustine Jr., to school in England, as did many of the Virginia gentry. After Augustine lost his first wife, he quickly married Mary Johnson Ball in 1731. They had a son, George, on February 22, 1732, and christened him in the Anglican Church.

On April 12, 1743, tragedy struck young George Washington when his father died. Due to Virginia's primogeniture laws favoring the eldest son, George inherited a smaller share of his father's property, including Ferry Farm and other properties. With the death of his father, George was dependent on the patronage of important men who saw it as a civic duty to help such a talented youth rise in society. His older brother Lawrence inherited Mount Vernon and helped George with introductions to the wealthy Fairfax family.[1]

George went often to Mount Vernon and Belvoir, the Fairfax family estate, to escape his overbearing mother and enjoy the entertainments of Virginia gentlemen—dancing, fox hunting, card playing, and fencing. Colonel William Fairfax was the master of Belvoir and took a liking to young George, frequently inviting him to Belvoir to instruct him on how to be a gentleman. Washington became a fixture at both family and formal social gatherings, where he learned the arts of manners, deference, and genteel conversation in colonial Virginia. Fairfax also helped to secure George a commission in the British navy, but his mother's intervention halted this early attempt at military glory.

Another source of character formation and civility in the

education of George Washington was copying and memorizing the *Rules of Civility and Decent Behavior,* a book of chivalrous guidelines of proper social manners that governed genteel society. He copied down rules concerning honor such as "Associate yourself with men of good quality if you esteem your reputation." He learned lessons that he would later instill in young soldiers under his command, including "Let your recreations be manful not sinful" and "Labor to keep alive in your breast that little spark of celestial fire called conscience." Following these rules would promote the practice of personal virtue for all and create a cohesive civil society.

In 1747, Lord Fairfax, cousin of the colonel, arrived in the colonies and opened up new opportunities for George. Lord Fairfax was impressed by his horsemanship and surveying skills, and he hired the young man to survey some of his vast tracts of land in the Shenandoah Valley. Over the next few years, George earned a respectable income with his surveying trips and acquired his own land by staking out claims himself. His surveying journeys took him far afield, including deep into the Ohio Valley, as far as what would later become Pittsburgh, Pennsylvania. His long-term goal was to amass enough land to become a wealthy planter with a large plantation rather than working for an income. At last, he was a rising gentleman with strong personal connections to the gentry through his brother, Lawrence, and the Fairfaxes.[2]

Lawrence was also rising through the social ranks but suffered from tuberculosis. In 1750 and the following year, he tried the cures at warm springs in the western part of Virginia, accompanied by his brother. In September 1751, the pair of brothers traveled to Barbados in the hope that the tropical air would bring Lawrence relief. George himself became deathly ill when he suffered smallpox but recovered and developed immunity. When he recovered, George sailed for home while Lawrence desperately tried to find a cure in Bermuda. In July 1752, Lawrence finally succumbed to the disease at home.[3]

Soon after Lawrence's death, George inherited Mount Vernon, which improved his social standing as a planter. He also angled to secure his brother's position in the Virginia militia. He called upon his relationships with the important gentlemen of the colony to lobby for the adjutancy of the Northern Neck. His hard work paid off. At twenty-one, without any military experience, George Washington became the adjutant general of the southern district, which carried a salary of £100. The following year, he secured the position for the Northern Neck. Finally, the fraternal Fredericksburg Masonic Lodge accepted Washington as a member, showing his rising social prominence and marking the beginning of his lifelong membership in this organization.[4]

But Washington was not just interested in becoming a landed gentleman who presided over an estate worked by slaves. He was a man of action who thirsted for military glory and lasting fame. Why the obsession with fame? For someone like Washington, it was priceless because it could be earned through merit rather than merely inherited. While an unbridled passion for fame could lead one to corruption and selfish ambition, a virtuous love of fame derived from courage in battle could lead to immortality in the annals of history.[5] This is what Washington longed for.

He did not have to wait long for a chance to win military glory, since the French were expanding into the contested Ohio Valley, where the British and the colonists, including the Ohio Company, had land claims.[6] In the spring of 1753, Virginia lieutenant governor Robert Dinwiddie learned of French incursions into the Ohio Valley and wrote alarming letters to the Earl of Halifax, president of the Board of Trade. Dinwiddie's warnings made it all the way to King George II and his cabinet by mid-August, and they immediately ordered the Virginia lieutenant governor to respond.[7]

The crown instructed Dinwiddie to warn off and, if necessary, to expel the French from the Ohio Valley. They emphasized, however, that the English should not be the aggressors and initiate hostilities.[8]

The colonists should build their own forts in English territory and only oust the French if they refused to leave.

When Washington heard rumors of the possible expedition, he traveled to Williamsburg and volunteered to deliver the message to the French. With pressure applied from Washington's political friends, Dinwiddie accepted. Dinwiddie dispatched the twenty-one-year-old surveyor to the area around Pittsburgh, where the French were building a fort at the Forks of the Ohio River. The young emissary was to deliver Dinwiddie's message warning them off, wait for an answer, and return. While waiting, he was to assess the French army and inspect the strength of their fortifications. Dinwiddie expressed his "especial trust and confidence in the ability, conduct, and fidelity" of the young man, who had won the powerful patronage of the royal governor.[9]

Armed with the letters to the French and a letter for safe passage, Washington and his growing party reached the Forks of the Ohio on November 22, where he assessed the area. In his journal, Washington wrote that it was "extremely well situated for a fort; as it has the absolute command of both rivers."[10] The following day, he traveled another seventy miles to meet the French at their settlement in Venango.[11] On December 4, at Venango, the half-Seneca French officer, Captain Philippe-Thomas de Joncaire, politely greeted the members of Washington's expedition. Washington explained his mission to Joncaire, who patiently listened but stated he had no authority to accept such a letter from Dinwiddie. He advised Washington to continue on to Fort Le Boeuf where there was an officer of sufficient authority to receive Washington and his message.

With that, Washington tramped farther north through the countryside, guided by a couple of French troops. On December 11, the party reached Fort Le Boeuf after sundown and was officially received the following morning. The French commandant scanned Dinwiddie's letter with displeasure. Dinwiddie was instructed by King George II to "require your [the French] peaceful departure."[12] On the evening of

December 14, the French commandant Jacques Legardeur finally gave Washington an answer. In short, Legardeur claimed that the "country belonged to [the French]; that no Englishman had a right to trade upon those waters; and that he had orders to make every person prisoner who attempted it on the Ohio, or the waters of it."[13] The same reply was made to the royal governor: "As to the summons you send me to retire, I do not think myself obliged to obey it. Whatever may be your instructions, I am here by virtue of the orders of my general."[14] Legardeur promised to forward the communication to Marquis Duquesne, the governor general of New France.

Washington and his party set off for home, and on January 16, 1754, he arrived in the capital and immediately sought an audience with Lieutenant Governor Dinwiddie, delivering Legardeur's hostile response. The young man also offered his journal of the trip to the governor, which he hoped would "be sufficient to satisfy your honor with my proceedings; for that was my aim in undertaking the journey…throughout the prosecution of it."[15] Dinwiddie asked Washington to prepare it hurriedly for publication, and it soon appeared in print throughout the English-speaking world, bringing the kind of recognition he was seeking. The governor also demonstrated his trust in Washington by authorizing the adjutant general to enlist one hundred militiamen to march to the Forks to defend the newly constructed fortifications against the French.

In Washington's absence, the governor had sparred with the Virginia General Assembly over funds to mobilize for war. Dinwiddie called the body into session on February 14 and delivered the French response as well as Washington's journal to persuade the assembly to appropriate money. The Burgesses hotly debated the governor's proposals, and several members thought he was simply pursuing the private interests of the Ohio Company rather than the good of the colony. They finally voted a hefty £10,000 to protect the frontier but stipulated that a committee would decide how the money would be spent.[16] Before disbanding, the Burgesses had voted Washington £50, which he thought an insulting pittance for his services.

With rumors swirling that the French and their Indian allies were on the march, Dinwiddie ordered Washington to "march what soldiers you have immediately to the Ohio."[17] On April 2, the newly commissioned lieutenant colonel Washington departed and a week later met up with Captain Adam Stephen and his recruits at Winchester. The frontiersman Christopher Gist met the force there and alarmed Washington with word that the French were expected shortly at the Forks, where a small group of men pleaded for reinforcements. Washington was too far away to reach them in time. On April 17, the new French commandant, Captain Contrecoeur, and his men paddled up to the Forks in canoes with upward of one thousand men and eighteen cannon and seized the strategically important point. The French immediately tore down the colonial stockade and began construction of Fort Duquesne.

Throughout early May, Washington proceeded toward the fort. The column chopped their way through the wilderness, and Washington's exasperation boiled over as he wrote Dinwiddie, lamenting about the difficulties of the expedition: "I find so many clogs upon the expedition, that I quite despair of success."[18] The governor, perhaps regretting making the green young colonist the leader of such an important mission, soon wrote back, shrugging off the complaints and expressing his disappointment that the officer he trusted was engaging in "complaints in general so ill-founded."[19]

Despite his complaints, Washington continued to perform his duty. He happily received Tanacharison, "Half-King," sachem of the Six Nations, with some warriors and reached Great Meadows, which his men started to clear and "prepared a charming field for an encounter," even though it was in a bowl surrounded by wooded high grounds.[20] While the soldiers were digging trenches and hastily erecting a stockade, Washington learned from Half-King and Gist that the French were advancing on them. The young officer presumed that the enemy had hostile intentions and sent out scouting parties to find them. Contrecoeur had indeed sent out a diplomatic mission of a few dozen men under Ensign Jumonville to find the English column and warn their leader off French territory, much like the young Virginian had unsuccessfully attempted the previous winter. Washington led four dozen men to Half-King's camp, rounded up the Indian leader and his warriors, and went to find the French. Since he considered them spies or worse, Washington and his allies stealthily crept up on their enemy with muskets drawn.

The French were startled by the sudden appearance of the English and Indians armed to the teeth. They reached for their own arms, and although the French may or may not have been able to squeeze off a round first, the English loosed a lethal volley in their direction at point-blank range. There was another exchange of gunfire, and as many as thirteen or fourteen French lay wounded or dead while Washington's force suffered only a few casualties. At some point, the Indians apparently went on a rampage and massacred the wounded, including Jumonville. Shocked, Washington did nothing (and probably could have done little) to prevent the Indians from scalping the French. After the grisly deed was done, he stopped any further bloodshed.[21]

Washington realized the gravity of the massacre and immediately sought justification for his actions to preserve his honor and reputation. He sincerely believed that the French were spies and deserved what they got—which was not an unreasonable assumption. He described the event in several letters to the governor to exonerate himself from any perceived wrongdoing. The French claim that they were ambassadors, Washington wrote, "is a mere pretense, they never designed to have come to us but in a hostile manner."[22] Instead of being treated as diplomats, they ought "to be hanged for spies of the worst sort."[23]

Washington was eager to prove his worthiness to Dinwiddie: "If the whole detachment of the French behave with no more resolution than this chosen party did, I flatter myself we shall have no great trouble in driving them to the d[amned] Montreal."[24] He told the governor that he was guided by unselfish, patriotic intentions: "The motives that led me here were pure and noble. I had no view of acquisition, but that of honor, by serving faithfully my King and Country."[25]

Washington was more candid about his youthful exuberance and romantic view of the battle when he wrote to his brother Jack: "I fortunately escaped without a wound, though the right wing where I stood was exposed to and received all the enemy's fire and was the part where the man was killed and the rest wounded." Despite the horrors of witnessing men with agonizing wounds being scalped, he boasted that "I can with truth assure you, I heard bullets whistle and believe me there was something charming in the sound."[26] When the letter was published in London, King George II retorted that "he would not say so if he had been used to hear many."[27] Washington's words may have been those of an overeager young man, but he was gaining invaluable experience and knowledge about war and empire.

In late May and early June, Washington ordered his army to dig trenches and reinforce the palisades in case the French attacked in retaliation. Indeed, it did not take long for the survivor of the skirmish to make his way back to Fort Duquesne and inform Contrecoeur of the death of Jumonville and a dozen others. Washington dubbed his defenses "Fort Necessity," acknowledging their relative weakness. Half-King disdainfully dubbed it "that little thing upon the meadow."[28] Meanwhile, Washington pressed for additional forces to march quickly and reinforce the small number of men at Fort Necessity.[29]

Lieutenant Governor Dinwiddie praised Washington for his role in the Jumonville affair and wrote, "I heartily congratulate you, as it may give a testimony to the Indians that the French are not invincible."[30] He promoted the young man to colonel, and Colonel Washington soon received reinforcements, but he still had reason to be troubled. Half-King had brought mostly women and children with him and would soon flee, fearful that the fort would fall quickly to the enemy. The reinforcements were untrained men of no better quality than the ragtag group of men Washington had originally raised. Finally, while some British regulars who arrived were more experienced soldiers, they scoffed at serving under a mere colonist like Washington, regardless of his official rank. To make matters worse, the promised supplies never arrived, and the men quickly consumed all of their meager provisions of flour and bacon. Washington was fighting with one hand tied behind his back, though a more experienced and prudent leader might have decided to leave until better equipped to face the French.[31]

On July 2, during a steady rain, Washington set some pickets to keep watch, arrayed the soldiers around the fort, and prepared to defend against the imminent assault. Only 284 out of the 400 troops in the fort were fit enough to report to duty. They did not have long to wait, because a force of roughly six hundred French and Canadian troops and one hundred Indian warriors under the command of Captain de Villiers, the older brother of Jumonville, arrived late the next morning. The French and Indians advanced in three columns, dispersed amid the cover of the woods, where they poured heavy fire into the defenders. This continued throughout the afternoon and into the evening as horrendous casualties mounted and screams filled the air inside the surrounded fort. "They then from every little rising, tree, stump, stone, and bush kept up a constant, galling fire upon us," Washington later described.[32] During the late afternoon, the "most tremendous rain that [could] be conceived" deluged the fort and ruined the dwindling supplies of gunpowder, making it impossible to put up much resistance.[33] As many as one-third of Washington's army was killed or wounded, and the situation seemed hopeless. Virginians laid down their arms in the heat of battle and broke into the casks of rum rather than face death. Unbeknown to Washington, the French were themselves running low on ammunition and were fearful of a counterattack, so they called out for a parley in the growing darkness.

After some initial negotiations, Washington decided he had no choice but to surrender and accepted the French articles of capitulation. Washington thought the terms seemed generous as he listened to them translated by flickering candlelight in the rain. The English could depart in peace and take their belongings except for their munitions (which was subsequently struck from the agreement to allow the English to protect themselves against Indians on the march to Virginia). The French also took Washington's journal, which was subsequently published to embarrass him for his role in the killing of Jumonville. One clause required Washington to admit to the "death" or "killing" of Jumonville, but the French actually meant "assassination." By affixing his name to the articles, Washington inadvertently conceded that he had assassinated Jumonville, which was considered a gross violation of the written and unwritten laws of war. On July 4, Washington marched out his army in defeat. The young colonel was very concerned about the effect of the defeat on his public reputation. The survivors of the battle limped back, while some had died of their wounds and even more deserted the army and went home.[34]

Washington was humiliated but rushed to the capital to defend his reputation in the halls of power. He need not have worried. Despite the ignominious defeat, Williamsburg welcomed the colonel as a hero. The *Virginia Gazette* praised his killing of Jumonville and blamed the other colonies for the defeat at Great Meadows. The council met and gave Washington three hundred pistoles (gold coins) to reward his men for their service.

Lieutenant Governor Dinwiddie wanted to put the debacle behind him and go on the offensive against the French to drive them from Fort Duquesne, or at the very least build a fort for future operations at Wills Creek. Washington did not think this scheme very feasible, since it was unlikely that many men would sign up and there were no funds. The House of Burgesses eventually voted a substantial £20,000 for war, but Dinwiddie informed Washington that the Virginia Regiment was to be split up and his rank reduced to captain. Washington unhesitatingly resigned his commission two days later. He went to his newly acquired home at Mount Vernon (which he inherited from Lawrence's remarried widow). He spent the remainder of the year getting the plantation up and running.[35]

The British began mobilizing for war against the French when word of Washington's defeat and Dinwiddie's alarming messages reached London. They dispatched the vain and arrogant major general Edward Braddock and two regiments of redcoats to the colonies in December 1754. The French, meanwhile, prepared to send thousands of troops to New France to combat the perceived British aggression. A war for empire would play itself out on American soil, starting at the contested fort on the Forks of the Ohio.

On February 20, 1755, Braddock arrived in Hampton and traveled to Williamsburg to consult with Dinwiddie, who supplied the general with a sketch of Fort Duquesne, along with the most recent intelligence. Washington exchanged letters with the Braddock camp regarding a position on the general's staff. While Washington was offended that British regulars would outrank colonists, he was mindful of the fact that serving under a British general was a golden opportunity to advance his military career and secure a regular commission: "I have now a good opportunity…of forming an acquaintance, which may be serviceable hereafter, if I can find it worthwhile pushing my fortune in the military way."[36] Writing to influential men such as John Robinson, Speaker of the House of Burgesses, the trusted Fairfaxes, and William Byrd, Washington shared the news and sought their help with a commission: "If I am entitled to the least countenance and esteem, it must be from serving my country with a free, voluntary will; for I can very truly say, I have no expectation of reward but the hope of meriting the love of my country."[37]

Braddock knew of Washington's reputation and the "disagreeable" situation regarding rank. He instructed his aide-de-camp to inform Washington that the general would be "very glad of your company in his family."[38] Washington offered to serve as a volunteer without pay directly in service to Braddock, which would be seen as a sign of patriotic service and humility but without the humiliating disparity of rank.

In mid-April, the commander in chief of the British forces in North America met in Alexandria, Virginia, with the five powerful governors of Massachusetts, New York, Maryland, Pennsylvania, and Virginia to discuss the war. After debating the North American strategy and their respective roles, the governors agreed to contribute to the cost of the war but warned that their colonial legislatures would refuse to consent to establishing a common fund unless Parliament ordered it. Thinking that he had everything in order from the colonies regarding finances, supplies and transport, and manpower, Braddock departed to catch up to his marching army. He was mistaken, however, and his difficulties multiplied rapidly because he did not have enough wagons to transport the massive cannon and lengthy baggage train. When he arrived at Frederick, Maryland, on April 21, Braddock discovered that many of the provisions were rotten.[39]

On May 10, Washington officially joined Braddock's headquarters as an aide-de-camp, and the army began its march to Fort Duquesne a few weeks later. Time was of the essence, because the general had learned that the undermanned fort was to receive nine hundred French reinforcements. Braddock wisely sent a five-hundred-man force ahead to clear the road and set up a supply depot, but he was in for a rude awakening about how difficult it was to move an army through the frontier. The movement of heavy guns and a miles-long baggage train was abysmally slow as they crested several major ridges.

Braddock's trust in Washington's judgment and frontier experience was demonstrated when the general sought his advice on how to traverse the wilderness faster. Washington suggested that replacing the wagons with packhorses as well as sending back some of the superfluous guns would greatly increase mobility. Braddock accepted the suggestion and then sent off an advance column to move even faster. It was already mid-June.

By June 23, Washington would not be leading the vanguard of the column of troops as he was suffering from the "bloody flux" and a fever. In fact, Braddock had to order the sick young man to ride in a covered wagon (which was hardly more comfortable, considering the bumpy terrain). He waited for the tail end of the column before setting off again and agreed to this only because Braddock had given his word that "I should be brought up before he reached the French fort."[40] Washington was horrified at the prospect of missing the action and a chance at military glory because of the ignominy of being laid up by dysentery.

After another ten days of laborious forward movement, the army drew up about eight miles east of Fort Duquesne. Braddock and a council of war decided to attack the fort that night, crossing the Monongahela River, passing the mouth of Turtle Creek, and recrossing the river to land within a short distance of the fort. Washington was finally shuttled to camp that evening, while British lieutenant colonel Thomas Gage (who was destined to become one of the most hated men in America two decades later when he faced off against the very colonists with whom he was currently fighting) assembled several companies and some Indian guides and marched out at 2:00 a.m., followed two hours later by deputy quartermaster general, Lieutenant Colonel Sir John St. Clair in a relief column. The French and Indians departed Fort Duquesne at eight o'clock in the morning. The two armies were pointed right at each other.

The rival armies approached each other, with the British beating drums to march in columns and the French and Indians stealthily approaching and fanning out in the surrounding woods in half-moon formation. As the sun approached its zenith, war cries erupted suddenly from every direction, and an ineffective volley was loosed by the

French and Indians. The frightened British responded with their own volley and blindly fired at an unseen enemy. A French commander was struck down by a lucky shot, but another took over. The British, meanwhile, were routed almost from the start. Their enemy poured hot lead into their confused ranks and picked off several officers. The British responded with grapeshot from their cannon, but the shots were too random to be of much effect.

Braddock moved up hundreds of soldiers into the killing zone and attempted to rally the men when he arrived. The men were too panicked and bunched up, foiling his efforts to establish order in the ranks. Mass confusion reigned in the British ranks, which resulted in friendly-fire incidents. Some Virginians smartly rushed toward the woods to seize the high ground and use the same tactics as the unseen enemy, but Braddock and other officers ordered them back into line for a traditional counterattack.

Washington also rode up to Braddock and tried to persuade him to match the frontier-style tactics of their enemy as the only reasonable chance to survive the disaster. Braddock exploded in wrath, rebuking the colonist: "I've a mind to run you through the body! We'll sup today in Fort Duquesne or else in hell!"[41] The pair separated and did their best to rally the troops. Washington conspicuously rode through the ranks and was nearly killed. He had two horses shot out from under him and had his clothing shot through four times. Washington reportedly displayed "the greatest courage and resolution" throughout the slaughter.[42] Braddock demonstrated no less daring and had four horses shot out from under him in the thick of battle. Finally, Braddock went down with a grave wound to his lung.

The British lines soon collapsed, and the men flew to the rear in their pell-mell retreat. Washington and others rescued Braddock and carried him to the rear in a litter. The young man remained cool under fire and tried vainly to organize the retreating men, but fortunately for Washington, the enemy did not pursue the defeated army. They settled for scalping the fallen and looting the wagons and discarded arms. A few unfortunate British wounded would be taken prisoner and tortured to death by fire at Fort Duquesne.

The retreating army marched through the night to elude any pursuit. Its wounded and demoralized survivors inching their way in the darkness were a pitiable sight. Washington would later write, "The shocking scenes which presented themselves in this night's march are not to be described. The dead, the dying, the groans, lamentations, and cries along the road of the wounded for help…were enough to pierce a heart. The gloom and horror of which was not a little increased by the impervious darkness."[43]

The fatigued column limped along for a couple of days. On July 13, Braddock succumbed to his wounds and died. Washington officiated at the impromptu funeral and oversaw the wilderness burial. Wagons were driven and men marched over the site to hide its location from the enemy, because Washington was (justifiably) concerned that the Indians would seek out and desecrate the body.

The remnant of the army straggled to Fort Cumberland, where the wounded received medical attention. Washington traveled to Mount Vernon to recover from his illness and consider the outcome of the battle. The French and Indians had thoroughly routed the British army. The combined British and colonial forces lost an incredible two-thirds of their fifteen-hundred-man force and more than three-quarters of their officers on this tragic day. The French, on the other hand, suffered light casualties, including eleven dead and twenty-nine wounded. Washington mustered enough strength to write to Dinwiddie, expressing his admiration for the colonial troops under his command: "The Virginia companies behaved like men and died like soldiers." The regular British troops bore much of the blame due to their "dastardly behavior" and refusal to listen to Washington and other colonists who advised them in frontier tactics. Rather than a great military victory driving out the French from the Ohio Valley, the allied army was decimated, and Washington did not know whether there were enough troops "to guard our frontiers."[44]

The British viewed the defeat differently and blamed the provincials for the debacle. The British, contrary to Washington's advice, eventually hacked their way back to Fort Duquesne in 1758, only to find that the French had recently abandoned it anyway. The war was fought in more important theaters throughout North America, and after William Pitt became prime minister, he found a winning strategy that would defeat the French and expel them from the continent.

As the fighting shifted, Washington won command of the Virginia Regiment and led the troops for three and a half years. It was a frustrating period, because the assigned task of guarding the frontier against Indian raids was an extremely difficult one. Nevertheless, while he may have been more preoccupied by seeking a regular commission (which was never won) and political office in Virginia, he gained valuable experience in the art of command.

Washington experienced other frustrations during this period. He had a falling out with his patron, Lieutenant Governor Dinwiddie. When the governor criticized the failed war effort on the frontier as well as his character, Washington thought the British earned the lion's share of blame for the defeat and proudly defended his public service: "No man that ever was employed in a public capacity has endeavored to discharge the trust reposed in him with greater honesty."[45] He also lost an election to the House of Burgesses. Finally, he resigned from the army in disgust after another expedition to the Forks. These experiences helped Washington mature as he entered civilian life as a planter.

He then set his sights on more traditional means of advancement in colonial Virginia. In 1758, he stood for election again and won a seat in the House of Burgesses, where he sat for more than a decade and learned the art of politics, which would serve him well in the future as general and statesman. He also became a tobacco planter, though like many other planters, he struggled with large debts because of the unprofitable nature of tobacco planting, failed crops due to droughts, and his insatiable consumption of British luxury goods. To compensate, he wisely experimented with wheat and other crops and diversified his operations at Mount Vernon to become a successful planter.[46] He also expanded and renovated Mount Vernon to make it more suitable for a family.

Throughout the summer of 1758, Washington courted a wealthy widow, Martha Custis, and the two were married on January 6, 1759. With this marriage, Washington added substantially to his property and slaves.[47] Thinking about the new life he created for himself, Washington reflected, "I am now, I believe, fixed at this seat with an agreeable consort for life and hope to find more happiness in retirement than I ever experienced amidst a wide and bustling world."[48] Putting the war and his youthful adventures behind him, Washington was a happily married man, stepfather to Martha's two children, a wealthy planter, and a representative in the House of Burgesses.

In addition to achieving military glory through fits and starts, the French and Indian War taught Washington valuable lessons that would shape his leadership in the Revolutionary War. First, he learned the essentials of military command, such as discipline, strategy, and logistics. Second, he became seasoned in managing tensions of civil-military and wider intercolonial relations. Third, and most important to his world view, he learned about imperial relations with the British and developed an antipathy for them and their superior attitude, thereby helping to shape his sense of an American character. After leaving the army, his work as a planter helped him learn to manage a large-scale business. These experiences would aid him in molding and commanding the Continental army later, but if not for postwar British policies, he might have remained a provincial planter, politician, and forgotten war hero.

CHAPTER TWO

"I WISH THERE WAS A WAR"
YOUNG ALEXANDER HAMILTON

ALEXANDER HAMILTON GREW UP in an entirely different world than George Washington. The West Indies were an alluring paradise where individual and imperial wealth easily rose and fell. The islands stood at a key nexus in the Atlantic trade networks, which were jealously guarded by imperial monopolies and caused wars among European rivals for more than a century. This milieu was the platform that would launch the rise of a powerful young immigrant to the American colonies.

The childhood of Alexander Hamilton was far less idyllic than the crystal-clear waters and grand estates of the rich familial empires. His early life was one of constant struggle and represented the more difficult side of life in the West Indies. The sugar islands held out the allure of wealth that led many to migrate to the Caribbean for get-rich-quick schemes with a small investment. Some achieved middling success and scraped by; others were greatly disappointed and led reprobate lives amid their failures and dashed hopes. They wandered from island to island and lived a life of squalor in paradise.

Alexander Hamilton's mother, Rachel Lavine, did just this, living most of her adult life on the margins of society and engaging with such dreamers who went in search of riches and perennially ended up broke.

For her part, she appears to have adopted the loose sexual mores of the islands and engaged in several doomed extramarital affairs. At one point, Rachel took up with the Scotsman James Hamilton, a ne'er-do-well with big aspirations and no reasonable hope of achieving them. They lived on Nevis, one of the Leeward Islands, which, like most, was almost entirely devoted to the sugar industry and trade. The couple had two sons, James and Alexander, the latter born on January 11, 1755. The two children were quickly designated illegitimate, because Rachel had already left her first husband but had not immediately divorced him before she entered into the relationship with Hamilton.[1]

In 1759, Rachel's first husband returned and sued her for divorce. He accused her of having "given herself up to whoring with everyone" and said that she "had shown herself to be shameless, rude, and ungodly."[2] Although he was free to remarry under the law, Rachel was not, due to the inequitable laws of the time, and thus her sons were officially declared bastards. In 1765, James Hamilton moved his growing family to St. Croix and then abandoned them. Alexander, left with his mother and brother, never saw his father after the age of ten.

Rachel did the best she could to support her two sons. They lived in Christiansted, a sheltered harbor on the north end of the island and capital of St. Croix, an island the Danish had held since 1733, with fifty thousand acres of land divided into 381 sugar plantations. The capital was heavily fortified because of a century of wars among European imperial rivals for control of Caribbean sugar. The waterfront had the usual array of wharves, merchants, and lending houses related to the export of sugar and import of provisions that sustained the island economy. Outside of the harbor, on symmetrical streets, were government offices, small businesses, taverns, and houses of ill-repute.[3] Roughly six hundred private homes were interspersed among the businesses. Rachel rented out a home near the wharf and ran a small provisioning store. She supplemented her meager income by renting out three slaves inherited from her mother. She instructed young Alexander in running her provisioning business, which bought goods from a much larger nearby import-export firm, run by David Beekman and Nicholas Cruger. Through his mother's business ties, the experienced young man impressed Cruger, who hired Alexander as an apprentice. His brother was apprenticed to a carpenter.[4]

Though his formal schooling was sketchy at best and mostly practical in business transactions and management, Alexander Hamilton was a brilliant young man. At that time, educational opportunities were roundly deficient in the West Indies, and many commentators noted the lack of educational facilities or worthy schoolteachers. Most planters' sons traveled back to England for an education at its prep schools and universities.[5] Rachel, meanwhile, had a decent collection of some thirty-four books, which probably included the Bible, Shakespeare, Plutarch's *Lives*, Alexander Pope's poetry, and devotional tracts. Alexander read and reread this small shelf of classics as he awaited better educational opportunities.[6]

In February 1768, disaster struck the small family when Rachel and Alexander came down with a terrible fever. After a week of enduring primitive eighteenth-century ministrations, Rachel succumbed and died. Her son recovered shortly thereafter but was orphaned at only thirteen years old. To add insult to injury, Rachel's first husband swooped in and claimed her entire estate (the pittance she had) for their son, Peter. As if that were not bad enough, Alexander and his brother's guardian was a thirty-two-year-old cousin, Peter Lytton, who would end his own life within a year. The boys were left virtually alone and forced to strike out and support themselves in what seemed a very cruel world.[7]

Alexander Hamilton was fortunate to find a home quickly in Beekman & Cruger, which was well situated to trade in the Atlantic network and where Nicholas Cruger assumed the role of a surrogate parent and protector. He worked hard at the firm and quickly picked up essential knowledge in management, bookkeeping, currency exchange, and oceangoing trade. He also learned about the mercantilist policies of the European nations, which attempted to monopolize the trade from their colonies in order to keep money flowing to their own countries rather than flowing out to other empires. The West Indies were intertwined in the same web of imperial regulations as the American colonies and also in the wars that were commonplace during this time.[8] The practical experience gained by Hamilton during his time at Beekman & Cruger would be of inestimable value to this future military officer and secretary of the treasury.

However tied in he was to international business and a good job, even at fourteen, Hamilton had a burning ambition for greatness and to play a part in larger worlds. He confessed to his friend, Ned Stevens, who was studying at King's College in New York, that "my ambition is present that I [condemn] the groveling and condition of a clerk or the like, to which my fortune etc. condemns me and would willingly risk my life though not my character to exalt my station." He sought a way to "prepare the way for futurity," even if some thought that he was a foolish young man building castles in the sky. With little other path to win glory and fame, he concluded "I wish there was a war."[9] In late 1771, Cruger became ill and sailed to New York for five months to recover and entrusted the sixteen-year-old Hamilton with management of the firm. Hamilton was finally getting some taste of being in a position of greater authority to match his youthful ambition.

While Cruger was in New York, his precocious young protégé went into action, directing the firm as if it were his own. The adolescent authoritatively gave grizzled sea captains instructions for their voyages and firmly reminded them to bring their shipments in on time. "Remember you are to make three trips this season and unless you are very diligent, you will be too late as our crops will be early in," he reminded one captain.[10] The Thunderbolt was a fine ship, but despite its name, Hamilton said that she was "not so swift as she ought to be."[11] After a cargo of starving, half-dead mules appeared, he presumptuously dressed down the veteran captain, telling him to "reflect continually on the unfortunate voyage you have just made and endeavor to make up for the considerable loss therefrom accruing to your owners."[12] The young man was quickly learning the art of command.

Besides taking liberties ordering clients, customers, and employees around, Hamilton also assumed considerable responsibility for selecting goods, inspecting cargoes, haggling over costs, turning merchandise for a profit, navigating imperial trade regulations, dealing with imperial rivals, and ensuring that everyone lived up to his high standards. Returning to the island in March 1772, Cruger heartily approved of the job his brilliant surrogate performed. He was even pleased to hear that Hamilton had fired the company's attorney, because he was "very negligent in [my affairs] and trifled away a good deal of money to no purpose."[13] Seizing the unexpected opportunity, Hamilton deeply impressed his boss, who knew that the young man was meant for great things. But more importantly, Hamilton had learned a great deal about running an international business and imperial relations. Again, this knowledge would become an important asset to the nation's first treasury secretary.

Hamilton also daily witnessed the stark horror of the Atlantic trade networks—slavery. The vast majority of 11 million African slaves who endured the unspeakable terror of traversing the Middle Passage bound for the New World were brought to the sugar colonies in the Caribbean and South America where brutal forms of abuse awaited them. The workload, coupled with various diseases, caused shocking mortality rates and an average life expectancy of only seven years for the African arrivals. Sugar was such a valuable crop that the planters believed it was generally a better investment to work slaves to death than to provide for their well-being. Even though thousands arrived every year, the slave populations remained fairly stagnant because so many died. Hamilton's opposition to slavery was likely forged in these early years of his life as he witnessed grisly scenes of sickly, skeletal Africans trudging off the ships in chains by the hundreds to be auctioned off to the highest bidders, while pitiless punishments were meted out to any "obstinate" slaves.

While Hamilton worked for Beekman & Cruger and dreamed of bigger things, he met an important patron who was to help him get off the island and to America. Reverend Hugh Knox, a classically trained Scottish minister who attended the College of New Jersey (now Princeton University), had lived on the tiny West Indian island of Saba for seventeen years and, fortuitously for Hamilton, moved to St. Croix as the minister of the Christiansted Presbyterian Church in early 1772. He sought to evangelize the island's residents in the intense religious experience of the Great Awakening revival that had swept the American colonies in the previous decades.[14]

As pastor of the Presbyterian Church in the small town, Reverend Knox became acquainted with Hamilton. He recognized Hamilton's genius, while the younger man perceived the worlds that Knox could open for an ambitious person like himself. Knox's sermons and discussions with Hamilton fired his religious imagination and led the young man to become deeply and prayerfully devout. Knox admitted that he enjoyed being a patron, "drawing these incomparable geniuses out of obscurity."[15]

Knox also sought to develop the young man's intellect and opened his impressive library to Hamilton, who was delighted to read a much broader range of classics. The pair spent hours conversing over the great ideas found in those texts, and it's likely that Knox introduced Hamilton to the republican ideals of the Scottish Enlightenment. Only a few years later, Hamilton would fill his own revolutionary tracts with the ideas he first learned from Knox. Though the pair spent only a few months together before Hamilton would depart the island, their friendship would impact the young man's ideas and actions for the rest of his life as an American statesman.

The patrons in Alexander Hamilton's life conspired to give him the opportunity to fulfill his ambitions by sending him to the American colonies for a real education and other advantages that the small island simply could not offer. Cruger had familial and business ties that would pave the way for Hamilton to go college. Knox wrote numerous letters of introduction to his associates in New York and New Jersey so that his protégé might study there. The pair took up a collection from wealthy merchants, ship captains, and officials in their circle who donated a generous sum for the cost of the young man's education. Knox might have had a tinge of regret in losing the company of the bright youth, but he would later write to Hamilton that "I have always had a just and secret pride in having advised you to go to America, and in having recommended you to some [of] my old friends there."[16] It is not clear how Hamilton reacted to these acts of generosity, but one can assume that he was likely delighted to seek larger worlds and greater challenges.

In October 1772, Hamilton boarded a ship for North America with few earthly belongings and never returned to the West Indies. His saga was to become one of the first great immigrant stories in American history, though his origins would sometimes be mocked by his political enemies. He landed in Boston, the center of the resistance to British taxes, and quickly made his way to New York where his contacts and college funds were waiting.

In New York, Hamilton went to Kortright and Company, where Cruger had deposited Hamilton's money. Cruger had been in New York only a year before Hamilton arrived, and he planned to replenish the college fund with future sales from barrels of sugar. Hamilton's good friend, Ned Stevens, was studying at King's College, and Alexander quickly befriended Hercules Mulligan, one of the leaders of the New York Sons of Liberty and brother of Hugh Mulligan, one of the partners at Kortright. Hercules was an Irishman who owned a tailor shop.[17]

Besides rekindling old friendships and making new ones, Hamilton made the rounds with prominent associates of Cruger and Reverend

Knox. The young man also became acquainted with William Livingston, a former New York lawyer and politician who had become a landed New Jersey gentleman and trustee of Princeton. He was widely known as a Whig (supporter of government by consent) and Presbyterian dissenter who abided by principles of liberty. Hamilton also became friends with Elias Boudinot, another lawyer, devout Presbyterian, and Whig. He had parents who hailed from the West Indies, and he took an instant liking to the talented youth who could benefit from study at Elizabethtown Academy, which Boudinot helped to found, and at Princeton, where he was a trustee alongside Livingston. Other figures in Livingston's circle who Hamilton met were Aaron Burr, a graduate of Princeton, and William Duer, a former West Indian planter who similarly migrated to New York due to business ties.[18]

This circle of patrons was critically important in continuing to shape Hamilton's political and religious outlook where Reverend Knox left off on St. Croix. They were firmly committed to the Whig cause of liberty, though at this point, they still hoped that the British would reconcile with their American colonists. These fierce Presbyterian Christians were highly individualistic in their religious world view, which was inextricably linked to their politics.

Hamilton greedily inhaled the rhetoric of liberty that surrounded this group of patriots. He learned a great deal from listening to their political conversations and having access to the impressive libraries at Livingston's Elizabethtown "Liberty Hall" mansion. Because the plan for Hamilton since he left the Caribbean was to attend Princeton, the group set up an interview for him with Reverend John Witherspoon, a Scottish Presbyterian and Whig who was then president of the university.[19]

Any ordinary prospective college freshman might have been intimidated by Witherspoon. Under his guidance, Princeton had become a breeding ground for republican ferment. John Adams would later call Witherspoon an "animated son of liberty."[20] Witherspoon advanced philosopher John Locke's ideas of social compact theory when he taught that God endowed all humans with natural rights and that the purpose of government was to protect those rights. He would later write that "God grant that in America true religion and civil liberty may be inseparable, and that the unjust attempts to destroy the one, may in the issue tend to the support and establishment of both."[21] Reverend Witherspoon also taught that religion was the basis for virtue and that virtue was the basis for republican self-government.[22] Hamilton had been informally educated in these principles under Reverend Knox and Livingston and would presumably find a very comfortable intellectual setting at Witherspoon's Princeton.

After only a year of intense study at a prep school in the classics to make up for his educational deficiencies, Hamilton applied to Princeton. Mulligan claimed to have accompanied Hamilton, who supposedly told his friend that he preferred Princeton because it "was more republican" than the loyalist King's College in New York. Mulligan thought he was instrumental in setting up the interview with Witherspoon for Hamilton, though Livingston and Boudinot certainly may have played a more significant role. Hamilton, however, presumptuously demanded as a condition that he be allowed to pursue an accelerated program of study. He would attend only "with the understanding that he should be permitted to advance from class to class with as much rapidity as his exertions would enable him to do."[23] Reverend Witherspoon hesitated, either because James Madison had recently completed an accelerated program, finishing his undergraduate education in two years before studying for an advanced degree, and had a nervous breakdown, or else the president simply thought the precocious young man was not extremely well prepared. Witherspoon promised he would take up the matter with the trustees, and two weeks later, Hamilton received a letter rejecting his request and wishing him luck at another school. He promptly applied to King's College in New York, even though it was a center of Anglicanism and Tory (Americans who supported the

British) sentiment and distinctly at odds with the principles he had learned over the previous two years.[24]

Hamilton moved to New York and attended King's College (which would become Columbia University). The city was much larger than anything Hamilton was used to in St. Croix, with roughly twenty thousand inhabitants, but it had a familiar diversity of ethnicities, languages, and religions. The port city had several wharves that housed an international business community with ties all over the Atlantic. New York was an excellent place for Hamilton to attend college and make connections for his rise.

Dr. Reverend Myles Cooper, who was loyal to Great Britain amid the fury of the patriot movement, was the president of the college. Though he was a loyalist who would not promote patriotic principles of religious and civil liberty the same way as Reverend Witherspoon, Dr. Cooper offered his students a similarly rigorous classical education that included modern philosophy and writers of the Enlightenment.

Hamilton thrived at King's and made an easy transition, surrounded by friends such as Mulligan and fellow students Ned Stevens and Robert Troup. The friends, inspired by their broad reading and example of their professors, started their own debating club at King's. The purpose of the club was "our improvement in composition, in debating, and in public speaking." Troup related that Hamilton demonstrated "richness of genius, and energy of mind."[25] Hamilton would use these skills when he entered public life during his time as a student.

Alexander Hamilton had come a very long way from the difficult childhood on St. Croix. Much like George Washington, he owed his success to the benefit of having many patrons who created opportunities. But he also had the innate genius and strong work ethic to seize the opportunities that were presented to him. His prospects for fame and glory would increase even more dramatically with the outbreak of war in the American colonies. The Revolutionary War would provide the historic occasion for George Washington and Alexander Hamilton to become national figures and forge a fruitful collaboration in the cause for liberty and self-government.

CHAPTER THREE

"WE MUST ASSERT OUR RIGHTS"
THE GROWTH OF REVOLUTIONARY IDEOLOGY

THE DECADE FOLLOWING THE end of the French and Indian War in 1763 was marked by increasing American resistance to British taxation and the growth in popularity of revolutionary ideas like liberty and self-government for the colonies. Amid this tumultuous atmosphere, George Washington and Alexander Hamilton quickly emerged as leaders of the patriot movement within their respective colonies, although they did not meet until the start of the Revolutionary War. They argued that the colonists had the traditional rights of Englishmen under the unwritten British constitution and the universal natural rights of all humans. But it was the embracing of these radical ideas and resistance to British tyranny in the streets and statehouses of the colonies that would eventually put Washington and Hamilton on a path to form their indispensable alliance.

George Washington's Virginia was one of the leading centers of American resistance to British taxes. As an important planter, member of the House of Burgesses, and military hero, Washington was at the center of the deliberation over the American response to the British. At first, he was moderate in the defense of liberty while young radicals and established conservatives fought over how to resist British policies in Virginia. Washington, however, emerged as one of the leaders of the patriot cause. He would never be mistaken for a firebrand radical like Patrick Henry, but he was nonetheless among the first Virginians who saw that further debate would not bear fruit and contemplated war as a solution to British tyranny.

Alexander Hamilton's New York was also an epicenter of colonial resistance. Hamilton made an immediate splash in the movement despite his youth, immigrant status, and late arrival in the American colonies. He joined the opposition in the street as a speaker and added his pen to the cause, writing some of the most important pamphlets of the early revolutionary era. His daring and profound intellect would bring him to the attention of revolutionary leaders in New York politics and eventually in the Continental army. The college student had much less to lose than the established planter Washington, but Hamilton had more obstacles to overcome in becoming a leader in the Revolutionary War. Opposition to British tyranny and the beginning of the American Revolution would provide both with an opportunity to enter into a larger national stage, fighting for principles of liberty and self-government.

★ ★ ★

THERE WERE MANY FACTORS that caused the American Revolution, but foremost among these was the fact that the French and Indian War added significantly to the British national debt. In 1764, it had reached a staggering £129 million with a burdensome annual interest payment. As a result, Parliament took a series of steps that fueled revolutionary sentiment in the colonies, passing the first tax on the American colonists, the Sugar Act, in April 1764. The British also established new admiralty courts to prosecute smuggling, which rankled Americans because their right to a trial by jury was stripped away, and they were left at the mercy of royally appointed judges rather than friendly local juries.[1]

During the spring of 1764, in the midst of the furor over the Sugar Act, Prime Minister George Grenville told the House of Commons that "it may be proper to charge certain stamp duties in the said colonies."[2] He intimated to the American agents in London and indirectly to the colonial legislatures that he expected their assent to the new taxes. He was to be sorely disappointed and quickly disabused of the notion. Although the tax did not take shape for nearly a year, the opposition quickly coalesced.

When asked by the ministry to gauge the anticipated American reaction to the proposed stamp tax in July 1764, Jared Ingersoll of Connecticut explained that the minds of Americans were "filled with the most dreadful apprehensions from such a step taking place…without the consent of the legislature of that country and in the opinion of most of the people contrary to the foundation principles of their natural and constitutional rights and liberties."[3] It was the first of many arguments based upon the idea of "no taxation without representation."

Williamsburg was to be one of the centers of resistance to the stamp tax. The Virginia General Assembly convened on October 30, 1764, and one of the members of the House of Burgesses, George Washington, was present at the Capitol during the session. On December 18, Washington and the other members of the assembly unanimously resolved that "it [is] a fundamental principle of the British constitution, without which freedom can nowhere exist, that the people are subject to any taxes but such as are laid on them by their own consent, or by those who are legally appointed to represent them." The proposed tax was subversive of their constitutional and natural rights, and they argued for the "freedom which all men, especially those who derive their constitution from *Britain*, have a right to enjoy."[4] Parliament scoffed at the Virginians and refused to hear their petition, because it would "not suffer a petition that should hint at questioning the supremacy and authority of Parliament to impose taxes in every part of the British Dominions."[5]

On February 6, 1765, Prime Minister Grenville finally introduced the stamp tax bill before the House of Commons. On March 22, the king signed the act into law. Word of the act crossed the Atlantic rapidly and arrived in the colonies in April. By May, the act was published in newspapers across the colonies. The new act levied taxes on almanacs, newspapers, legal documents, and even playing cards.

In early May, George Washington read about the Stamp Act in the *Virginia Gazette* and heard the buzz in the Williamsburg taverns as he traveled to the capital for the meeting of the Virginia General Court and House of Burgesses. He then wrapped up his personal business, and with the legislature session winding down, he went home to oversee the spring planting at Mount Vernon. Consequently, he missed the fireworks that erupted over the Stamp Act in the Capitol at the end of the month.[6]

On May 29, a twenty-nine-year-old freshman burgess, Patrick Henry, rose to offer five resolutions protesting the Stamp Act scribbled on the blank leaf of an old law book. Only 39 of the 116 burgesses were present, since most had gone home to their plantations. With fiery rhetoric, Henry introduced the resolutions, which expressed the commonplace ideas of taxation by consent and colonial self-government. These ideas spread to the other colonies and solidified the growing opposition to parliamentary taxes. They sparked riots, most notably in Boston, and numerous pamphlets and letters denouncing British tyranny.

George Washington weighed in on the issue privately in the fall of 1765, explaining the American reaction to the Stamp Act to some correspondents in England. He said that most colonists viewed the act as an "unconstitutional method of taxation as a direful attack upon their liberties, and loudly exclaim against the violation." Washington thought the act imprudent and could not judge "what may be the result of this—and some other (I think I may add) ill-judged measures." He correctly predicted that the "advantage accruing to the mother country will fall greatly short of the expectations of the ministry."

Since he was deeply involved in the imperial trade with Great Britain, Washington knew that whatever "contributes to lessen our importations must be hurtful to their manufactures." The people could adopt more frugal, virtuous ways and stop purchasing British luxuries. The greatest consequence in Washington's opinion was that "our courts of judicature must inevitably be shut up; for it is impossible (or next of kin to it) under our present circumstances that the act of Parliament can be complied with were we ever so willing to enforce the execution." He guessed that the "merchants of Great Britain trading to the colonies will not be among the last to wish for a repeal of it." In short, he asked, "Where then lies the utility of these measures?"[7] Washington criticized the Stamp Act from a constitutional as well as practical view that it would ruin trade with America and that the decline in trade would be far greater than any increase in revenue—which was precisely what happened. Washington's opposition to the Stamp Act was adopted by colonists across America and even the entire British Empire.

Many colonists in the West Indies shared Washington's concerns, including young Alexander Hamilton some sixteen hundred miles away (almost a decade before he moved to America). Hamilton heard about resistance to the Stamp Act on the islands as well as distant opposition in North America from islanders and ship captains. On October 31, a large mob in the capital of St. Kitts marched to the home of the deputy stamp distributor, John Hopkins, and burned the stamps they found within. Then the angry crowd threatened him and the Stamp Act distributor, William Tuckett, who was hiding in fear of being "suspended" on a gibbet, into resigning their positions. Several other sites around the capital, including the customs house, were searched for stamps, which were discovered and summarily burned. When Tuckett escaped to Nevis and imprudently began to "distribute those badges of slavery," St. Kitts' Sons of Liberty chased him unsuccessfully but burned more stamps and a couple of homes. In the coming weeks, mobs burned effigies of Tuckett and permanently forced his resignation, prevented any more stamps from landing, and made toasts to "liberty, property, and no stamps." One observer noted, "there is hardly a man among them from the highest to the lowest who does not openly show his hearty abhorrence of the Stamp law."[8] There is no written record of Alexander Hamilton's reaction to the resistance to the taxes on the islands, but it may have helped to shape his view of the British Empire during his formative years.

Events eventually moved in the direction Washington had foreseen, with both houses of Parliament repealing the act and the king assenting. Washington learned about the repeal from one of his merchants in London, who wrote to him only a few weeks after the fact: "We congratulate thee and all our friends in America upon the repeal of the Stamp Act." They reminded him that they "used our best endeavors" to prevent the act and agitated constantly to repeal it.[9] On June 9, Lieutenant Governor Fauquier officially notified Virginians that Parliament repealed the reviled tax to great popular acclaim.[10] In July, Washington rejoiced in the news of the repeal because the consequences of Parliament obstinately enforcing the Stamp Act would have been "more direful than is generally apprehended both to the mother country and her colonies." He cordially thanked all of the merchants "who were instrumental in procuring the repeal."[11]

The American jubilation at the defeat of the stamp tax was short-lived. The British were still in debt and looked to the American colonists to pay a fair share for the annual cost of stationing troops on the American frontier (£400,000). The Rockingham ministry had fallen, and the king called upon William Pitt, Lord Chatham, to form a new government. Armed with the authority embodied in the Declaratory Act, the chancellor of the exchequer, Charles Townshend, proposed a new round of taxes on the Americans. On June 29, 1767, Parliament agreed to levies on glass, paint, paper, and tea, which would take effect in November. The government also decided to enforce customs more strictly with a new American Board of Customs headquartered in

Boston and new vice-admiralty courts to try offenders. Moreover, the redcoats on the frontier were relocated in eastern cities to restore law and order and were to be quartered in American homes. All of these actions roused even fiercer American resistance than the Stamp Act. The Townshend Acts also led to the rise of George Washington as a prominent figure in the resistance movement in Virginia.[12]

On April 2, 1768, George Washington was at Mount Vernon when the burgesses started considering their response to a circular letter from Massachusetts protesting the Townshend Acts. On April 16, they adopted petitions seeking revocation of the acts. The burgesses claimed the right of Englishmen to govern themselves by their own consent. Washington missed this critical vote, arriving a week later and participating in routine legislative business, but he firmly supported the position of his fellow burgesses.

In late October 1768, Virginians, including George Washington, welcomed a new governor, Norborne Berkeley, also known as Lord Botetourt. Washington traveled to the capital for court days and participated in the gala events. Even though the patriot movement protested British taxes, they were still Englishmen who mostly respected royal authority. Washington and several gentlemen dined at the palace with the governor, who called for a new election for the spring session and invited the gentry to a grand ball. The festivities would give way to conflict during that session of the assembly. Unbeknown to the gentlemen, Botetourt had been instructed to "converse with, the members of our...council in [Virginia], separately and personally, as also with the principal persons of influence...and endeavor to lead them...to disclaim the erroneous and dangerous principles which they appear to have adopted."[13]

On the afternoon of April 2, 1769, George Washington hosted several Maryland merchants at a dinner at Mount Vernon. His guests brought copies of their colony's nonimportation agreement and a letter encouraging Virginia to join the movement.[14] Washington was impressed by what he read, and on April 5, after riding around his plantation all day, he sat down in his study and composed a letter to his Fairfax County neighbor George Mason of Gunston Hall, which revealed his adherence to liberty and willingness to act. Washington believed that the British ministers were conspiring to destroy the freedom of their American colonists. It seemed to him that "something should be done to avert the stroke and maintain liberty which we have derived from our ancestors."[15]

Washington argued that acting to defend the colonists' endangered liberties was a matter of moral principle. Moreover, even at this early date, he actually considered the possibility of taking up arms against the British: "That no man should scruple, or hesitate a moment to use arms in defense of so valuable a blessing, on which all the good and evil of life depends." But war with Britain could not be lightly undertaken and would only be a last resort. Washington believed that petitioning the crown and Parliament had been ineffective and would yield no further gains, years before others gave up. "Their attention to our rights and privileges is to be awakened or alarmed by starving their trade and manufactures," he told Mason.[16]

Washington started working out on paper what the nonimportation association for Virginia might look like. He praised the northern associations but feared that self-interest would prevent some Virginians from joining the association unless they were "stigmatized, and made the objects of public reproach." The more he thought about the scheme, the "more ardently[he] wish success to it." He thought that the plan would have some additional advantages beyond repealing the taxes, such as developing American manufacturing and encouraging planters to live more frugally within their means. All he and Mason needed to do was work out the details and timing.[17]

Mason wrote back to his neighbor the very same day. He proposed that they draw up a plan for Washington to present at the approaching assembly session when "a number of gentlemen, from the different parts of the country, will have an opportunity of conferring together, and acting in concert." Mason promised to complete and send over a proposal he had worked on before he was laid low by illness—perhaps a bout of gout. "The little inconveniencies and comforts of life, when set in competition with our liberty, ought to be rejected…with pleasure," Mason wrote. He agreed that the plan should be based upon a republican simplicity that abstained from "all manner of superfluities" and a boycott that would "distress the various traders and manufacturers in Great Britain," who would again pressure the government for repeal.[18]

On April 17 and 18, Washington served as a local justice for the Fairfax County court and returned to Mount Vernon "in the evening with Mr. Mason." Using the plans of other colonies as their model, Washington and Mason discussed the nonimportation association and hammered out the details of the proposal that they would lay before the House of Burgesses.[19] On April 30, Washington rode out for Williamsburg with the association plan safely tucked away in his saddlebags, while his neighbor recuperated at Gunston Hall.

On May 8, Lord Botetourt received the newly elected burgesses, and the legislative session began. When the house assembled, Speaker Peyton Randolph addressed the thought on all of their minds when he informed his colleagues that the Virginia circular letter had been sent to the other colonies and replies were received. He laid these on the table so that they might be examined by the members, who spent the next week individually considering the responses.[20]

On May 15, the chief political question of the day was openly confronted when the burgesses assembled as a committee of the whole to "consider the present state of the colony."[21] On May 16, after much animated deliberation, the House of Burgesses passed some relatively uncontroversial resolutions that the "sole right of imposing taxes on the inhabitants…[is] legally and constitutionally vested in the House of Burgesses," and that the Englishmen were entitled to the basic rights of petitioning the king and a trial by jury.[22]

Governor Botetourt angrily learned of the resolves and sought to follow his instructions to the letter. The next day, he convened the burgesses in his second-floor chamber of the Capitol and informed them, "Mr. Speaker, and Gentlemen of the House of Burgesses, I have heard of your Resolves, and augur ill of their Effect. You have made it my Duty to dissolve you; and you are dissolved accordingly."[23]

The burgesses marched a short distance down the main thorough-fare, Duke of Gloucester Street, to the second-floor Apollo Room of Raleigh Tavern to consider "their distressed situation." Speaker Randolph was selected to preside over the extralegal assembly, and Washington was selected to chair a committee appointed to prepare a plan of nonimportation because of his work with Mason. The committee worked late into the evening and revised the Washington-Mason plan. In the morning, Washington and the committee members presented the nonimportation plan for discussion. After it was "read, seriously considered, and unanimously approved," the association was signed by eighty-eight of "the principal Gentlemen of the Colony," who thereby pledged not to import from a list of goods related to the Townshend Acts.[24]

The signers of the Virginia Nonimportation Association resolved to risk their lives and fortunes opposing the "late unconstitutional act" that was "destructive to liberty" and had the effect of "reducing us from a free and happy people to a wretched and miserable state of slavery." The purpose of the resolutions was to "induce the good people of this colony to be frugal in the use and consumption of British manufactures" and prod British merchants "from motives of interest, friendship, and justice" to exert themselves on behalf of the colonists by winning another repeal. The association was to take effect on September 1, which would allow planters to rush out their tobacco shipments ahead of the deadline. Besides a list of enumerated goods that included a wide variety of foodstuffs, clothing, and manufactured items, the Virginians also agreed not to import any human cargo from Africa. "That they will not import any slaves, or purchase any imported, after the first day of November next, until the said acts of Parliament are repealed," it read.[25] On May 20, Washington departed for Mount Vernon, an emerging leader of the opposition to British taxes and tyranny.[26]

During the summer and fall, Washington and his neighbors adhered to the boycott of British goods. Washington's order of goods from his factor, Robert Cary & Company, dropped to less than a quarter of previous purchases. In late July, he informed Cary that "if there are any articles contained in either of the respective invoices (paper only excepted) which are taxed by Parliament for the purpose of raising a revenue in America, it is my express desire and request, that they may not be sent, as I have very heartily entered into an association… I am there- fore determined to adhere religiously to it, and may perhaps have wrote for some things unwittingly which may be under these circumstances."[27]

In November 1769, Washington went to Williamsburg to attend the next session of the House of Burgesses and received very welcome news. Governor Botetourt made some important opening remarks to the house, pledging his support for repeal of England's taxes except for the one on tea. He relayed the news to the burgesses that he had received a letter from Lord Hillsborough, secretary of state for the colonies, who informed him that Parliament would probably repeal the existing duties and that there would be no more taxes for the purposes of raising a revenue. The burgesses were appeased by his speech but continued the association until final word of the repeal was heard.[28]

In early 1770, Lord Botetourt's prediction that the Townshend Acts would be repealed came to fruition. The taxes had generated very little revenue and severely affected colonial trade, with American imports from Great Britain falling dramatically from £2.2 million to £1.3 million in 1769. With merchants again clamoring for repeal, the ministry responded to their appeals. In January 1770, a new chancel- lor of the exchequer, Frederick Lord North, took office and urged Parliament to repeal the acts, which it did in March. The Tea Act, however, was retained, Lord North explained, "as a mark of the supremacy of Parliament, and an efficient declaration of their right to govern the colonies."[29]

The civility that reigned in Williamsburg stood in marked contrast to tensions in Boston. Ever since the redcoats had occupied the city, they clashed with the townspeople. Although the officers sought to maintain discipline and punish any mistreatment of civilians, problems ensued. Boston workers resented British troops moonlighting in their off-hours for extra income. Exchanges of heated words led to drunken brawls in taverns that spilled into the streets and calls for reinforcements on both sides. Armed mobs wielding clubs, cutlasses, and shovels patrolled the streets and routinely fought soldiers with bayonets. One British lieutenant was slain, and a sympathetic local jury acquitted the accused, Michael Corbet. The city was a powder keg, and radical patriots such as Samuel Adams were ready to supply a match.[30]

In late February, events came to a head when a mob crowded before the home of a merchant, Theophilus Lillie, who violated the nonimportation agreement and was thus considered a traitor to the patriot cause. The multitude screamed threats: "Come out…I'll have your heart, your liver out!" When a neighbor, Ebenezer Richardson, left the safety of his home to warn off the mob, the throng pelted him with rocks, sticks, and eggs. Richardson armed himself in fear of his life as the tension grew. Tragically, the frightened Richardson fired into the crowd and mortally wounded an eleven-year-old boy, Christopher Seider, in the chest and abdomen. When he announced, "I don't care what I've done," he was seized, dragged through the streets, beaten, and nearly hanged. Samuel Adams used the boy's funeral as a massive propaganda tool to decry British tyranny for the thousands who attended.[31]

But the worst was yet to come. On the chilly evening of March 5, Private Hugh White was posted as the lone sentry by the customs house on King Street. He was taunted relentlessly by a group of hostile boys and pelted with an assortment of projectiles. Private White responded by smashing the butt end of his musket into one of their faces. Captain Thomas Preston learned of the disturbance and marched out a relief party of six privates and a corporal to come to White's aid. They attempted to disperse the crowd, but fire bells tolled throughout the town, and citizens came running out of their homes. The growing mob challenged the redcoats to fire and bombarded them with snowballs, chunks of ice, and cobblestones. Skirmishes broke out, and a soldier was knocked down by a club. A weapon was discharged, whether in fright or by accident, and a volley erupted along the line, striking eleven Bostonians, five of whom bled to death in the street. Preston ordered his men to hold their fire and prudently marched them off before they were in turn slain by the shocked mob. Lieutenant Governor Thomas Hutchinson helped restore calm and even sent some of the troops out of the city to defuse the situation.

Patriots made the most of the killing and published gruesome, one-sided accounts of the Boston Massacre. Paul Revere published his engraving showing the troops slaughtering innocent civilians in cold blood. Samuel Adams organized an even larger funeral procession that dwarfed the earlier one. Eventually, John Adams defended the soldiers to confirm the importance of the rule of law and American belief in trial by jury. Most of the troops were acquitted, with two receiving a thumb branding for manslaughter.[32]

Curiously, for such a watershed event in the struggle against British tyranny, Washington did not acknowledge the event publicly or even in private correspondence or his diary. Although the event represented the greatest American loss of life in the decade of resistance, it did not galvanize American resistance, which ebbed over the next few years. During the lull in rebellious activity, Hamilton traveled to America and took up his studies, and Washington was consumed by mostly personal concerns. However, national events would soon pull Washington away from his domestic cares.

In May 1773, Parliament pursued a course of action that would lead to war and the rise of Washington and Hamilton. The financially ailing East India Company was deeply in debt and received a government bailout to the tune of £1.4 million. The Tea Act kept the three-pence tax on tea but gave the company a monopoly on the tea trade, which cut out American merchant middlemen and allowed the company to dump its surplus tea on American shores. George Washington and other Americans saw through the plan and characterized it as tyrannical.[33]

The Tea Act set off a firestorm of protest in American ports, most notably in Boston. On the evening of December 16, one day before the legal deadline for landing the tea, several thousand townspeople assembled at Old South to demand the return of the ships. The governor sent an inflammatory message to the crowd that read "I warn, exhort, and require you and each of you thus unlawfully assembled, forthwith to disperse and surcease all further unlawful proceedings at your utmost peril." The self-governing citizens at the town meeting went apoplectic when they heard the warning. Samuel Adams warned that nothing more could be done to save American liberties, while John Hancock was heard to yell, "Let every man do what is right in his own eyes." The frenzied crowd screamed "Boston harbor a teapot tonight!" and "The Mohawks are come!" while a war whoop signaled the "Mohawks," men dressed like Indians, to march down to the waterfront to destroy the tea.[34] Thousands followed the Mohawks as they marched down to Griffin's Wharf, where they boarded the three ships. They hoisted 342 casks of tea on deck, where they broke them open and dumped their contents into the harbor.[35]

Washington saw the Boston Tea Party in a measured way. On one hand, he recognized that the principles of self-government and the British constitution were at stake. On the other hand, he disapproved of mob rule where passion predominated over reason and prudence. "Not that we approve their conduct in destroying the tea," he wrote. Washington supported a constitutional rule of law for leaders and the people alike.[36]

The British learned of the Boston Tea Party at the end of January 1774. The destruction of the tea elicited much consternation in the ministry and in Parliament, where even those usually sympathetic to the American colonies condemned their actions. Benjamin Franklin noted the "torrent of clamor against us," though he agreed with Washington's condemnation of the "act of violent injustice on our part," destroying private property.[37]

The cabinet met and decided to take certain measures to "put an immediate stop to the present disorders" and for "better securing the execution of the laws, and the just dependence of the colonies upon the Crown and Parliament of Great Britain." On March 14, Lord North presented the Boston Port Bill to the House of Commons, which would close Boston Harbor on June 1 to all commerce until restitution was made to the East India Company for the entire value of the tea. He argued that since Boston "has been the ringleader of all violence and opposition to the execution of the laws of this country...Boston has not only therefore to answer for its own violence but for having incited other places to tumults."[38] He also stated that Parliament would not "sit still and see America" flaunt British authority and become "totally independent."[39]

During the spring, Parliament passed an additional wave of punitive laws to punish Boston for the tea party. The Massachusetts Government Act banned town meetings—and thus democratic self-government— and changed the colony's charter to allow greater royal control over who would serve on juries or committees of correspondence. The Impartial Administration of Justice Act permitted British officials in the colonies accused of a crime to be tried in England. Bostonians labeled this the "Murder Act," because soldiers could escape American justice after a capital crime. The Quartering Act allowed the quartering of troops in taverns and unoccupied private homes. Finally, the Quebec Act granted Canada the frontier land between the Ohio and Mississippi Rivers as well as freedom of religion to Roman Catholics.[40]

On May 10, 1774, the storm broke when Bostonians received official word of the Boston Port Act, closing Boston Harbor to all commerce, which would be utterly destructive to their economy. On May 12, Samuel Adams and the members of the committee of correspondence wrote a letter to the Virginia committee, informing them of the Port Act, which he called a "stroke of vengeance." Adams pleaded for a unified response that would frustrate the designs of the "cruel act" and help Bostonians endure the "severe trial," which they could not do alone.[41] On May 13, irate citizens gathered for a town meeting at Faneuil Hall and called on the other colonies to agree on an immediate joint boycott of British goods by all the colonies "till the act for blocking up this harbor be repealed" for the "salvation of North America and her liberties."[42] The following day, the committee dispatched the indefatigable rider, Paul Revere, on the first of his many important missions to Philadelphia and Annapolis to distribute the letters to colonial committees to the south.[43]

In the middle of this explosive situation, General Thomas Gage arrived in Boston on May 13, with orders from the king "to repel force and violence by every means within his reach." Gage replaced the defeated Thomas Hutchinson and had additional instructions to arrest patriot leaders John Hancock and Samuel Adams. Four regiments of redcoats were placed at Gage's disposal and were sailing for America. Gage arrived with the mission of enforcing the Coercive Acts with military force and quelling the tumult in riotous Boston.[44]

George Washington did not know of this dramatic turn of events when he left Mount Vernon for Williamsburg on May 12. Over the next week, Peyton Randolph, Edmund Pendleton, a young Thomas Jefferson, and the other members of the committee of correspondence received the letters from Boston with additional communications from Philadelphia, Baltimore, and Annapolis. They decided to lay them before the House of Burgesses that week for consideration.[45]

Events were indeed moving to a head elsewhere, and a shared

consensus on a united American reaction was building. On May 20, in New York, Alexander McDougall and radical Isaac Sears organized a gathering that created the Committee of Fifty-One, representing the radical Whigs. On May 22, after receiving Revere's pleas from Boston and letters from Philadelphia calling for support of Boston, the committee wrote to Boston, supporting the "common cause." They proposed that "a congress of deputies from the principle colonies is of the utmost moment; that it ought to be assembled without delay, and some unanimous resolution formed in this fatal emergency, not only respecting your deplorable circumstances, but for the security of our common rights." A few days later, Revere carried this letter back to Boston.[46]

In Virginia, on the evening of May 23, while Washington dined with Attorney General John Randolph, a group of others, including Thomas Jefferson and Patrick Henry, met in the empty council chamber of the Capitol and scoured through its fine library of books. There, in the words of Jefferson, they "cooked up a resolution" attempting to rally the people from their recent "lethargy."[47] The following day, the burgesses passed the resolution, unanimously calling for a day of fasting, humiliation, and prayer" on June 1, in support of their brethren in Boston.[48]

On May 25, Washington dined with the governor, and the following day, when the call for a day of fasting and prayer was printed in the *Virginia Gazette*, he rode out to Governor Dunmore's farm. He returned in time for the 11:00 a.m. start of the meeting of the House of Burgesses, which examined the several letters from the other assemblies and committees of correspondence.[49] Later that day, Dunmore learned of the resolution for a day of fasting and called the burgesses to his chamber, where he informed them that he was dissolving the body: "Mr. Speaker and Gentlemen of the House of Burgesses. I have in my hand a paper published by order of your house, conceived in such terms as reflect highly upon his Majesty and the Parliament of Great

Britain; which makes it necessary for me to dissolve you; and you are dissolved accordingly."[50]

Washington thought that the governor's order dissolving the house was an unnecessarily harsh measure condemning a moderate call for a day of fasting and prayer. He revealed that the burgesses were prepared to act much more radically: "This dissolution was as sudden as unexpected for there were other resolves of a much more spirited nature ready to be offered to the House which would have been unanimously adopted respecting the Boston Port Bill as it is called but were withheld till the important business of the country could be gone through."[51]

As they had done previously, the burgesses reassembled at the Apollo Room at Raleigh Tavern. On May 27, they agreed to a resolution that attacked the violation of American liberties, expressed solidarity with the people of Boston, called for a boycott of tea, and called for a general congress of the colonies. It read:

We are further clearly of opinion, that an attack, made on one of our sister colonies, to compel submission to arbitrary taxes, is an attack made on all British America, and threatens ruin to the rights of all, unless the united wisdom of the whole be applied. And for this purpose it is recommended to the committee of correspondence, that they communicate, with their several corresponding committees, on the expediency of appointing deputies from the several colonies of British America, to meet in general congress, at such place annually as shall be thought most convenient; there to deliberate on those general measures which the united interests of America may from time to time require.[52]

After meeting for a few additional days, on May 30, Speaker Randolph led the remaining burgesses to agree to meet within ninety days to discuss how to respond to Boston's plea for aid. Washington signed the resolution that day, stating that Virginia would join the other colonies seeking measures for the "preservation of the common rights and liberty of British America," especially a boycott. Although the governor was responsible for convening the assembly, they would meet on their own authority as a convention of the people's representatives. It was a dramatic act of self-government. The delegates signed their names to a dispatch written by Randolph: "We are sending dispatches to call together the late representatives to meet at Williamsburg on the first day of August next to conclude finally on these important questions."[53] The time would allow Virginia to receive more news from Massachusetts and give planters time to deliberate on the "alarming crisis" and develop "speedy, united councils of all those who have a regard for the common cause."[54]

On June 1, at ten o'clock, Speaker Randolph led the procession that included Washington to Bruton Parish Church to hear prayers and sermons on the day of fasting. Thomas Jefferson described the results: "The people met generally, with anxiety and alarm in their countenances, and the effect of the day through the colony was like a shock of electricity, arousing every man and placing him erect and solidly on his center."[55] Washington recorded simply in his diary: "Went to Church and fasted all day."[56] That night, he wrote his factors in London about tobacco shipments and orders of goods but doubted whether commerce would continue, since "it seems to be a matter of very great doubt at present."[57]

Over the next two months, Washington wrote a series of letters in which he reflected on the nature of the Coercive Acts and systematically developed his constitutional arguments. He believed he found indisputable evidence for a British conspiracy against American liberty. They were "endeavoring by every piece of art and despotism to fix the shackles of slavery upon us."[58] He asked, "Does it not appear, as clear as the sun in its meridian brightness, that there is a regular, systematic plan formed to fix the right and practice of taxation upon us? Does not the uniform conduct of Parliament for some years past confirm this?... Is not the attack upon the liberty and property of the people of Boston...a plain and self-evident proof of what they are aiming at?"[59]

For Washington, the dispute was rooted in the moral principle of consensual self-government, not economic self-interest: "For sir, what is it we are contending against? Is it against paying the duty of 3 pence per pound on tea because burthensome? No, it is the right only...setting forth that, as Englishmen, we could not be deprived of this essential, and valuable part of our constitution." The American colonists were only claiming a "right which by the law of nature and our constitution we are, in my opinion, indubitably entitled to." With a common-sense example, Washington explained, "I think the Parliament of Great Britain hath no more right to put their hands into my pocket, without my consent, than I have to put my hands into yours, for money."[60]

Washington thought that although he could not foresee the outcome, the colonies were united in resisting British tyranny: "The ministry may rely on it that Americans will never be taxed without their own consent, that the cause of Boston...is and ever will be considered as the cause of America (not that we approve their conduct in destroying the tea) and that we shall not suffer ourselves to be sacrificed by piecemeal though God only knows what is to become of us."[61] The time for choosing between liberty and death, freedom and slavery, was at hand. He stated, "the crisis is arrived when we must assert our rights, or submit to every imposition that can be heaped upon us; till custom and use, will make us as tame, and abject slaves, as the blacks we rule over with such arbitrary sway."[62] Washington thought that petitions had been tried and their time was at an end, and he countenanced the consideration of the use of force: "Ought we not, then, to put our virtue and fortitude to the severest test?"[63]

While George Washington contemplated going to war for American rights and liberties, on July 4, 1774, the New York Committee of

Fifty-One met and selected delegates to the approaching congress, which included a blend of moderates and radicals. Two days later, Alexander McDougall organized and led a public meeting that endorsed the chosen delegates, condemned the Boston Port Bill, supported the common cause with Boston, proposed nonimportation and nonexportation, sought aid for Boston, and instructed the delegates to the congress. Some New York conservatives thought this was a rump session with no legal standing, but the patriots thought differently, and the people gave it legitimacy.[64]

Alexander Hamilton reportedly attended the meeting and addressed the crowd as his first public act for the patriot movement. He attacked the Boston Port Act and called on his fellow New Yorkers to support "our brethren" in Boston who were "now suffering in the common cause of these colonies." He urged the various boycotts to win "the salvation of North America and her liberties" from the "fraud, power, and the most odious oppression." If the colonies united in the defense of their liberties, they would "rise triumphant over right, justice, social happiness, and freedom." The crowd was apparently astounded that such a young man addressed them with such eloquence and yelled, "It's a collegian!" Hamilton was making a name for himself, protesting British policies.[65]

Hamilton would later criticize other punitive laws, especially the Quebec Act. As with several other Founders, equating Roman Catholicism with tyranny crept into his thinking. Hamilton feared that it would establish "arbitrary power, and its great engine the Popish religion." The primacy of continental civil law over English common law was another reason he opposed the act. "While Canada was under the dominion of France," he wrote, "the French laws and customs were in force there; which are regulated in conformity to the genius and complexion of a despotic constitution." Under the English, however, there had been the "milder influence of the English laws; and his Majesty, by proclamation, promised to all those who should settle there, a full enjoyment of the rights of British subjects."[66]

Washington thought the Quebec Act was oppressive for different reasons. As a large speculator in western lands, he had a strong interest in his investments and in the promised bounty of land from commanding troops in the French and Indian War. In fact, he never let political events in Virginia interfere with lobbying the governor by letter or dinner to fulfill the decades-old promise that was frustrated by the Proclamation of 1763 and now seemed a dead letter with the Quebec Act. It violated his property rights and frustrated his designs to remain a wealthy and independent planter, as well as his vision of a strong continental empire.[67]

On July 14, Washington went back to Alexandria and was elected to the Virginia Convention. An English visitor described the election and the ball Washington threw afterward: "The candidates gave the populace a hogshead of toddy (what we call punch in England). In the evening the reelected burgess gave a ball to the freeholders and gentlemen of the town. This was conducted with great harmony. Coffee and chocolate, but no tea. This herb is in disgrace amongst them at present."[68]

On July 17, Washington attended church services, and "Col. Mason came in the afternoon and stayed all night." Since Mason was a member of the Fairfax resolutions committee, they probably spent this Sunday afternoon and evening perfecting a draft of the Fairfax County Resolves, which they posted for public consumption the following day.[69]

Washington went back to Alexandria and attended a meeting where his committee drafted the Fairfax Resolves. At the general meeting of the people, Washington found a "perfect satisfaction, and acquiescence to the measures proposed."[70] The resolves were adopted at this meeting. They were a vigorous defense of natural and constitutional rights as well as American self-government against British tyranny.[71]

The Fairfax County Resolves stated that the people were entitled to the rights of Englishmen and the "natural rights of mankind." Extorting taxes without the consent of the people was an "encroachment of despotism and tyranny," "diametrically contrary to the first principles of the constitution," and "totally incompatible with the principles of a free people." Arbitrary government was a calculated attempt to "reduce us, from a state of freedom and happiness, to slavery and misery."

The Fairfax County citizens also resolved to take certain measures to fight tyranny and oppressive government. First, they would take up a subscription to "purchase provisions, and consign them to some gentleman of character in Boston, to be distributed among the poorer sort of people there." They recommended a general congress of deputies from all the colonies to develop a common plan for the "defense and preservation of our common rights." They would adopt the classical republican ideals of "temperance, fortitude, frugality and industry," opposed to the luxury and indulgence characteristic of the monarchical government. They signed a nonimportation and nonexportation agreement, completely boycotting British goods. They agreed not to import slaves and leveled a withering critique of the slave trade with the influence of George Mason: "No slaves ought to be imported into any of the British colonies on this continent. And we take this opportunity of declaring our most earnest wishes, to see an entire stop forever put to such a wicked, cruel, and unnatural trade." Finally, implicitly promoting the use of force as Washington had done privately, they promised "we will use every means, which Heaven hath given us, to prevent our becoming its slaves."[72]

On July 28, Washington traveled to Williamsburg to participate in the first meeting of the delegates to the Virginia Convention, which was assembling to "take under their consideration the present critical and alarming situation of the continent of North America."[73] On August 1, the representatives probably met in the Capitol rather than Raleigh Tavern, despite the extralegal character of their meeting. Washington and more than one hundred delegates would meet for several days through August 6 and make momentous decisions regarding Virginian resistance to British policies.[74] He reported that "we never before had so full a meeting of delegates at any one time, as upon the present occasion."[75]

The planter-statesmen selected Peyton Randolph as the moderator of the convention. On the very first day of the meeting, the delegates called a "general congress of deputies from all the colonies" to assemble as quickly as possible "to procure redress for the much injured province of Massachusetts-Bay, to secure British America from the ravage and ruin of arbitrary taxes, and speedily as possible to procure the return of that harmony and union, so beneficial to the whole empire, and ardently desired by all British America."[76] On August 5, the delegates voted to select the members who would represent Virginia at the general congress in Philadelphia. Peyton Randolph, Richard Henry Lee, George Washington, Patrick Henry, Richard Bland, Benjamin Harrison, and Edmund Pendleton were the seven delegates who received the most votes.[77] Two anecdotes have survived related to Washington's military reputation. Thomas Lynch, a South Carolina delegate to the Continental Congress, attended the convention and heard, as he related to John Adams, Washington deliver a "most eloquent speech" asserting that "I will raise 1,000 men, subsist them at my own expense, and march myself at their head for the relief of Boston."[78] This would have been an uncharacteristic burst of passion in public deliberations where Washington was normally reserved and aloof. Virginian Edmund Randolph asserted that Washington was chosen to attend the Philadelphia meeting "to command an army, if an army should be raised," but this was many years after the fact and overestimates the extent to which many were contemplating war.[79]

On August 6, the members of the Virginia Convention agreed to a nonimportation and nonexportation association to protest the "unconstitutional" and "ill-advised regulations" that had caused "the deepest anxiety" and "most alarming apprehensions" of Virginians and across the colonies. The nonimportation agreement banned several goods and slaves and was scheduled to take effect on November 1. It sought to achieve "the strictest economy and frugality, and the exertion of every public virtue" in Virginia. The signers agreed to adhere religiously to the association until they achieved a "redress of all such American grievances." In deference to the tobacco planters, the nonexportation of tobacco would take effect later, on August 1, 1775, to allow them to ship one last crop. The association members also agreed to appoint enforcement committees, boycott tea, and support Boston with contributions.[80]

The historic Virginia Convention adjourned after signing the association agreement and delivering instructions to the seven chosen delegates to the general congress. The convention told the delegates to obtain a redress of American grievances so that the colonies might return to a "constitutional connection with Great Britain" and a "return of that intercourse of affection and commercial connection that formerly united both countries."[81] With a great deal of weight on his shoulders, Washington had much to contemplate as he departed for home on August 7.[82]

As Washington prepared for his trip to Philadelphia, he wrote to his friend, Bryan Fairfax. The letter reflected the deepening of Washington's thinking about the principles at stake in the dispute with Great Britain. The British taxes were clearly "subversive to the laws and constitution of Great Britain," but Washington also reflected that "an innate spirit of freedom first told me, that the measures which administration hath for sometime been, and now are, most violently pursuing, are repugnant to every principle of natural justice." Since the British were pursuing a plan to violate the natural rights of their subjects, he continued to wonder where the line "ought to be drawn." For Washington, "the crisis is arrived when we must assert our rights, or submit to every imposition that can be heaped upon us." Nothing, he stated, but "firmness" could prevent this intolerable situation from happening.[83] Washington went to Philadelphia believing in liberty or death as a moral principle.

On August 31, Edmund Pendleton and Patrick Henry arrived at Mount Vernon to pick up Washington for the journey to Philadelphia.

George Mason came to see his friends off. After dinner, they set out for Philadelphia, and according to Pendleton, Martha Washington gave them a Spartan-like admonition to stand firm in their demands against the British ministry. After taking rest in Annapolis and other towns along the way, the three Virginia delegates arrived in Philadelphia on September 4 and dined at the City Tavern.[84]

Washington and the other gentlemen of Virginia impressed their fellow delegates. John Adams described them as "the most spirited and consistent, of any."[85] Connecticut's Silas Deane thought that Washington had a "hard" countenance but an "easy, soldier-like air and gesture."

On September 5, Washington and forty-two other delegates (out of the fifty-six) assembled at Carpenter's Hall. During the first day, they unanimously elected Virginian Peyton Randolph, who enjoyed a continental reputation as a politician that probably exceeded Washington's as a war hero, as the chairman of the First Continental Congress.[86]

Although other members of various assemblies engaged in rhetorical debates displaying their grand eloquence and dramatic flair, George Washington remained relatively silent during the proceedings. He usually listened carefully and offered the gravity of his character rather than brilliance in debate—and this Congress was no different. While the Congress was debating its economic and political future and in between nightly dinners and entertainments, Washington reflected on current events privately in a letter. He wrote that the "most essential and valuable rights of mankind" were being violated, and every day "fresh proofs of a systematic assertion of an arbitrary power" were found. He did not believe that the "people of Massachusetts are rebellious, setting up for independence," but promised that "none of them will ever submit to the loss of those valuable rights…without which, life, liberty, and property are rendered totally insecure." The Congress included strong advocates for liberty who wished that "peace and tranquility, upon constitutional grounds" be restored and that the "horrors of civil discord [be] prevented."[87]

On October 14, the delegates agreed upon a Declaration of Rights and Grievances that trod familiar ground of American rights and liberties. They protested taxation without consent, standing armies in time of peace, and the Coercive Acts. They claimed the rights of mankind and of Englishmen and argued for a limited government that could not violate those rights: "That they are entitled to life, liberty, and property, & they have never ceded to any sovereign power whatever, a right to dispose of either without their consent."[88]

On October 20, the Congress agreed on a Continental Association based upon the model of Washington and Mason's Fairfax Resolves. It established a nonimportation agreement that would take effect almost immediately on December 1, and in deference to tobacco planters, the nonexportation ban would begin in September 1775. The association included a ban on slavery, as did the Fairfax Resolves.[89]

When the Congress concluded its work in late October, Washington traveled home, hoping for reconciliation but preparing for war if it came to that. John Adams and the Massachusetts delegation traveled through New York on the way home and met with the Sons of Liberty. We do not know if the relatively unknown Alexander Hamilton saw the delegation return home, but in the coming months, he would advance the patriot cause in New York in defending principles of liberty and self-government and the work of the First Continental Congress.

In late November, a pamphlet titled *Free Thoughts on the Proceedings of the Continental Congress*, signed by "A. W. Farmer," appeared in New York. It was an attack on the Continental Congress and the radical Whigs who met in Philadelphia and rioted in New York City. The author was Samuel Seabury, an Anglican priest, Tory, and graduate of Yale. Painting himself as a common farmer, he argued that the boycotts and other radical machinations of the Congress would primarily hurt ordinary people and benefit greedy, wealthy merchants. The Whigs were causing much ado over a trifling tax on tea that the upper classes could easily afford. Lumping together the Congress, associations, and mobs in the street, he railed, "a plague on them all."[90] Seabury warned that "the farmer that is in debt will be ruined: the farmer that is clear in the world will be obliged to run in debt to support his family: and while the proud merchant and the forsworn smuggler riot in their ill-gotten wealth, the laborious farmers, the grand support of every well-regulated country, must all go to the dogs together.—Vile! Shameful! Diabolical device!"[91]

Only three weeks later, Hamilton published a reply to Seabury titled *A Full Vindication of the Measures of the Congress*, in which he confidently entered the public debate over the Congress. He defended the Congress and anchored his reasoning in the ideas of John Locke and the compact theory of government, in which government was established to protect the natural rights and liberties of the people: "That Americans are entitled to freedom, is incontestable upon every rational principle. All men have one common original: they participate in one common nature, and consequently have one common right. No reason can be assigned why one man should exercise any power, or pre-eminence over his fellow creatures more than another; unless they have voluntarily vested him with it."[92] He argued that the Congress was driven to adopt boycotts by British actions. Like Washington, Hamilton considered the possibility of going to war but thought that that ultimate measure should be averted. Although further petitions would be fruitless, boycotts had forced Parliament to alter its policies several times over the past decade and would do so again. Besides, the Americans would reap additional benefits of becoming economically self-sufficient and developing their own manufactures.

Seabury did not let his anonymous adversary go unanswered and replied quickly with another pamphlet, *View of the Controversy Between Great Britain and Her Colonies*. Cutting to the quick, Seabury argued that Parliament had the power to regulate the American trade, taxes, and internal policies. He warned the people that the representatives in the Congress were not really chosen by the democratic people but by the radical Whigs and therefore were not truly representative of the common man.

In early February 1775, Hamilton published the lengthy rejoinder, *Farmer Refuted*, showing that he had mastered a wide variety of natural law and natural rights political thinkers at King's College. Hamilton asserted that "the origin of all civil government, justly established, must be a voluntary compact between the rulers and the ruled, and must be liable to such limitations as are necessary for the security of the absolute rights of the latter… To usurp dominion over a people in their own despite, or to grasp at a more extensive power than they are willing to entrust, is to violate that law of nature which gives every man a right to his personal liberty, and can therefore confer no obligation to obedience."[93] He quoted jurist Sir William Blackstone, who stated, "'The principal aim of society is to protect individuals in the enjoyment of those absolute rights which were vested in them by the immutable laws of nature.'"[94]

In the pamphlet, Hamilton wrote an eloquent statement of the rights of mankind and their inviolability that arguably rivaled the Declaration of Independence: "The sacred rights of mankind are not to be rummaged for, among old parchments, or musty records. They are written, as with a sun beam, in the whole volume of human nature, by the hand of the divinity itself; and can never be erased or obscured by mortal power."[95]

Washington had reached Mount Vernon on October 30 and did not have the luxury of writing pamphlets, since he bore the heavy weight of preparing for war. Although he conducted normal business at his plantation, he stated that the "times are ticklish," and he was distracted by larger events.[96] On November 13, he met with men from Prince William County and accepted the command of its independent military company. In the coming months, he accepted the command of four other independent companies in Fairfax, Fauquier, Richmond, and Prince William counties. In mid-January 1775, he reviewed the Fairfax County company and drilled the men. He also chaired the county committee, acting as local government, which taxed each citizen three shillings to pay for gunpowder and organized the militia. The committee resolved that a "well-regulated militia, composed of gentlemen, freeholders, and other freemen, is the natural strength and only staple security of a free government."[97]

Washington corresponded and met with a number of people regarding other martial preparations. They sent him military treatises on discipline and strategy for him to study. They purchased fifes and drums, flags, uniforms, muskets, bayonets, cartridges, and pouches for the men under his command. Washington hosted Charles Lee, a retired British officer and veteran of the Braddock Expedition, at Mount Vernon to discuss military matters.[98]

On February 20, Washington traveled to Alexandria for the elections to the Second Virginia Convention that was convening in Richmond in March.[99] He was elected, and his resolve to serve was strengthened a few days later when he learned of King George III's address to Parliament. Washington thought the speech "prognosticate[s] nothing favorable to us," and the speech and other correspondence he received from London convinced him that "there is reason to believe, the ministry would willingly change their ground, from a conviction the forcible measures will be inadequate to the end designed. A little time must now unfold the mystery, as matters are drawing to a point."[100]

With the threat of war looming ever closer, on March 15, Washington set out for the Second Virginia Convention in Richmond and reviewed several militia companies along the way. On March 20, he arrived in Richmond and joined the other delegates in the tense Virginia Convention at St. John's Church. The following day, Washington and his fellow delegates to the First Continental Congress formally reported on the proceedings in Philadelphia the previous fall. The Virginia Convention endorsed the resolutions of the Continental Congress and thanked the delegates for their "unremitted endeavors to maintain and preserve inviolate the just rights and liberties of his Majesty's dutiful and loyal subjects in America."[101]

On March 23, radical Patrick Henry rose from his seat and railed that British armies in America were stripping away their cherished liberties. Coming to the same conclusions as Washington, Henry sought to persuade the convention that the time for petitions was past and the time for war had come. "I repeat it, sir, we must fight! An appeal to arms and to the God of Hosts is all that is left us!" He finished the speech with his famous words: "I know not what course others may take; but as for me, give me liberty, or give me death!" Dramatically, Henry plunged an imaginary dagger into his heart and slumped into his chair.[102] Afterward, Washington was among the men chosen for the resulting committee to "prepare a plan for embodying, arming, and disciplining such a number of men as may be sufficient for that purpose."[103]

A few days later, Washington and the other six delegates to the First Continental Congress were selected again to represent Virginia at the Second Continental Congress that was scheduled to meet in Philadelphia in May. The convention also authorized a militia, provided for its ammunition, and stated that each man would be armed with a "tomahawk, one pound of gunpowder, and four pounds of ball" and clothed "in a hunting shirt by way of uniform." On March 31, Washington returned to Mount Vernon with his colony even closer to war.[104]

That spring, Alexander Hamilton also showed that he was firmly dedicated to the patriot cause, but much like Washington, he opposed the destruction of lives and property engendered by mob rule. When a "murderous" mob of hundreds marched through the night on the home of Reverend Myles Cooper, possibly bent on tarring and feathering the college president, Hamilton and Robert Troup saved Cooper from the vicious punishment against Tories. Hamilton supposedly harangued the mob by shouting they would "disgrace and injure the glorious cause of liberty" and caused them to reconsider their actions, thus buying Cooper precious seconds to escape. He may have simply awoken Cooper and whisked him away to a friend's house near the Hudson. Either way, Cooper found refuge on a British warship and fled America.[105]

In a later episode, Connecticut militiamen advanced against Tories in New York, captured Samuel Seabury, and marched on the print shop of James Rivington, the Tory printer who had printed Seabury's pamphlets (though he also published those of patriot Hamilton). They seized the type and smashed the press. Hamilton was said to have given this group a tongue-lashing as well. Even though he thought Rivington's press was "dangerous and pernicious," he opposed riotous mobs: "In times of such commotion as the present, while the passions of men are worked up to an uncommon pitch, there is great danger of fatal extremes. The same state of the passions which fits the multitude, who have not a sufficient stock of reason and knowledge to guide them…very naturally leads to a contempt and disregard for all authority."[106]

During the spring, the Tory-dominated New York legislature was disbanded. After the people formed the New York Provincial Congress and elected their chosen representatives, they selected delegates to the Second Continental Congress.[107] Hamilton, of course, was still relatively unknown and not a leader in the New York patriot movement, so he was not considered. But the impending war would propel him to a continental stage in the army that dwarfed provincial politics.

In Virginia and New York, delegates were preparing to depart for Philadelphia for the meeting of the Second Continental Congress. Whether the outcome would be war or peace, no one could foresee. Meanwhile, militias in both states—and around the American colonies—prepared for the war that seemed imminent. When the redcoats marched on Concord to seize a cache of weapons, war did erupt. And an alliance was forged in the crucible of that war—one that would create a new nation.

CHAPTER FOUR

REVOLUTIONARY BAND OF BROTHERS

THE AMERICAN REVOLUTION WAS the pivotal event that shaped George Washington's life and secured his reputation as the "Father of His Country." While General Washington lost more battles than he won, he possessed a preternatural fortitude in the face of repeated setbacks that would have broken most men. Over time, he came to grasp the central truth of the American war effort: the success of the "glorious cause" rested entirely on his ability to keep his army alive. Similarly, the upstart college student Alexander Hamilton was fiercely dedicated to the patriot cause and played a central role as Washington's aide-de-camp. As with Washington, the war was the seminal event in Hamilton's life and provided him with an opportunity to showcase his considerable talents.

The pair met for the first time on the battlefields of New York as the unseasoned Continental army narrowly escaped destruction against the larger, better trained and equipped British forces. Washington and Hamilton labored to hold the army together and find a way to defeat the British, becoming intimates who shared the horrors of war and the decisions that determined military success. There were times when the declining fortunes of the army and their different characters strained their friendship and in fact broke it once, during one of the darkest hours of the war.

Washington and his lieutenants confronted a unique challenge, one not seen since the ancient Roman republic and the early modern Venetian and Florentine republics, in that they led a republican army that existed at the grace of Congress. The general set an example of respect for civil-military relations as he endured the miserly, self-interested policies of the Congress and states with as much fortitude as he brought to his command against the British. Although continually frustrated by the civilian government, his deference to its republican authority never flagged. At the end of the war, Washington voluntarily surrendered his commission, offering a startling contrast to the numerous historical examples of heroes who had succumbed to ambition and set up a dictatorship. Thus he earned the reputation for republican virtue that he had worked so hard to cultivate.

For his part, Hamilton immediately joined the patriot cause. He acted courageously under fire and commanded Washington's attention during the Battle of New York and the retreat across New Jersey. Washington invited the brilliant young man to join his staff of trusted advisors. Hamilton earned the confidence Washington placed in him but also sought military glory on the battlefield, something he had desired since the age of fourteen. This yearning contributed to the breaking of their indispensable relationship during the war. Hamilton finally won command at Yorktown and stormed the British defenses during the decisive battle of the war.[1] No one might predict what would become of their relationship, but as the war ended, Washington and Hamilton shared a belief in republican government but with a national outlook and stronger national government—if that new nation were to last.

★★★

As the crisis with Great Britain steadily worsened in the spring of 1775, Washington and Hamilton each made preparations for war. In Virginia, Washington, hero of the French and Indian War two decades before, was chosen as commander of the five regiments that were raised in the colony. He also purchased several items for war, including a tomahawk and books on military science. New Yorkers mobilized for war as well, raiding the city arsenal for weapons in their defense. Hamilton was an inexperienced if enthusiastic youth who poured over military books and joined the Corsicans, a volunteer militia company that had revolutionary slogan "Liberty or Death" stitched into their clothing.

Neither Washington nor Hamilton was present on the night of April 18 when British general Thomas Gage sent infantry through the Massachusetts countryside to seize colonial weapons caches and capture the prominent rebels Samuel Adams and John Hancock at Concord and Worcester. A battle ensued on the Lexington Green and at Concord Bridge, with the two sides exchanging fire until the British formed ranks and marched back to Boston. The Americans pursued the British and fired at them from behind buildings and nearby woods, harassing the exhausted redcoats the entire way. There was no turning back at this point; the American Revolution had begun.[2]

Word of the fighting to the north quickly spread throughout the colonies. On May 4, Washington left for Philadelphia, intent on commanding the army as men grabbed their muskets and headed to New England. Congress convened on May 10 and busily mobilized for war. The members of the Congress appointed Washington to several military committees due to his combat experience. On June 14, 1775, Congress approved a plan to raise a Continental army made up of troops from all of the colonies to support Boston. The next day, Congress selected Washington as the commander of "all the continental forces, raised, or to be raised, for the defense of American liberty."[3]

There was little doubt that Washington would be selected to lead the Continental army. The famous hero of the French and Indian War pulled out his musty uniform and wore it conspicuously while attending sessions in Congress, all the while possessing a martial dignity and remaining silently above the political fray.[4] He was a known supporter of republican liberties yet was not seen as an unpredictable firebrand. A fellow member of Congress was deeply impressed by Washington and described him as "discreet and virtuous, no harum scarum ranting swearing fellow but sober, steady, and calm. His modesty will induce him I dare say to take and order every step with the best advice possible to be obtained in the army."[5]

As a Virginian, Washington was a symbol of intercolonial unity. Expressing a common sentiment in Congress, Massachusetts delegate John Adams viewed Washington as "a gentleman whose skill and experience as an officer, whose independent fortune, great talents, and excellent universal character would command the approbation of all America and unite the cordial exertions of all the colonies better than any other person in the Union."[6] As a member of the House of Burgesses and experienced war commander, Washington was familiar with civil-military relations, and this convinced Congress that it could entrust him with power over a continental army. Nonetheless, because of the republican fear of standing armies and tyranny, Congress reminded him of his subordination to its civilian authority. It directed him to follow "such orders and directions from time to time as you shall receive from this or a future Congress of the said united colonies."[7]

Washington was the unanimous selection of a Congress that was sharply divided on many issues. He accepted his new commission with a sense of gravity and great humility, telling Congress:

I am truly sensible of the high honor done me in this appointment, yet I feel great distress, from a consciousness that my abilities and military experience may not be equal to the extensive and important trust. However, as the Congress desires it, I will enter upon the momentous duty and exert every power I possess in their service and for the support of the glorious cause. I beg they will accept my most cordial thanks for this distinguished testimony of their approbation...I, this day, declare with the utmost sincerity, I do not think myself equal to the command I am honored with.[8]

Further, he refused the proffered salary because he did not wish to profit by service to his country and asked only that his expenses be reimbursed. John Adams admired this selfless act and observed, "His views are noble and disinterested."[9]

Nevertheless, Washington was apprehensive that poor leadership on his part or a humiliating defeat would ruin his honor. The famous physician Dr. Benjamin Rush related that Washington bemoaned the potential consequences of his appointment to fellow Virginian, Patrick Henry: "Remember, Mr. Henry, what I now tell you: From the day I enter upon the command of the American armies, I date my fall, and the ruin of my reputation."[10] On the other hand, Washington feared that refusing the appointment would demonstrate a dishonorable lack of patriotism.

In letters home, Washington asked for the assistance of Providence in performing his new duties. He thought he had the characteristics necessary for good leadership: a firm belief in the cause for liberty, a faithful adherence to his duties, and integrity. Also, he had a chance to secure immortal fame by leading the patriot army.[11] At the same time, he distanced himself from any accusation of being motivated by selfish ambition: "It is an honor I by no means aspired to—It is an honor I wished to avoid as well as from an unwillingness to quit the peaceful enjoyment of my Family, as from a thorough conviction of my own incapacity and want of experience... May God grant therefore that my acceptance of it may be attended with some good to the common cause and without injury to my own reputation."[12]

Meanwhile, on June 17, the war in Boston proceeded without knowledge of the new American army or its commander when the British made three costly assaults on Breed's Hill against entrenched American militia who had marched up and silently occupied the hill the night before. Americans celebrated their great moral victory in the battle they named Bunker Hill and took away the lesson that their fervent desire for liberty would defeat the more disciplined, professional British army. Their new general would seek to disabuse them of this naïve notion.[13]

On June 23, Washington left Philadelphia for Boston to assume command of the army. In New York, he received an address from the Provincial Congress expressing a hope that at the end of the conflict, he would "cheerfully resign the important deposit committed into your hands, and reassume the character of our worthiest citizen." The fear of a large standing army ran deep among a republican people fighting for their liberty, but the Continental Congress had chosen the right man as commander in chief. Washington promised the state assembly that when American liberty had been firmly established, he would return to his "private station in the bosom of a free, peaceful, and happy country."[14] Soon after this, he wrote to British general Thomas Gage, "I cannot conceive any more honorable [rank], than that which flows from the uncorrupted choice of a brave and free people—the purest source and original fountain of all power."[15] Throughout the war, Washington would defer to Congress as representative of the sovereign people, even when it damaged the war-making abilities of the army, which it did on multiple occasions.

On July 3, the Massachusetts assembly sent Washington a message, cautioning him that the army's discipline was a work in progress. He was a realist regarding human nature and assured the assembly that the "course of human affairs forbids an expectation that troops formed under such circumstances should at once possess the order, regularity, and discipline of veterans." However, when he took command of the army, he saw that the assembly's concern was, if anything, understated. Washington told numerous correspondents that his "great concern" was to establish discipline in the army or "general confusion must infallibly ensue."[16] And it would be difficult to establish discipline in an army while facing an enemy encamped only a mile away.

Much of the discipline problem stemmed from the democratic spirit of the people of Massachusetts. The citizen-soldiers of the militias had a strong streak of independence, as could be seen in their practice of democratically electing their officers from among the soldiers. Washington put an end to this practice, because it tended to make the officers "curry favor with the men" rather than strictly enforce orders. It did not help that the states also had a great deal of control over the appointment of officers, which he begged Congress to change.

Washington issued various orders to the army with instructions that they were to maintain the strictest discipline. To that end, he forbade cursing and drunkenness and emphasized the need for cleanliness in order to prevent outbreaks of sickness in camp. He urged the men to attend religious services "to implore the blessings of heaven upon the means used for our safety and defense."[17] The general even issued orders for his men to cease skinny-dipping in front of ladies and other passersby. The Continental army was to be a disciplined, moral army under Washington's command.

Washington had many other problems to contend with while establishing his army. He begged Congress and nearby states to supply his army with adequate weapons, gunpowder, food, and clothing, and he did not stop doing so until the war ended. Smallpox and other illnesses plagued his army and reduced its strength, causing him to lay down rules pertaining to the cooking of food and digging latrines. One of the most serious problems confronting the general was that his army lost men when their short enlistments expired and they walked home. He warned Congress that unless it acted to lengthen the terms of service, his army would simply dissolve.

Perhaps Washington's greatest concern at this time was creating a truly continental army. The soldiers considered themselves citizens of the states from which they hailed, and inculcating a devotion to the common cause and creating a national allegiance was a daunting challenge. As Washington told John Hancock, he wanted to find a means of abolishing "those provincial distinctions which lead to jealousy and dissatisfaction."[18] He commanded his army to join Boston in a day of thanksgiving and prayer for liberty and to "strengthen the harmony of the United Colonies."[19] On August 5, 1775, Washington informed the army that "the regiments of the several provinces that form the Continental Army, are to be considered no longer in a separate and distinct point of view, but as parts of the whole army of the United provinces."[20]

In more candid letters, Washington expressed a great deal of frustration with the army he led and his low opinion of New Englanders generally. He stated, "The people of this government have obtained a character which they are by no means deserved—their officers generally are the most indifferent kind of people I ever saw… They are an exceeding dirty and nasty people."[21] By November, a kind of malaise grew in Washington's mind. He thought there was "a dearth of public spirit and want of virtue" and noted that a "dirty, mercenary spirit pervades the whole." These problems led him to regret his decision to lead the army: "No consideration upon Earth should have induced me to accept this command."[22]

Militiaman Alexander Hamilton remained in New York far from the action, spending some of his time helping to bolster the city's defenses. War had not yet come to New York, but the warship *Asia* demonstrated British naval superiority and New York's vulnerability when it patrolled unchallenged around the surrounding waters. The Provincial Congress was concerned that the British might seize its guns at the tip of the battery, thereby rendering the city almost defenseless against the might of the British navy. Young Hamilton's recklessness almost got him killed when he came under fire trying to preserve the city's fortifications. He and his comrades at King's College rescued several cannon from the battery while a barge from the *Asia* bombarded them. They were forced to depart when the barrage became too heavy. When his friend Hercules Mulligan left Hamilton's musket at the fort, Hamilton foolhardily went back for it "with as much unconcern as if the vessel had not been there" and recovered his weapon.[23]

In the coming months, Hamilton would have to settle for a war of words as he penned a series of essays under the pseudonym "Monitor." He urged Americans to act boldly in the face of British tyranny and invasion: "In public exigencies, there is hardly anything more prejudicial than excessive caution, timidity and dilatoriness, as there is nothing more beneficial than vigor, enterprise and expedition." He warned against "a humble submission to arbitrary rule." He also continued to study and attend class despite the war. Besides the brief exhilaration of protecting the city's guns, Hamilton drilled with the militia and dreamed that he might participate in the glorious cause for liberty soon. He was eager to get into the fight but was frustrated that he had still not fired a shot.[24]

During the fall of 1775, the two armies faced each other in Boston for months in a monotonous standoff. Washington believed that the American army had to engage the enemy if he was to keep his soldiers inspired, especially before their enlistments expired, but his generals argued against such an attack. He trusted their judgment and listened when they advised him to occupy Dorchester Heights in order to utilize the artillery that the obese but vigorous Henry Knox miraculously dragged hundreds of miles across frozen rivers and over mountains from Fort Ticonderoga to Boston in the middle of winter. On the night of March 4, 1776, the Americans surprised the British by occupying the heights and putting up barricades of furniture and bales of hay because the ground was too frozen for digging trenches as at Bunker Hill. With American artillery now stationed on higher ground and British troops and vessels vulnerable, General William Howe decided to depart. Seeing British preparations to withdraw, Washington dispatched General Charles Lee to reinforce New York in case the British attacked there. Washington kept troops stationed in Boston, because he was unsure about British intentions and feared they might return. He was indecisive about the best course of action.[25]

While General Washington watched the British army put to sea, the New York Provincial Congress raised an artillery company to provide for the defense of New York. Alexander Hamilton's friend, Alexander McDougall, was in charge of raising the New York regiment and recommended him for a captaincy of the artillery in February. Hamilton's only qualifications for the position were a deep reading in books on artillery, some drill, and a patriotic thirst for glory. Hamilton mustered a company of men and immediately set to outfitting them properly and instilling military discipline in the ranks. He lobbied the Congress a number of times for better pay and rations equal to those of the Continental army, because he recognized that his men would be guided by their interest to seek better pay there. He was training his men when the Continental army marched into New York, and the strapping young captain whipping his men into shape appears to have caught the attention of Nathaniel Greene, a general close to Washington. Greene was supposedly impressed by the young man when they dined together. If true, Washington might have heard about the young patriot from Greene, whom he deeply admired.[26] Hamilton may have also been offered a position as an aide to Brigadier General Lord Stirling, which he turned down. He desperately wanted to be in the middle of battle and would now get his chance. In April, General Washington arrived in New York City and immediately prepared for an expected British invasion.

Washington struggled over how to defend New York against the

British, whose unchallenged naval supremacy permitted them to land troops at any point of their choosing. He was unsure about where to place his troops and eventually split his forces between Long Island and Manhattan, a critical mistake. At the end of May, he wrote, "We expect a very bloody summer... I am sorry to say that we are not, either in men or arms, prepared for it." The Continental army was outnumbered, outgunned, and outgeneraled. Washington prepared the best he knew how and hoped that Providence would bless his army because its cause was just.[27]

On July 2, the British landed unopposed on Staten Island with a vast armada of hundreds of ships and more than thirty-two thousand British and Hessian troops—against less than twenty thousand for the Continental army. That day, Washington tried to rouse his men's spirits with an appeal to the moral vision of why they were fighting: "The time is now near at hand which must probably determine whether Americans are to be free men or slaves; whether they are to have any property they can call their own; whether their houses and farms are to be pillaged and destroyed, and they consigned to a state of wretchedness from which no human efforts will probably deliver them. The fate of unborn millions will now depend, under God, on the courage and conduct of this army."[28] While it is difficult to determine whether the soldiers were moved by Washington's words, they prepared their defenses and stood ready to fight against a larger, more powerful foe.

Meanwhile, in Philadelphia, John Adams and John Dickinson had just completed an epic debate over American independence. That day, Congress adopted Richard Henry Lee's motion from the previous month that "these United Colonies are, and of right ought to be, free and independent States."[29] On July 4, the delegates adopted Thomas Jefferson's eloquent Declaration of Independence, asserting the natural rights of mankind, the social compact of consensual government, and the list of grievances that compelled Americans to seek independence.[30] Around the colonies, thirteen toasts were drunk, church bells tolled, and

the king was burned in effigy. On July 9 in New York, the announce-
ment that America had declared its independence from Great Britain
was met with enthusiastic approval by a mob, including soldiers, who
toppled a statue of King George III and melted the lead into 42,088
bullets for use against the British. Washington told his troops that he
hoped "this important event will serve as a fresh incentive to every
officer and soldier to act with fidelity and courage."[31]

Washington tried to bolster the strength of the army by promoting
their unity. In the wake of the Declaration, he entreated his men to
support the noble cause in which they were engaged with "one hand
and one heart." He told them that "the honor and success of the army
and the safety of our bleeding country depends upon harmony and
good agreement with each other." He was slowly molding a continental army and promoting a national union through it.[32]

Washington built his defenses on Brooklyn Heights and waited.
Meanwhile, on July 12, Admiral Richard Howe sent the heavily armed
Phoenix and the *Rose* to terrorize soldiers and civilians on Manhattan
and to test the defenses, especially at the battery. Captain Hamilton and
his artillery company weakly returned fire and ended up blowing up
some of their own guns, killing several men in the process. Washington
described the event as "proof of the incompetence of [our] batteries."[33]
After demonstrating the weakness of American defenses, the warships
sailed up the Hudson River unopposed. It was an inauspicious start for
Hamilton, though Washington soon suffered an even greater blow.

On August 22, the massive British army began rolling toward the
American defenses on Brooklyn Heights. The next day, Washington
tried to bolster his men with patriotic words: "Remember officers and
soldiers that you are freemen, fighting for the blessings of liberty—that
slavery will be your portion, and that of your posterity, if you do not
acquit yourselves like men... Those who are distinguished for their
gallantry and good conduct may depend upon being honorably noticed
and suitably rewarded...and acquire to themselves immortal honor."[34]

Despite such inspiring words, the British flanked the American army and routed it, launching a three-pronged attack with Generals William Howe, Henry Clinton, and Charles Cornwallis wheeling around to the right and smashing through a gap in the Continental lines at the Jamaica Pass. A feint by British ships forced Washington to keep half his men on Manhattan rather than reinforce the lines on Long Island. Moreover, Washington had had to replace the ill General Nathaniel Greene at the last minute with General John Sullivan.

The battle was disastrous for the Americans. Hundreds of men were killed, with scores slain by Hessian bayonets even after surrendering. Hundreds more were captured, including Generals Stirling and Sullivan. To Washington's consternation, those Americans who were not encircled retreated all along the line. He reinforced his crumbling Long Island army with three regiments to prevent total disaster.

On August 28, a hastily convened council of war convinced him to pull the army of ten thousand back to Manhattan. The experienced sailors of the Massachusetts regiments heroically accomplished this mission overnight without losing a single man. Washington personally took command of the crossing, and it was completed less than an hour before the British forces arrived. A dense fog had rolled in and covered the retreat, causing many to think they saw the hand of Providence at work.[35]

The British initially paused but then landed on Manhattan a few weeks later and continued to drive the Americans into a headlong retreat. American soldiers deserted by the hundreds, and those who remained were filled with despair and confusion. It was an embarrassing scene for Washington, who allegedly took to cursing and horse whipping his men as he could no longer contain his famous temper. Unable to control the chaos, he wailed, "Are these the men with whom I am to defend America?" In the midst of this outburst, Washington failed to notice the close proximity of the enemy and barely escaped capture. He was confounded by a mobile army that could land troops anywhere and flank the Continentals.[36]

Hamilton, by contrast, albeit with significantly less responsibility, coolly led his men as his artillery company covered the retreating army while it fled to Harlem Heights. In their haste, his company was forced to abandon all but two of their artillery pieces. Exhibiting great courage in the heat of battle, Hamilton was one of the last Americans to reach Harlem and organized the building of a defensive earthen work redoubt. Behind these defenses, the Americans repulsed a British attack on September 16. Washington probably noticed Hamilton's leadership during the retreat. Hamilton's son later claimed that Washington invited Hamilton to the command tent for a conversation, although no firm evidence exists to prove this. Nevertheless, Hamilton's company was incorporated into the Continental army and placed under the command of General Henry Knox. Washington pulled back to White Plains, where Hamilton's artillery pounded the British and Hessian troops as they attacked across the Bronx River.

In calmer moments, Washington finally recognized that retreat was necessary. The British had too many soldiers and too many advantages, including the world's finest navy and far more experience than the Americans. Washington told John Hancock that experience had proven that America should fight a defensive war, or a war of posts, and the two men had a running debate over whether Washington was going to abandon and even burn New York to deny it to the British (as Washington preferred). Although constant retreat left the army discouraged, wisdom dictated that Washington should delay a direct confrontation with the British army until the time was ripe.

The troops were not the only ones becoming dejected over the army's retreat. Washington himself was increasingly subject to bouts of self-doubt. He wrote home, "If I were to wish the bitterest curse to an enemy on this side of the grave, I should put him in my stead with my feelings... I do not know what plan of conduct to pursue. I see the impossibility of serving with reputation, or doing any essential service to the cause by continuing in command... In confidence I tell you that

I never was in such an unhappy, divided state since I was born."[37] It is a measure of his character and leadership that he managed to rally his own spirits and that of his men to persevere during their retreat.

Bitter experience had led Washington to conclude that depending on militias was no way to fight the war. They were too poorly disciplined and trained, and their short enlistments meant that inexperienced soldiers were constantly rotated into the ranks of fluctuating regiments. The militias, Washington feared, "will totally ruin our cause."[38] He advocated the creation of a standing army, despite republican fears, but he now recognized that the greater threat to liberty was defeat.

Compounding matters, the ambitious general Charles Lee was furious with Washington for allowing "absurd interference" by the "cattle" in Congress and wanted him to menace the body into granting him greater powers.[39] Rejecting this advice out of hand, Washington remained steadfast in his deference to civilian authority. As his army disintegrated around him, he made requests to the Massachusetts, Pennsylvania, and New Jersey legislatures for more troops. When they failed to meet his requisitions, he begged even more.

On November 12, 1776, unsure of British intentions and confused about his own, Washington divided his forces and withdrew over two thousand men across the Hudson. Forts Washington and Lee were sentinels that were supposed to impede the enemy from sailing up the Hudson. In reality, the British navy continued to travel the river unopposed. Against Washington's better judgment, a council of war decided to hold Fort Washington under Greene's command. The commander wondered to General Greene, "What valuable purpose can it answer to attempt to hold a post from which the expected benefit cannot be had?"[40] On November 16, General Howe attacked the fort with thirteen thousand troops, and it capitulated in hours within sight of a dejected Washington and Greene. Almost three thousand men surrendered and were taken prisoner, along with supplies that the Americans could ill afford to lose.[41]

As the Continental army retreated across New Jersey over the next month, its situation remained grim. Washington marched his army through Hackensack and Newark with the British in hot pursuit. He finally received a thousand New Jersey militiamen in late November and another thousand from Philadelphia, but on December 1, he lost another two thousand militiamen from New Jersey and Maryland whose enlistments expired. Hundreds of other dispirited soldiers simply deserted. Washington slowly augmented his army, but he expected to lose more men when their enlistments expired at the end of the year.

He also failed to convince General Charles Lee and his fifty-five hundred men to reinforce his beleaguered army. The imperious Lee was highly critical of Washington, writing that "a certain great man is damnably deficient."[42] Washington tried to cajole his generals into obedience and hesitated in issuing a direct command to Lee to merge his forces with the main body of the army. In late November, Washington wrote Lee, "I would have you move over by the easiest and best passage."[43] A week later, Washington wrote, "My former letters were so full and explicit as to the necessity of your marching as early as possible…that I confess I expected you would have been sooner in motion."[44] Still, Lee did not bring his army, because he was intent on pursuing his own glory. On December 12, Lee was rewarded for his hubris when the British captured him in a tavern.

During these desperate times, Washington and his officers noticed Hamilton's actions with great interest. On December 1, Washington led his army across the Raritan River at New Brunswick, one step ahead of the British. Because it was shallow, the river afforded many crossing places for the advancing enemy. Since Washington's army did not have adequate numbers to make a stand, he decided to continue the retreat, and Hamilton's artillery provided covering fire for the patriots to make good their escape.

In a letter to Congress, Washington indirectly praised Hamilton, writing that the British had appeared "in several parties on the heights opposite Brunswick and were advancing in a large body towards the crossing place. We had a smart cannonade while we were parading out men but without any or but little loss on either side."[45] One contemporary source explained that Washington "was charmed by the brilliant courage and admirable skill" that Hamilton exhibited when he delivered his fire into the British ranks.[46] This account seems plausible, since Washington would have witnessed and applauded individual courageous actions by his men in such a small army.

However brave, the Continental army was suffering horribly. The soldiers lacked winter clothing, blankets, and often shoes as they marched through snow and across rivers. There was little hope of enticing the soldiers to reenlist for a losing cause when the year ran out. Near Trenton, Washington's army crossed the Delaware River and destroyed the unused boats for miles around to deny the British pursuit. In response, General Howe marched most of the British forces to winter quarters in New York and left a small Hessian mercenary force guarding Trenton.

Washington decided on a bold attack to raise his army's spirits and prevent it from crumbling on January 1 when enlistments ended. Revolutionary financier Robert Morris scrounged up money and supplies for the distressed army. The army was reinforced by the arrival of two thousand of Lee's soldiers under Sullivan. Thomas Paine, who was then traveling with the army, contributed stirring words in his pamphlet, *The American Crisis*, to bolster the men's spirits: "These are the times that try men's souls. The summer soldier and the sunshine patriot will, in this crisis, shrink from the service of their country; but he that stands it now, deserves the love and thanks of man and woman."[47]

In the dark hours of Christmas night, Washington led the Americans across the ice-choked Delaware River through a storm of sleet and snow. Henry Knox once again accomplished what seemed impossible when he ferried the artillery across the river, capitalizing on the talents of his Massachusetts watermen. Washington split his army into two columns; he and Greene led one and Sullivan the other. Shoeless men left trails of blood in the snow as they marched; a few dropped dead from exposure.[48]

The Continental army surprised the sleeping Hessians, and when the alarm was finally sounded, the groggy Hessians hastily grabbed their arms, entered the streets, and attempted to launch a counterattack. They could not form up under the withering fire and lost their commander, Colonel Johann Rall. Hamilton was in the vanguard of the attack and set up his artillery on King Street, the main thoroughfare. He kept his men steady as his company engaged in an artillery duel with the Hessians and poured whiffs of grapeshot into their ranks to cut them down. Sullivan led a bayonet charge into the enemy ranks. While some Hessians escaped, they lost one hundred men, and almost one thousand surrendered within an hour of the battle commencing. An astounding two Americans were killed in battle, and a handful were wounded, including Washington's fellow Virginian, James Monroe. Reflecting on the victory, Washington thought that "we should rather exert ourselves, and look forward with hopes, that some lucky chance may yet turn up in our favor."[49] It was decisive action rather than luck that gave Washington (and Hamilton) a great victory as the army recrossed the Delaware.

Washington agonized over what to do next. He savored the victory, but it was not enough to hold the army together. Moreover, General Cornwallis had marched some eight thousand men from New York, presenting Washington with an opportunity should he prove as bold as at Trenton. He set the wheels in motion for another crossing and attack.

Fearful of the proximity of the enemy, Congress fled Philadelphia in disarray. Before it left, it temporarily invested Washington with dictatorial powers to do what was necessary to fight the war. The general wrote Congress and explained that "instead of thinking myself freed from all civil obligations, by this mark of their confidence, I shall constantly bear in mind that, as the sword was the last resort for the preservation of our liberties, so it ought to be the first thing laid aside." He quickly deferred to the civil control of his army and surrendered these dictatorial powers.

On December 29, under even more dangerous conditions than on Christmas Eve, the army again moved back across the Delaware into Trenton, where it received reinforcements and an emergency enlistment bonus from Robert Morris in Philadelphia. Though it still lacked adequate supplies, the army's morale was bolstered by its victory at Trenton. On December 30, Washington prepared for another daring assault, this time on Princeton. First, he had to persuade a New England regiment to stay for one more chance at glory. Washington appealed to the hesitant men to remain in the army and fight again, even though their enlistments were set to expire. He told them, "My brave fellows, you have done all that I asked you to do, and more than you could be reasonably expected, but your country is at stake, your wives, your houses, and all that you hold dear."[50] He then asked them to stay and fight for just another month, rendering their service "to the cause of liberty and to your country." Realizing that patriotic appeals were not enough, Washington offered them a generous bonus of ten dollars to remain and told Morris that, with liberty at stake, "I thought it no time to stand on trifles."[51] The entire regiment decided to remain for six more weeks and fight for their liberties.

General Cornwallis raced from New York to central New Jersey to engage the unexpectedly active Continental army. On January 2, 1777, Cornwallis arrived in Trenton with fifty-five hundred soldiers and lined up opposite Washington across the Assunpink Creek. After three bloody assaults on the bridge failed, Cornwallis settled for taking the Americans in the morning. "We've got the old fox safe now," Cornwallis reputedly said. "We'll go over and bag him in the morning."[52] As darkness settled over the armies, Washington left a rearguard in camp to build roaring fires and make noise to trick Cornwallis into thinking that the whole army was there. Meanwhile, he stealthily slipped away through the night to Princeton on a forced march of twelve miles, with several of his soldiers marching shoeless through the ice or falling asleep from exhaustion. Briefly surprised yet prepared, British regiments held the line against the American assault. After several initial attacks failed, Washington rallied his men to victory from atop his horse, calling, "Parade with us, my brave fellows. There is but a handful of the enemy, and we will have them directly!" As the tide turned, he shouted, "It's a fine fox chase, my boys!"[53] Amid the rout, Hamilton's artillery company again brought their guns to bear in the victory, and he supposedly fired off a shot that beheaded a portrait of King George II hanging in Nassau Hall at Princeton University.

By this point in the war, Washington and his officer corps had taken note of the young artillery commander. One of Washington's officers is said to have observed "a youth, a mere stripling, small, slender, almost delicate in frame, marching…with a cocked hat pulled down over his eyes, apparently lost in thought, with his hand resting on a cannon, and every now and then patting it, as if it were a favorite horse or a pet plaything." Another reported that Hamilton's company "was a model of discipline. At their head was a boy and I wondered at his youth, but what was my surprise when that slight figure…was pointed out to me as that Hamilton of whom we had already heard so much."[54] Hamilton himself later proudly looked back at the dramatic victory: "Trenton and Princeton…[were] the dawnings of that bright day which afterwards broke forth with such resplendent luster."[55] The armies retired into winter quarters, giving Washington time to take stock and prepare his strategy for the spring.

The respite also gave Washington and Hamilton the opportunity to cement their relationship. The commander in chief had been suitably impressed by Hamilton's leadership and courage under fire. In January, at winter quarters in Morristown, Washington officially invited Hamilton into his inner circle as an aide-de-camp. Hamilton probably weighed the decision for some time, since he desperately wanted a military command to win the glory he sought. He later wrote, "When in the year 1777 the regiments of artillery were multiplied, I had good reason to expect that the command of one of them would have fallen to me had I not changed my situation and this in all probability would have led further."[56] On March 1, he was officially promoted to lieutenant colonel and thus gained some influence over the direction of the army. He had rejected similar offers from lesser generals but accepted this one from the commander in chief. This decision was momentous, for it led to a relationship with Washington that helped to forge the American republic in war and in peace.

Washington desperately needed someone with Hamilton's skills and talents on his staff. He wanted to delegate certain tasks that would free him up to concentrate on finding a winning strategy in the face of the previous year's routs. Problems of supply and organization plague every military commander, but they were particularly acute for General Washington because of a weak Congress and the recalcitrant states. He needed staff officers who could find the necessary supplies to fit his army for operations and simultaneously respect the civil authority of Congress and the states.[57]

But as Hamilton soon discovered, Washington was a demanding and at times hot-tempered taskmaster who expected loyalty, industry, and perseverance from his staff officers. He wanted men who were capable of being "confined from morning to evening, hearing and answering...applications and letters."[58] They had to share his republican vision, yet he was open to different opinions regarding specific decisions. He brooked differences but not with those who harmed the war effort, which was now so closely tied to his personal honor. Thus, a diversity of views and talents coexisted within a unified command.

Hamilton, for his part, fit Washington's needs perfectly. His administrative genius contributed to greater organization in the army, and his keen mind and uncanny ability to articulate ideas quickly and persuasively made him one of Washington's most trusted officers. When

Washington received his nightly dispatches, he allegedly uttered the command, "Call Colonel Hamilton!" to write the appropriate reply. Fellow aide Robert Troupe noted, "The pen for our army was held by Hamilton; and for dignity of manner, pith of manner, and elegance of style, General Washington's letters are unrivalled in military annals."[59] Hamilton was the author of many of Washington's letters. Their shared philosophy of the struggle for liberty allowed Hamilton to express Washington's thoughts perfectly, whether in orders to generals or letters to civilian authorities. Soon, Washington trusted Hamilton so much that he was allowed to pen letters and sign Washington's name to them.

Hamilton also shared Washington's own capacity for hard work and personal sacrifice. They worked together for many hours daily in close quarters. Hamilton and the other advisors were expected to be available day and night, and though the demands were heavy, the two men developed an intimacy rather quickly. They ate their meals together and slept under the same roof, sharing fleeting moments of respite or joy. They also pored over maps, discussed upcoming battles, and made decisions that determined the fate of young men under Washington's command. They personally led these men through the horrors of war, with Hamilton emerging as Washington's "principal and most confidential aide." The two were so close that the general referred to Hamilton as "my boy."[60]

Despite their close relationship, there were some limits to its depth. Washington was an aloof commander who followed an ethic of leadership that disdained too much familiarity. He publicly spoke with his soldiers and officers and made magnanimous gestures to them, treating them as worthy patriots. But he was also formal and upright, believing this was the way to win their respect and preserve the dignity of his command.[61] Complicating their relationship was the fact that Hamilton was ambitious for honor and disliked being subordinate to anyone. The Marquis de Lafayette later told Hamilton, "I know the General's friendship and gratitude for you, my dear Hamilton. Both are greater than you perhaps imagine."[62] This must have deeply impressed Hamilton, for Lafayette had Washington's complete trust and confidence.

In exchange for their dedication, Washington offered his advisors patronage in the form of advancement and his unbounded confidence in their ability to make decisions for the army. Washington created a meritocracy in which talent and virtue, rather than aristocratic birth, led to promotion and influence. Thus, Hamilton found a perfect vehicle for upward mobility to match his energy, ability, and ambition.[63]

Hamilton shared Washington's ardor for the rightness of their cause. As they suffered the hardships of war, often at the hands of their own national and state governments, they never wavered. They developed a continental outlook that America needed an adequate national government and union to govern itself, since a weak Congress and sovereign states had proven unequal to the task.

The next few years of the war brought the Continental army few victories and not a few frustrations. General Howe did not move the British army out of New York until July 1777, when he sailed up the Chesapeake Bay with eighteen thousand men. He landed in Maryland with his sights set on Philadelphia because of its trade and symbolic importance as the American capital. After Washington marched through Philadelphia to bolster civilian morale, the two armies met at Brandywine Creek on September 11.[64] Washington gave battle at the creek and arrayed his forces along its length in a seemingly excellent position on the high ground and woods. However, while he feinted with a frontal attack by Baron Wilhelm von Knyphausen, General Howe sent Cornwallis north with more than eight thousand men to cross the creek at another ford. Cornwallis discovered an unprotected flank in the American lines and unleashed a brutal attack. Washington immediately dispatched Lord Stirling to reinforce General Sullivan, and they barely held the line and prevented encirclement. Washington was outgeneraled again, and the Continental army suffered over one thousand casualties, with the remaining

American forces fleeing in disarray. Among the wounded was one of Washington's newest young advisors, the Marquis de Lafayette, who was shot in the leg.

While the army was licking its wounds, Washington entrusted Hamilton with two vitally important missions. First, he ordered Hamilton and "Light-Horse Harry" Lee to take a contingent of men to burn flour mills along the Schuylkill River to deny them to the enemy. Hamilton barely escaped with his life when advance elements of the British army fired on him as he crossed the swelled river in a flatboat after completing his task. As his men were being killed and wounded all around him, he led the survivors into the water to swim for safety. After escaping, Hamilton sent a message to John Hancock, imploring the Continental Congress to evacuate Philadelphia.[65]

Washington then ordered Hamilton into Philadelphia with extraordinary powers to commandeer supplies and horses for the army and simultaneously prevent them from falling into British hands, since they were on the verge of taking the city. Hamilton was on a delicate mission, and he had to walk a fine line between respecting the republican citizenry and keeping the war effort alive. Washington told Hamilton that it was a painful if necessary mission and ordered, "This you will do with as much delicacy and discretion as the nature of the business demands." Washington's trust in Hamilton was repaid when he secured the provisions while scrupulously making an accounting to the citizens and avoiding giving offense. The British took the city but were denied the supplies.[66]

In October, Washington kept up the pressure and attacked the main British army at Germantown, suffering another defeat and another thousand casualties. His planned four-prong attack was hopelessly complex and began with a fifteen-mile overnight march, which was confounded by a dense early morning fog. An impenetrable obstacle emerged when the Americans wasted valuable time and resources assaulting a stone house. Even Knox's artillerymen could not bring the small contingent of redcoats inside to surrender the stronghold. The attack foundered, and Washington ignominiously withdrew again.

As success eluded Washington and his army, American forces won a stunning victory in upstate New York. During the summer, British General John Burgoyne marched south from Canada along the shores of Lake Champlain with a force of eight thousand, while General Barry St. Leger sailed down the St. Lawrence River and General Henry Clinton sailed up the Hudson from New York. The British sought to cut the colonies in two and isolate New England, hoping to stamp out the Revolution in one stroke. An American army under the command of General Horatio Gates confronted Burgoyne's forces at two separate battles at Saratoga, New York, in September and October 1777. Burgoyne surrendered on October 17, handing over fifty-eight hundred British prisoners as well as arms and supplies. The victory was one of the turning points in the war and encouraged France to recognize American independence and send desperately needed loans, supplies, and army and naval forces. An ecstatic Benjamin Franklin negotiated the treaty of alliance on February 6, 1778.

In November 1777, Washington sent Hamilton on another important mission, this time to visit General Gates to take control of most of his troops, despite his great victory. Washington wanted more troops for what he considered the main theater of battle, especially since the British threat to the north had just been nullified. He instructed Hamilton that Gates's men should "be immediately put in motion to join this army."[67] Hamilton's mission included meeting with Gates personally and bargaining with the experienced general to surrender a considerable number of troops under his command.

Hamilton's mission to Gates was indicative of Washington's trust in his young aide, who was granted a great deal of latitude. For good measure, Hamilton made a quick diversion to induce General Israel Putnam to part with hundreds of militia for Washington. Speaking in the name of General Washington, Hamilton demanded obedience to his orders.[68]

The resolute young man only managed to gain a promise of a single brigade from Gates. When Hamilton discovered that it was an under-manned brigade, he was furious at what he viewed as Gates's impudence. Hamilton wrote Gates that "I did not imagine you would pitch upon a brigade" and now demanded two brigades.[69] When Hamilton feared he had acted imperiously, Washington assured him that "I approve entirely of all the steps you have taken."[70]

While Hamilton contended with Gates, Washington brought his army into winter quarters at Valley Forge, Pennsylvania, where Hamilton rejoined them in January 1778. The soldiers built their own huts from the surrounding woods and suffered a deadly short-age of food and clothing. Congressional bungling led over twenty-five hundred men to starve or freeze to death, while over one thousand soldiers deserted and hundreds of officers resigned. Washington warned Congress that the "barefoot and otherwise naked" army was reaching its breaking point. He laid bare the possible consequences of the situa-tion: "Starve—dissolve—or disperse."[71]

Washington attempted to bolster his army's spirits with performances of his favorite play, Cato, which celebrated manly Roman virtue and service to the republic. Simultaneously, he maintained strict discipline to preserve order. He made Baron Friedrich Wilhelm von Steuben the army's inspector general, despite his questionable claims of experi-ence in European armies. In early March, Steuben drilled a company of one hundred men. He barked commands in French, which Alexander Hamilton helped interpret, and strings of curses, which the men loved, in broken English. The company practiced marching and loading weapons to instill discipline and regularity. The model company then separated and trained the entire army. Washington worked feverishly to send foraging parties to impress livestock and supplies from reluctant farmers and state governments. Amazingly, the army emerged from winter quarters with a renewed vigor and spirit. Washington's resolve had again held the army together and preserved their obedience to civilian authority.[72]

Nevertheless, with a humiliating string of defeats behind him and the results of the training yet to be seen, Washington's reputation reached its nadir during that winter. Whispers questioning his effectiveness began circulating in Congress and among his own army. At the center of the murmurings were Gates and Brigadier General Thomas Conway, the latter a bothersome narcissist with a penchant for scheming. Washington had a low opinion of Conway, whose "importance in the army, exists more in his imagination than in reality."[73] Hamilton had an even harsher assessment of Conway: "There does not exist a more villainous calumniator or incendiary."[74]

After Saratoga, Conway made disparaging comments about Washington's leadership to Gates, who reveled in his own recent prominence. Conway wrote a flattering letter to Gates, claiming that "Heaven has been determined to save your country or a weak general and bad counselors would have ruined it." A copy of this letter came into Washington's hands in November.

In a December 8 letter to Washington, Gates charged Hamilton with rifling through secret files to steal the letter: "I conjure your excellency to give me all the assistance you can in tracing out the author of the infidelity which put extracts from General Conway's letters to me into your hands. Those letters have been *stealingly copied*."[75] Washington informed both Conway and Gates that he knew of their correspondence and equated it with giving "a gleam of hope to the enemy" by causing dissension within the army.[76] To Gates, Washington labeled Conway a "secret enemy" and "dangerous incendiary," and he informed Gates that copies of the letter were on their way to Congress.[77] Once Washington let it be known that he knew of the incipient cabal, his reputation for integrity and a growing, albeit grudging admiration for his persistence among members of Congress led to its collapse. The affair dissolved with Washington's reputation and friendship with his loyal aide intact.

Washington was fighting a two-front war, dealing with intrigue behind his own lines while facing the world's greatest military. The latter reappeared at the Battle of Monmouth Courthouse when General Charles Lee encountered Lord Cornwallis's forces on June 28, 1778, in blistering ninety-degree heat. Lee's forces were routed, resulting in another chaotic retreat for American forces despite their recent training. Lee was acting strangely; at first, he refused to lead the probing advance guard, so Washington appointed General Lafayette to do the job, then Lee demanded his command back. When Washington witnessed the mayhem, he was beside himself with rage and cursed Lee. Washington confronted Lee, demanding to know "the meaning of this disorder and confusion!"[78] Lee gave a muddled reply that failed to placate Washington's anger, and he relieved Lee of his command on the spot. Once again, on horseback, Washington restored order in the lines and rallied his men until the two armies fought to a standstill. Hamilton marveled at how Washington's steadfastness turned the tide and saved the day. He wrote, "I never saw the general to so much advantage. His coolness and firmness were admirable. He instantly took maneuvers for checking the enemy's advance and giving time for the army, which was very near, to form and make a proper dispensation."[79] For his part, Hamilton was injured when his horse was shot out from under him, forcing him to retire from the battlefield. The British eventually made their way to Sandy Hook, where they sailed for New York.

General Lee demanded a court-martial to clear his name and was obliged with a guilty verdict and the loss of his command, thanks in large part to the testimony of Hamilton and other aides who maintained that Lee had been negligent in his duty.[80] Hamilton disliked Lee, describing him as "a driveler in the business of soldiership or something much worse."[81] When Hamilton's friend and fellow aide-de-camp John Laurens challenged Lee to a duel and wounded him slightly, Hamilton served as a second. More importantly, the Battle of Monmouth Courthouse was the last that Washington's forces fought in the North as the British shifted to a southern strategy. For two years, Washington encamped his army around New York, searching for ways to invade the city and reclaim it for the Americans.

While the general and his army watched the British garrison in New York, Washington and Hamilton were drawn into a controversy involving arming slaves in the South. Washington had grappled with this difficult subject throughout the war. Free blacks had fought for the ideal of liberty from the very beginning of the war at Lexington, Concord, and Bunker Hill. They had fought as courageously as any white soldier and earned accolades that they were "brave and gallant" soldiers. One general of the militia noted, "I look on them, in General, Equally Serviceable with other men, for Fatigue & in action; many of them have proved themselves brave."[82]

Being a slave owner from a large plantation in Virginia, Washington had looked askance at the presence of the black troops in the army when he arrived in New England. In October 1775, Washington and his officers decided to "reject all Slaves, & by a great Majority to reject Negroes altogether," though concessions were made to allow the reenlistment of "free Negroes who [already] have Served in this Army."[83] Washington's views were also shaped by events in his native Virginia since the royal governor, Lord Dunmore—whom Washington had labeled an "arch traitor to the rights of humanity" for his November 1775 proclamation offering freedom to the colony's slaves—had raised his infamous "Ethiopian Regiment," comprised of slaves who ran away and joined the British side in the Battle of Great Bridge in December.

In any event, Washington had received the pleas of many black soldiers that they be allowed to fight in the cause of liberty. He had some sympathy for their complaints, having witnessed their bravery first hand. Considering their passionate desire to serve, while at the same time struggling with the constant shortage of manpower that plagued the war effort and fearing that they might otherwise join the British, a remarkable change gradually took place in the mind of the master of Mount Vernon. At the end of the year, he wrote to Congress that "I have presumed to depart from the resolution respecting them and have given license for their being enlisted."[84] The republican general submitted the difficult issue to Congress, and by February 1776, a congressional committee endorsed his decision to keep black soldiers but not admit any new black recruits into the army. Even though states passed similar restrictions, both the national and state resolutions were observed more in the breach, usually a concession to the desperate necessity of raising enough men to fight.

The uneasy policy was followed for years, so the presence of black soldiers was barely noticed. As long as the Continental army and state recruiters focused on free blacks and did not press for the service of slaves, the equilibrium persisted. That is, until young, idealistic men surrounding Washington like Hamilton, Lafayette, and South Carolina's John Laurens urged arming slaves as a means to further schemes of emancipation. Washington was thus uncomfortably thrust into the middle of a controversy he very much wished to avoid.

Hamilton was inclined to use the opportunity of the war to arm slaves so that they could demonstrate their manhood and equality and fight for their freedom. He wrote to John Jay, the new president of Congress, plugging Laurens's plan and leadership: "I have not the least doubt that the negroes will make very excellent soldiers with the proper management and I will venture to pronounce that they cannot be put in better hands than those of Mr. Laurens." Hamilton believed that the degrading system of slavery was responsible for perceived inequality or want of courage on the part of blacks but that they would prove themselves in combat: "I think their want of cultivation (for their natural faculties are probably as good as ours) joined to that habit of subordination which they acquire from a life of servitude will make them sooner become soldiers than our white inhabitants." Finally, he encouraged Jay to support the enlightened plan because it "will give them their freedom with muskets. This will secure their fidelity, animate their courage, and I believe will have a good influence upon those who remain by opening a door to their emancipation... The dictates of humanity and true policy, equally interest me in favor of this unfortunate class of men."[85]

Washington received Henry Laurens's missive and knew of the passionate antislavery ideas of his young aides, but he refused to go along with the proposal. As a slave owner, he knew how much his fellow southerners would oppose the idea. With the war effort faltering and the general contending with countless other pressing problems with Congress and the states in supplying arms and men, he had little taste to stir up additional trouble by talking about arming and freeing slaves in places threatened by the British. With a touch of moderation that comes with age, though perhaps not of virtue in the eyes of those who wanted him to do more, Washington brushed aside the idealistic pleas of the young officers. He responded that the scheme might stir up trouble among slaves and generate a widespread discontent with slavery that would arouse the great antipathy of slave owners, some of whom were already lukewarm about the American cause. It was simply too divisive an issue to deal with at the moment. He feared that it would "render Slavery more irksome to those who remain in it" and "will be productive of much discontent in those who are held in servitude." Being perhaps a bit disingenuous, he averred that it was "a subject that has never employed much of my thoughts." He found the plan "laudable" but refused to give his approval as too imprudent at the moment.[86]

Understanding the revolutionary import of its actions, Congress nevertheless unanimously recommended the plan to "take measures immediately for raising three thousand able-bodied negroes" with compensated emancipation to the South Carolina and Georgia assemblies, where the outraged reaction was as bad as Washington predicted. Whatever the merits of the emancipation scheme in theory, the reality was that it was not palatable to the southern states. The dispute over the issue between Washington and Hamilton revealed their different cultural outlooks as well as their different levels of responsibility. This shaped their divergent views on the emancipation of slaves; however, their views would converge later in their lives.

Due in part to the southerners' reluctance to arm their slaves, disasters soon piled up in the southern theater for the commander in chief. In May 1780, the British captured Charleston, where General Benjamin Lincoln would accept any soldier, black or white, to defend the port city, and took over five thousand American prisoners. In August, General Gates lost two thousand men killed or taken prisoner at the Battle of Camden. Hamilton lamented, "Was there ever an instance of a general running away, as Gates has done, from his whole army?" He mocked Gates: "One hundred and eighty miles in three days and a half. It does admirable credit to the activity of a man at his time of life." Washington dispatched General Nathaniel Greene to take over the army from Gates.

In a blow worse than military defeat for a general who put a premium on loyalty and integrity, Washington soon discovered treason in his officer corps. In August, he commanded General Benedict Arnold "to proceed to West Point and take command of that post and its dependencies."[87] Arnold had led a difficult, ill-fated expedition to Quebec early in the war and had been wounded in the leg. He was also one of the heroes of Saratoga, and Washington sympathized with Arnold's frustration in being passed over for promotion. In April 1777, Washington had written to Arnold, "I confess I was surprised, when I did not see your name in the line of major generals, and was so fully of opinion that there was some mistake in the matter." However, he warned Arnold not to push the civilian authorities too hard in the matter and thanked him for his patience.[88] Arnold was later accused of using his military office for profit but received only a reprimand for his dealings.

Arnold contacted the British months before his treason was discovered and entered into negotiations over the price they were willing to pay for his planned treachery in handing over West Point along with capturing Washington, Hamilton, and the rest of the general's staff. The plan collapsed when a British officer, John Andre, was captured by American militiamen with the plans for West Point in his boot.[89]

On the morning of September 25, Washington and Hamilton arrived in West Point to inspect the fort and breakfasted at Arnold's house. Washington ate and left to make his inspection, while Hamilton remained. At the same time, Arnold learned of Andre's capture and began acting strangely. Unbeknown to Hamilton, Arnold fled at that moment, leaving incriminating papers and his Tory wife behind. Learning of her husband's flight, Mrs. Arnold went upstairs and broke into a hysterical fit when Washington arrived back at the house. Hamilton described the scene:

It was the most affecting scene I ever was witness to... The general went up to see her, and she upbraided him with being in a plot to murder her child. One moment she raved, another she melted into tears. Sometimes she pressed her infant to her bosom, and lamented its fate, occasioned by the imprudence of its father, in a manner that would have pierced insensibility itself. All the sweetness of beauty, all the loveliness of innocence, all the tenderness of a wife, and all the fondness of a mother showed themselves in her appearance and conduct.[90]

The pair reacted as one might expect from men devoted to an eighteenth-century conception of honor, trying to comfort her and taking great pity on her for her husband's actions. With a flourish of chivalry, Hamilton stated that he "wished myself her brother, to have a right to become her defender... Could I forgive Arnold for sacrificing his honor, reputation, and duty, I could not forgive him for acting a part that must have forfeited the esteem of so fine a woman."[91] Little did they know that they had been duped, because Peggy Arnold was only acting the part of a distressed wife. In reality, she had been deeply involved in the plot and was giving her husband time to escape to British lines.

Hamilton handed Washington a packet of papers exposing the treason. Washington emotionally choked out, "Arnold has betrayed us... Whom can we trust now?"[92] Washington dispatched Hamilton to intercept Arnold, but the traitor had already escaped. Hamilton had the wherewithal to write General Nathaniel Greene: "I advise you putting the army under marching orders and detaching a brigade immediately this way," since the British might be advancing to execute Arnold's plan.[93]

Meanwhile, Andre was in American custody and court-martialed for espionage. Since he was captured in civilian clothing, he was sentenced to be hanged as a spy. During visits with the prisoner, Hamilton became somewhat enamored of Andre, seeing him as a man of honor and refinement, despite his treason. Hamilton described Andre as "well improved by education and travel, [who] united a peculiar elegance of mind and manners and the advantage of a pleasing person."[94] Hamilton pleaded with Washington to have Andre shot honorably by a firing squad as befitted an enemy officer, but Washington refused, so Andre was hanged. Andre preserved his dignity, tightening his own rope and blindfolding himself. Hamilton romantically described his death: "I am aware that a man of real merit is never seen in so favorable a light as seen through the medium of adversity. The clouds that surround him are shades that set off his good qualities."[95]

Hamilton and Washington both lived by the code of honor, though it manifested itself differently in each. The Andre affair showed how honor could tear at their friendship. Hamilton was especially quick to defend his personal honor and came close to engaging in duels during the war because of the perpetual chip he seemed to have on his shoulder. One can scarcely imagine Washington doing the same, as he preferred to lead the army in an irreproachable manner and preserve his reputation as a man of prudence and moderation. Their personal differences soon led to an incident that created a rift between the pair after years of amity between them. In early 1781, Hamilton impetuously reacted to a slight against his honor when Washington failed to contain his explosive temper. After their falling out, Hamilton's desire for honor and military glory temporarily brought the two together at the Battle of Yorktown. But their relationship had suffered a major blow.

Hamilton related the split to his father-in-law, Philip Schuyler. Several times in the letter, Hamilton expressed a heartfelt desire to justify himself to Schuyler and keep his approval: "I wish what I have said to make no other impression than to satisfy you I have not been in the wrong."[96] He told Schuyler that there had been a significant altercation with Washington that would surprise Schuyler. Hamilton was correct.

Hamilton recounted the episode with the greatest objectivity that he could muster. He explained that one afternoon, he had passed Washington on a flight of stairs at their command headquarters. Washington said that he would like to speak with Hamilton, who responded that he would be able to talk right after he delivered an important letter. He was subsequently headed for Washington's office when he was detained by the Marquis de Lafayette momentarily to converse on some matter. Hamilton impatiently broke away from Lafayette and was on his way to Washington's office when:

Instead of finding the General as usual in his room, I met him at the head of the stairs, where he accosting me in a very angry tone, "Col Hamilton (said he), you have kept me waiting at the head of the stairs these ten minutes. I must tell you Sir you treat me with disrespect." I replied without petulancy, but with decision "I am not conscious of it Sir, but since you have thought it necessary to tell me so we part" "Very well

Sir (said he) if it be your choice" or something to this effect and we separated.[97]

After an hour, Washington sent an underling to apologize and make assurances of the general's confidence in Hamilton's abilities and integrity. Washington, who meticulously followed the propriety of command and hierarchy, deeply regretted his outburst and offered Hamilton a private, candid conversation, a unique opportunity to express his dissatisfaction with his superior's actions. Remarkably, Hamilton refused, because he was determined to part company with Washington. Not wishing to hamper the war effort, Hamilton agreed to remain silent about the affair and stay on Washington's staff until a replacement could be found. Hamilton resisted pressure from his friends to reconcile with Washington. "My resolution is unalterable," he stated.[98] The fissure was complete.

Hamilton was deeply wounded by the split with Washington, though he tried to shrug off their relationship. Although he used the term "family" to describe Washington's staff several times, he stated that he disliked his position of aide-de-camp "as unworthy of a courageous leader." He only accepted the position because he was "infected…with the enthusiasm of the times, an idea of the general's character." He even claimed, "For three years past I have felt no friendship for him and have professed none. The truth is our own dispositions are the opposites of each other and the pride of my temper would not suffer to profess what I did not feel. Indeed when advances of this kind have been made to me on his part, they were received in a manner that showed at least I had no inclination to court them."[99] To Major James McHenry, Hamilton explained the rupture and wrote nastily, "He shall for once at least repent his ill-humor."[100] In light of their close wartime collaboration, it is hard to read Hamilton's words as anything but the injured feelings of a young man.

Nonetheless, Hamilton had nagging doubts that he had acted too hastily in rebuffing Washington's contrite overture. He also wanted to make sure that in sharing the event with Schuyler he had not disappointed his father-in-law. Hamilton explained that it was not bitterness that guided his actions but rather, "It was the deliberate result of maxims I had long formed for the government of my own conduct."[101] In other words, honor.

Hamilton then thought about his options. He could take command of an artillery or light infantry company. If the war ended in the near future, he would lose his opportunity to display great valor. He began to regret joining Washington's staff due to the harmful effects this had on his chances for promotion as an artillery officer. He could not "think of quitting the army during the war," because he thirsted for military glory and fame.[102] Indeed, he had written to Washington the previous year itching with ambition for a military command: "Sometime last fall when I spoke to your Excellency about going to the southward [where the war had shifted], I explained to you candidly my feeling with respect to military reputation and how much it was my object to act a conspicuous part in some enterprise that might perhaps raise my character as a soldier above mediocrity."[103]

Schuyler responded with the gentle, guiding hand of a typical father-in-law. While professing support for the honor of Hamilton's actions, he also urged Hamilton to accept Washington's apology. Schuyler promised he did not "discover any impropriety in your conduct in the affair in question." Nevertheless, he was not going to remain silent and let Hamilton off the hook. Because Hamilton was such an important adviser to Washington, Schuyler bluntly stated, "Your quitting your station must therefore be productive of very material injuries to the public." He even thought that it would have a negative effect on the French alliance because it would show divisions in the highest levels of American leadership, not to mention Hamilton's essential translating skills. Schuyler wondered, "How will the loss be replaced?" He knew that only an appeal to the national honor might impel Hamilton to overlook his own personal honor and reconcile with Washington.

Schuyler advised Hamilton to forgive Washington, since he had acknowledged his blame and quickly repented. Indeed, Schuyler taught Hamilton an important lesson about friendship: "It falls to the lot of few men to pass through life without one of those unguarded moments which wound the feelings of a friend." Schuyler thought Hamilton should "impute them to the frailty of human nature." Schuyler lauded the principles and maxims by which Hamilton chose to live his honorable life, but there were occasions when "times and circumstances sometimes render a deviation necessary and justifiable." Since the good of his country was at stake, Hamilton should make a sacrifice and reconcile with Washington.[104]

Hamilton did not follow his father-in-law's advice and pursued a commission instead. Contact with Washington was limited to formal letters that betrayed none of the former relationship they had shared. In April, Hamilton boldly offered his services and hoped to know "in what manner you foresee you will be able to employ me in the ensuing campaign."[105] Washington wrote back, barely containing his anger at Hamilton's impertinence. In the language of eighteenth-century men of honor, Washington wrote, "Your letter of this date has not a little embarrassed me." He would not be pressured into giving Hamilton a choice command to the ire of others in line.[106] In July, Hamilton implicitly resigned, cheekily sending Washington his commission. On July 31, Washington responded charitably and gave Hamilton a light-infantry command.[107] After raising a battalion of New York troops, Hamilton had trouble securing enough shoes for his men. He asked Washington to push through the requisition from Continental supplies, and Washington eventually promised the requested shoes would be coming.[108]

On August 15, at his headquarters on the Hudson River, Washington learned that a French fleet was sailing under Admiral

François-Joseph-Paul de Grasse for the Chesapeake with twenty-eight warships and three thousand infantry. De Grasse offered to provide naval aid to America until October, when he had orders to sail to the West Indies to confront part of the British navy. Washington had to strike while the opportunity presented itself.

Washington seized the occasion for several reasons. De Grasse's fleet would give the Franco-American forces temporary naval superiority in North America. In July, Washington's attacks on heavily fortified New York had been easily repulsed, and his probes showed that a major attack would be suicidal. Most importantly, Washington desperately needed a victory to hold the army together. Congress was not satisfactorily paying or supplying his army. Desertions and poor morale troubled the army. Soon, he might not have an army with which to fight.

Since New York seemed to be impregnable, General Cornwallis made an attractive target for Washington. That spring, Cornwallis had handily defeated Continental forces in Virginia. Cornwallis's army drove General Lafayette from Richmond and General von Steuben from Point Fork. Virginia governor Thomas Jefferson and the Virginia legislature took flight from Charlottesville in disgrace, with British colonel Banastre Tarleton in hot pursuit. In June, Cornwallis was camped in Williamsburg with orders to reconnoiter the area for a naval base. At the end of July, Cornwallis settled on Yorktown and fortified the area against attack.[109]

After deciding on a joint Franco-American campaign against Cornwallis in the Chesapeake, Washington faked preparations for an attack against New York. The British general, Sir Henry Clinton, took the bait and remained in New York. Washington then marched his army to Virginia with all deliberate speed and secrecy. A large contingent of French troops from Rhode Island under General Rochambeau followed closely behind. Washington's forces passed through Philadelphia on September 2 and Mount Vernon on September 8. With his arrival imminent, he ordered Lafayette to besiege Yorktown.

Simultaneously, de Grasse cruised into the Chesapeake Bay, landed three thousand marines, and arranged for transport for the converging allied armies. British admiral Thomas Graves sailed a smaller fleet down to the Chesapeake to confront de Grasse's fleet of thirty-six ships. The European fleets exchanged broadsides and killed hundreds of men. The naval battle ended inconclusively, but significantly, Graves was driven back to New York and could not relieve Cornwallis's forces.

A worried Cornwallis warned Clinton of the untenable position at Yorktown: "This place is in no state of defense. If you cannot relieve me very soon, you must be prepared to hear the worst."[110] Regardless, Clinton didn't try to rescue the army nor did Cornwallis make any serious attempt to escape. Washington and his allies were a better model of coordination with both land and sea forces. Washington met de Grasse, who promised the general that he would stay until late October. The French admiral would block any attempt by the British to break in or out of Yorktown. Rochambeau and his engineers were ready to assist Washington in battering British defenses and assaulting the fortifications.

Hamilton had joined his forces with the advance guard of the army. Before he disembarked for Yorktown, he tried to console his wife and ease her worry: "Cheer yourself with this idea, and with the assurance of never more being separated. Every day confirms me in the intention of renouncing public life, and devoting myself wholly to you. Let others waste their time and their tranquility in a vain pursuit of power and glory: be it my object to be happy in a quiet retreat with my better angel." Nonetheless, he marched off to battle for one last chance at fame. His forces sailed around Annapolis and landed near Williamsburg on September 20. By September 28, the Franco-American army of about sixteen thousand troops formed up and marched on Yorktown.[111]

With a large Continental force approaching and a French fleet blocking escape on the York River, Cornwallis dug in and prepared for the assault. He sank a few ships in the York River to prevent a landing in the rear. On September 30, he abandoned his outer defenses around the town and awaited the impending siege.

The Continental forces swarmed into the outer British defenses. Directed by French engineers, American sappers furiously improved the trench system in a zigzag pattern five hundred yards from the British lines. Washington suddenly appeared to some of the men one night, encouraging the troops and even lending a hand with a pickax. Washington was also on hand and lit the first fuse when allies launched an artillery barrage against British defenses on October 9. The twenty-foot-high British earthen works repulsed the American bombardment, while British marksmen picked off the Americans. The Continentals, however, gave as good as they received, as the artillery duel killed and wounded many British, forced Cornwallis to seek refuge in a subterranean cave, and reduced the British troops to subsisting on putrid rations. The Continentals inched closer to enemy lines to prepare for the final assault.

With the looming attack, Hamilton pleaded with his friend Lafayette to grant him the honor of leading the charge. Lafayette agreed to present the request for Washington to decide. After a few minutes conferring in Washington's command tent, Hamilton emerged and exclaimed to one of his men, "We have it! We have it!"[112]

On October 14, Hamilton led the American forces against redoubt number 10 in a courageous initial charge to seize artillery batteries simultaneous with a French assault on redoubt number 9. With bayonets fixed, Hamilton and his men courageously forced their way through a barricade of sharpened sticks. He then leapt onto the shoulders of another man and launched himself onto the enemy parapet with his saber slashing. His forces linked up with the successful French attackers, and they established a new trench from which to bombard and assault the British.[113]

On the night of October 16, Cornwallis attempted to sneak across the river into Gloucester to escape to New York, but a squall prevented the movement. Surrender was inevitable. The next day, Cornwallis sent an officer to parley with Washington, and the British army formally surrendered on October 19. The British and German troops stacked their weapons. Cornwallis sent a subordinate, Brigadier General Charles O'Hara, to offer his sword to the American commander. Washington refused to accept it and sent General Benjamin Lincoln in his stead. Whatever the final theatrics and insults, Washington bagged approximately eight thousand British prisoners. When he heard of the defeat, King George III exclaimed, "It is all over."[114]

Washington and Hamilton emerged from the Yorktown battlefield with a heroic victory that brought them instant fame and glory. Though their friendship was not quite healed, the rift was not beyond repair either. Concerned about the national union, they set to work individually at first to create a stronger national government. With their British foe for all practical purposes defeated, the struggle to create an American republic began.

CHAPTER FIVE

A CONTINENTAL REPUBLIC

WHILE ELATED OVER THE American victory at Yorktown, both Washington and Hamilton believed that there was something deeply flawed with the way the American government, to the extent that there was one, conducted the war. The suffering at Valley Forge was just one example of the mismanagement that plagued the American war effort. Washington contended with Congress and the states for men, supplies, and money to carry out his war effort. Although the civilian authorities infuriated him, Washington nonetheless maintained his respect and deference even as they marred the war effort. He tried to prod them into action and expressed his frustrations, but he did not threaten the civilian government that granted him his power. As a member of Washington's inner circle, Alexander Hamilton shared Washington's exasperation with Congress and the states.

During the war, Washington and Hamilton mostly kept silent about the ineptitude of the civilian authorities except in their private correspondence. Washington was especially opposed to any ideas that smacked of disloyalty to the republican government for which he was fighting. Hamilton, on the other hand, began to despair and countenance extreme ideas about creating a stronger national government. At the end of the war, both penned public statements airing their views. Thus, they stood at the forefront of a movement of nationalists who favored centralizing government power.[1]

In addition to their words, they showed their character through their actions. An opportunity to prove their respect for the republican government came when a group of dissatisfied officers and their men made threats against Congress. Washington never wavered in his support of the republic. Hamilton, however, was sympathetic to this group of dissenters. Although both sought the same end of a republican government, their different methods of achieving it showed the fissure between the pair as their friendship reached its lowest point.

★★★

THE AMERICAN EXPERIENCE UNDER British rule had caused fear of centralization and the creation of a weak national government during the war. As a result, Congress lacked adequate powers to coerce the states to meet their supply and manpower quotas or pay their tax obligations. Moreover, the states often failed to send delegates to Congress, so that body could not assemble a quorum and simply could not administer the war. At other times, the states were outright defiant of the Congress and ignored its requisitions, perniciously keeping supplies for their own war effort. In fact, the obedience of the states was often directly proportional to the presence of the enemy on their own soil. This was made painfully evident to Washington and Hamilton at Valley Forge, and they increasingly took note of it throughout the war. They both thought that the common good necessitated a stronger national government instead of a government controlled by the narrow, self-interested states.

It would not be easy though. Hamilton wrote, "We must secure our union on solid foundations; a Herculean task and to effect which mountains of prejudice must be leveled."[2] Washington complained that

the "states separately are too much engaged in their local concerns."[3]
Since he was the commander in chief of a republican army, the virtuous Washington bent over backward to cajole the states into sending
provisions. For instance, Washington wrote to New York governor
George Clinton in 1778, deferentially requesting that "you can perhaps
do something towards [our relief]; and any assistance, however trifling
in itself, will be of great moment at so critical a juncture."[4]

That did not mean that Washington accepted the situation
lightly. He could quite angrily denounce the foolishness of Congress
and the states to friends, though he always tried to keep a polite tone
with the civilian authorities, even in times of great distress. He told
George Mason:

Friends and foes seem now to combine to pull down the
goodly fabric we have hitherto been raising at the expense of so
much time, blood, and treasure—and unless the bodies politic
will exert themselves to bring things back to first principles—
correct abuses—and punish our internal foes, inevitable ruin
must follow... I cannot refrain lamenting however in the
most poignant terms, the fatal policy too prevalent in most
of the states, of employing their ablest men at home in posts
of honor or profit, until the great national interests are fixed
upon a solid basis.[5]

At the Constitutional Convention of 1787, Benjamin Franklin
would later use the metaphor of a two-headed snake that died of thirst
when each head wanted to go a different way when stopped by a twig.
Washington used similar language to describe the disunity that animated
the states during the war. The Union was a "many headed monster, a
heterogeneous mass, that never will or can, steer to the same point. The

contest among the different states now, is not which shall do most for the common cause, but which shall do least."[6]

Hamilton, fearful that the national honor was at stake, was more willing to lecture state officials for hoarding their soldiers and supplies for their own defense when the British threatened their particular territories. He also wrote to Governor Clinton, noting that "however important it is to give form and efficiency to your interior constitutions and police; it is infinitely more important to have a wise general council; otherwise a failure of the measures of the union will overturn all your labors for the advancement of your particular good and ruin the common cause."[7] Hamilton was frustrated that the states could decide whether or not to contribute to the general cause. They seemed to be fair-weather friends of the army.[8]

Privately, Hamilton used even harsher language to describe the actions of the states. In 1780, he wrote, "Our countrymen have all the folly of the ass and all the passiveness of the sheep in their compositions. They are determined not to be free and they can neither be frightened, discouraged, nor persuaded to change their resolution." He even claimed to be understating the case: "Don't think I rave; for the conduct of the states is enough most pitiful that can be imagined."[9] He was deeply perturbed by the lack of united action by his fellow citizens.

Toward the end of the war, Washington and Hamilton thought that one of the problems was that the most virtuous and enlightened men of the early Revolution had either returned to their states to manage local affairs or gone abroad as diplomats, leaving the Congress bereft of talent. Thomas Jefferson, Benjamin Franklin, and John Adams all spent years in Europe as diplomats. Early leaders of the Revolution, such as Patrick Henry and Samuel Adams, served in state offices. Washington wondered, "Where is Mason, Wythe, Jefferson?" He did not want men of virtue and talent to "content themselves in the enjoyment of places of honor or profit in their own country, while the common interests of America are mouldering and sinking into irretrievable ruin."[10] Hamilton agreed, arguing that "each state in order to promote its own internal government and prosperity, has selected its best members to fill the offices within itself, and conduct its own affairs. Men have been fonder of the emoluments and conveniences, of being employed at home, and local attachment, falsely operating, has made them more provident for the particular interests of the states to which they belonged."[11] During the war, they thought that enlightened statesmen could make up for deficiencies in the structure of government.

Both men concurred that the weak national government was responsible for seriously hampering military operations. Several times, Washington informed Congress with no exaggeration that the honest result of its policies would be the destruction of the army and its glorious cause. He also warned state officials, including Benjamin Harrison, Speaker of the Virginia House of Burgesses, that "if the states will not, or cannot provide me with the means; it is in vain for them to look to me for the end, and accomplishment of their wishes. Bricks are not to be made without straw."[12] Writing to General Greene after Yorktown, Washington examined the course of the war and thought that future generations would not believe the conditions under which the Continental army fought and won the war, "by numbers infinitely less, composed of men oftentimes half starved; always in rags, without pay, and experiencing, at times, every species of distress which human nature is capable of undergoing."[13]

Hamilton also warned of the damaging effects of reducing the army to such a desperate situation. He wrote, "At this very day there are complaints from the whole line, of having been three or four days without provisions." The impact on the morale of the army was plain: "Desertions have been immense, and strong features of mutiny begin to show themselves. It is indeed to be wondered at, that the soldiery have manifested so unparalleled a degree of patience as they have. I know not how we shall keep the army together or make another campaign."[14] The system of state influence on the Continental army was simply an untenable policy. Only the Congress should control the army's promotions and provisions. The states "should have nothing to do with [the army]." This was the "cement of the Union."[15]

Even common citizens were to blame for the suffering of the army. Farmers and others patriotically supported the American cause while they endured their own privations, including a dearth of food and rampant inflation. It is not surprising that their patriotism waned over the course of the war. They hoarded goods out of self-interest, angering Washington. Conversely, he was frustrated that he was reduced to commandeering necessary supplies from the republican citizenry and handing out receipts for the goods, redeemable for worthless currency: "We must assume the odious character of plunderers instead of the protectors of the people."[16] He was nonetheless scrupulous in accounting for the supplies he took out of respect for the republican citizenry.

Washington informed Congress of the distresses of the army several times. The results would either be the dissolution of the army, or worse, mutiny. Indeed, several regiments did mutiny during the war, protesting their wretched condition. Washington was caught in an extraordinarily difficult situation. He had to convince Congress that it needed to supply the army adequately while at the same time preserving the loyalty of his army to the government. By 1781, he notified Congress that "the patience of the army from an almost uninterrupted series of complicated distress is now nearly exhausted; their discontents matured to an extremity, which has recently had very disagreeable consequences, and which demonstrates the absolute necessity of speedy relief."[17] He simultaneously warned the army that mutinies such as had recently occurred in the New Jersey line would be summarily put down and no leniency shown. He counseled patience with the civilian government because there was no doubt "the public will in the event do ample justice to men fighting and suffering in its defense. But it is our duty to bear present evils with fortitude."[18]

When thinking about the suffering of the army, Hamilton

overturned the conventional wisdom regarding the causes of tyranny. Whereas most Americans thought that governments should be strictly limited to prevent them from destroying liberty, he argued that there was a "greater risk of having a weak and disunited federal government, than one which will be able to usurp upon the rights of the people." A decentralized government would cause the army to collapse, and Americans would lose all of their freedoms.[19]

Washington and Hamilton were clear about the solution to their problem. They wanted Congress to have greater power and to develop a national character in the American people. If the states failed to vest the national government with sufficient power, the war effort, union-ism, and republican government itself would collapse. Washington keenly understood the inevitable consequences: "Certain I am that unless Congress speaks in a more decisive tone; unless they are vested with powers by the several states competent to the great purposes of war, or assume them as a matter of right; and they, and the states respec-tively, act with more energy than they hitherto have done, that our cause is lost. We can no longer drudge on in the old way."[20]

Elsewhere, Washington used an Enlightenment metaphor from Newtonianism to explain the collapse of the republic because of the myopia of the states: "I think our political system may be compared to the mechanism of a clock; and that our conduct should derive a lesson from it for it answers no good purpose to keep the smaller wheels in order if the greater one which is the support and prime mover of the whole is neglected."[21] Washington advocated the growth of a national public spirit in pursuit of a common cause: "If we would pursue a right system of policy, in my opinion, there should be none of these distinc-tions. We should all be considered, Congress, army, etc., as one people, embarked in one cause, in one interest; acting on the same principle and to the same end."[22] He wrote that "unless the states will content themselves with a full, and well chosen representation in Congress, and vest that body with absolute powers in all matters relative to the great purposes of war, and of general concern…we are attempting an impossibility."[23] Congress must exercise the powers of a sovereign nation if the United States were to become one and must make laws for the nation that the individual states were compelled to follow. He thought that Congress, "after hearing the interests and views of the several states fairly discussed and explained by their respective representatives, must dictate, not merely recommend."[24]

Hamilton agreed, arguing that the needs of the Union superseded those of any particular state. He warned of the dangerous "consequences of having a Congress despised at home and abroad," when the new nation was trying to establish its sovereignty.[25] The United States would thus face anarchy domestically and constant attacks from nations that would not fear reprisals. This was no way to build a great nation. Washington agreed, fearing that the government would be just as weak in peace as it had been during the desperate moments of the war.[26]

Hamilton was at odds with his countrymen regarding how much power he was willing to grant the central government. Even before the Articles of Confederation were ratified by the states, creating the first framework of an American national government, he proposed "calling immediately a convention of all the states with full authority," of vesting Congress with complete sovereignty over all matters relating to war, peace, finance, trade, and foreign affairs.[27]

Both men thought that the economic institutions of the country were woefully inadequate to fund the long war, though Hamilton possessed greater insight on this matter. Washington saw clearly that the financial weaknesses of the confederation could affect the outcome of the war. He wrote, "In modern wars the longest purse may chiefly determine the event… [The English] system of public credit is such that it is capable of greater exertions than any other nation."[28]

Hamilton had more extreme remedies in mind. During the war, he read the works of several economists and argued for a national bank to establish a national currency and put the public credit on a solid footing.

He was weary of the indecision of deliberative bodies: "It is impossible such a body, numerous as it is, constantly fluctuating, can ever act with sufficient decision." Only a strong executive could act with the kind of energy and vigor that he thought necessary to administer the government. In thoughts that would become fodder for his opponents throughout his political career, he proposed to "blend the advantages of a monarchy and republic in our constitution."[29]

Indeed, he became more radical as the war became more desperate. By late 1780, he was willing to argue, "Necessity must force [reforms] down; and that if they are not speedily taken the patient will die." In accusatory, unrepublican rhetoric, he bemoaned to his friend, John Laurens, "'Tis in vain you attempt to appease; you are almost detested as an accomplice with the administration." Hamilton became quite despondent about the chances for success. He was ready to give up and wrote with great disgust: "I hate Congress—I hate the army—I hate the world—I hate myself. The whole is a mass of fools and knaves."[30]

While he was attempting to secure a command in 1781, Hamilton authored the first installments of a series of six "Continentalist" essays that were published by the *New-York Packet*. In the essays and in his private correspondence, he described the problems that afflicted the Union during the war and made several proposals for specific reforms that fit into his general vision for a strengthened republic. He wanted to grant the national government greater powers that would allow it to govern an emerging empire. The essays gave him an opportunity to lay out his ideas for a better framework of government.

In these essays, Hamilton reviewed the problems of the confederacy and the need for a stronger Congress to control the power of the states. The reason was plain. If the states acted so selfishly during the perils of war, "what are we to expect in a time of peace and security?"[31] He observed, "The great defect of the confederation is, that it gives the United States...no revenue, nor the means of acquiring it." He also thought the national government should have the power of regulating trade, especially through tariffs for revenue. Finally, the public credit was sinking and caused a rapid depreciation of the currency, and the country assumed a massive debt during the war. Only a national bank could help put the national finances on a firm footing.[32] Lacking sufficient revenue and powers, the national government existed in name only. Establishing a sound government was a matter of national honor.

The states finally ratified the Articles of Confederation in 1781, after years of wrangling and delay. The government was a far cry from meeting Hamilton and Washington's continental vision, for it lacked a judiciary and independent executive. The states continued to be sovereign and retained great control over taxation and raising armies. Laws, treaties, and amendments often had to win large majorities or unanimity, which was virtually impossible among the divided states. Washington joined Hamilton in arguing for revising the Articles at a new constitutional convention because the government they created was unworthy of a sovereign people and an enduring republic.[33]

In early 1782, Hamilton was on furlough from the army and lived at the Schuyler mansion in Albany, pondering his life after the war, and he settled on pursuing a career in the law.[34] With a successful start, Hamilton retired from the military in the spring. He renounced a pension but retained his rank in case he had to answer "the call of the public."[35] He could not keep his hand out of public affairs, however. Robert Morris offered Hamilton a position as receiver of continental taxes for New York, which he at first rejected but later accepted when Morris made it more lucrative. This gave him firsthand evidence of the workings of the enfeebled Union. In the summer, he drafted a series of resolutions that the New York legislature passed, calling for a convention to revise the Articles of Confederation.[36]

Whatever leanings General Washington had for strengthening the Union, he absolutely rejected any suggestion that he might take more power for himself. He was a steadfast defender of the republic and would not countenance any talk of dictatorship or hint of Caesarism in America.

In May 1782, Washington received a letter from a young officer named Lewis Nicola. Nicola had the audacity to write to Washington and suggest that he should overthrow the Congress and become king. Nicola was frustrated with the plight of the army caused by the civilian authorities. He wrote to Washington that "this war must have shown to all, but to military men in particular the weakness of republics… The same abilities which have led us through difficulties apparently unsurmountable by human power to victory and glory, those qualities that have merited and obtained the universal esteem and veneration of an army, would be most likely to conduct and direct us in the smoother paths of peace."[37] In other words, only a military dictatorship could achieve the desired order and stability—even if at the expense of liberty.

In May 1782, Washington wrote Nicola a scathing letter that showed the general's outrage at his suggestion and sternly rebuked him. Washington was greatly pained that "such ideas exist[ed] in the army." Knowing the virtue of his own character, he was "at a loss to conceive what part of my conduct could have given encouragement to an address which to me seems big with the greatest mischiefs that can befall my country… You could not have found a person to whom your schemes are more disagreeable." He conveyed some sympathy for Nicola's frustration but advised that it be expressed "in a constitutional way." He finished his letter with advice to "banish these thoughts from your mind" if Nicola had any "regard for your country, concern for yourself or posterity, or respect for me."[38]

As always throughout his military career, Washington's public character and selfless service to his country would remain unblemished. He repeatedly rebuffed efforts to enhance his power at the expense of republican government, perhaps most importantly during the Newburgh conspiracy. As the nation's finances teetered on the edge of bankruptcy, Congress learned that Virginia had revoked its ratification of an amendment allowing a national five-percent tax on imports, while Rhode Island doggedly opposed the tax and any strengthening of the national government vis-à-vis the states. In this tense situation, the unpaid Continental army, led by a small group of conspirators, posed what was potentially the greatest threat to the fledgling American republic. The plotters comprised a group of nationalists who used the army to menace the civilian government to achieve a stronger political and economic union.[39]

Alexander Hamilton played a sordid role in the Newburgh conspiracy. Frustrated by years of congressional impotence in prosecuting the war, it seems he finally decided to use the threat of force, though not its actual use, to gain the desired end of continental American power. His role in the affair was arguably the most dishonorable act of his public career and provided grist for his opponents to tar him as a conniving character who could not be trusted with power. Although he intended to strengthen the republican government, he foolishly believed that he could incite the army and then rein it in. If the army had actually mutinied, it might have destroyed the young republic that he and Washington had fought and sacrificed for eight years to establish. It was a dangerous game to play.

On the other hand, George Washington displayed moderation throughout the entire affair. He recognized that both the army and Congress had legitimate viewpoints that must be considered in formulating a reasonable national policy for compensating the army. He thought that prudent discussion of the problems would work to the benefit of all parties—Congress and the states would meet their obligations to those who fought, the army would receive its pay, and an effectual scheme for funding the national government would be found. He would not, however, use threats to bully a republican government that was founded on the consent of the governed. As he had done so often throughout the war, Washington would act with untarnished respect for civilian government. Thus, in single-handedly destroying the conspiracy, he proved himself to be the great republican general who protected his country from enemies, both foreign and domestic. He was an American Cincinnatus, not a Caesar. Hamilton and Washington were never farther apart in their public actions than in this nefarious affair. They were in constant contact, and although they did not openly confront each other, they played very different roles, according to their positions.

The origins of the affair date to late 1782, when the Continental army was stationed in winter quarters on the Hudson at Newburgh, New York. The army grew restless since its soldiers had not been paid in months and, in many cases, years. The officers were especially concerned that peace would come and the army would be disbanded before a 1780 congressional promise of a half-pension for life would be fulfilled. They knew that the chances that Congress would act were few. Congress could not raise the revenue to pay the soldiers because of the reluctance of the states to meet the demands of the national government under the Articles and pass the impost tax.

Although Washington pined for Christmas at Mount Vernon, he refused to leave his command while his army was discontented. On December 14, 1782, he wrote, "The temper of the army has become more irritable than at any period since the commencement of the war. This consideration alone prevented me…from requesting leave to spend this winter in Virginia, that I might give some attention to my long neglected private concerns."[40] For many months, he had pleaded with Congress to honor its promised pension to the officers. If the debts to the soldiers were not met, Washington was fearful that "a train of evils will follow of a very serious and distressing nature."[41] Consequently, he was obliged to "stick very close to the troops this winter and to try like a careful physician to prevent if possible the disorders getting to an incurable height."[42]

In December, the officers sent a three-man delegation to petition Congress with a compromise demand for a lump-sum payment in lieu of the pension for life. General Henry Knox drafted the petition and worked with Secretary at War Benjamin Lincoln to lobby Congress on its behalf. In the petition, the officers told members of Congress of their exasperation with serving unpaid: "We have borne all that men can bear—our property is expended—our private resources are at an end, and our friends are wearied out and disgusted with our incessant applications." For their suffering and honorable service, the officers believed they were entitled to a just compensation. They went on to make thinly veiled threats against the civilian government. If they did not receive that pay, they warned, "any further experiments on their patience may have fatal consequences."[43]

Hamilton had been elected to Congress earlier in 1782 and started attending its sessions in November. He met other nationalists such as James Madison who shared his frustrations. Madison regretted that at such a critical period, "the civil institutions of America [are] cursed with the impotence of old age, when they should enjoy the vigor of youth."[44] Hamilton led a group of congressional nationalists who were outraged over the failure of the impost. He joined with his fellow New Yorkers Superintendent of Finance Robert Morris and Representative Gouverneur Morris to pressure Congress to approve the impost.

On January 6, 1783, the officer delegation warned members of Congress of an impending mutiny. The officers wanted to frighten Congress into approving a plan that would place the country's economic system on a permanently firmer footing, thereby strengthening the national government.[45] One officer told Congress of what might happen if the army was left unpaid: "The temper of the army was such that they did not reason or deliberate coolly on consequences, and therefore a disappointment might throw them blindly into extremities." Robert Morris then met with members of Congress and played his role expertly. The superintendent of finance warned that the army would not be paid "until certain funds should be previously established," trying to goad them to pass the impost tax.[46] He also threatened to resign if Congress did not act. As a result, Congress appointed Hamilton and other representatives to a committee to consider the petition. By the end of the month, a tense Congress promised to secure funding to pay the soldiers their salaries as well as a lump-sum pension, but several states actually voted down the measures.

When word arrived in February from Paris that a preliminary peace with Britain was signed, the conspirators made overtures to important men to support their cause. The ambitious general Horatio Gates, the hero at the Battle of Saratoga, had the support of some radical officers who might really have wanted to overthrow the government. Contrarily, Washington's aide, General Henry Knox, was approached but refused to join the cabal and ruin the reputation of the army: "We should even suffer wrongs and injuries to the utmost verge of toleration rather than sully it in the least degree."

Hamilton's machinations necessitated the participation of General Washington, since his opposition would destroy the plan. On February 13, 1783, Hamilton wrote to Washington, obliquely enlisting his help in the plot in a letter filled with duplicitous intentions. He explained that a decisive moment had arrived that required action in Congress. Since he believed that Congress was "a body not governed by reason or foresight," he admitted that he wanted to press the Congress hard: "The claims of the army urged with moderation, but with firmness, may operate on those weak minds which are influenced by their apprehensions more than their judgments, so as to produce a concurrence in the measures which the exigencies of affairs demand."

Hamilton cautioned Washington that it would be difficult to keep the suffering army from taking immoderate action and advised that he should take control. Yet he feared that Washington might calm the army too much, thereby deflating its influence. Hamilton suggested that Washington should "guide the torrent, and bring order perhaps even good, out of confusion." He then craftily intimated to Washington that some thought he had lost the confidence of his army. He claimed not to believe it personally, but he relayed this rumor in order to encourage Washington's leadership in the affair.

Hamilton explained his motive at the end of the letter: "The great *desideratum* at present is the establishment of general funds, which alone can do justice...restore public credit and supply the future wants of government. This is the object of all men of sense; in this the influence of the army, properly directed, may cooperate."[47] What Hamilton did not tell Washington was that Hamilton was attempting to use his friend to force the hand of Congress with carefully measured threats from the military.

Washington responded prudently and refused to take Hamilton's bait to lead such a scheme. He feared that the consequences of a general mutiny "would at this day be productive of civil commotions and end in blood. Unhappy situation this! God forbid we should be involved in it." He blamed the discontent of the army on designing men, such as his old nemesis Horatio Gates, who operated "under the mask of the most perfect dissimulation and apparent cordiality." Washington hoped that justice would prevail before events spiraled out of control. He still had reason to believe that the Congress and the state legislatures would meet the just demands of the army. "The states cannot, surely," he wrote, "be so devoid of common sense, common honesty, and common policy as to refuse their aid." Likewise he remained confident that the army would be reasonable in pressing its claims. He shared Hamilton's desire for a more powerful federal government, though not his means of achieving it.[48]

Only a few days later, the brewing tempest exploded. On March 8, the officers stationed in Newburgh gathered to read the anonymous Newburgh Address that made overt threats to the Congress. The author (John Armstrong Jr.) told the officers that they had together "felt the cold hand of poverty without a murmur, and [had] seen the insolence of wealth without a sigh" in the service of their country. He told them "faith has its limits, as well as temper; and there are points beyond which neither can be stretched, without sinking into cowardice, or plunging into credulity." They would suffer at the hands of their own government no more. Even though the army had beaten the British, the Congress failed to thank their sacrifice with "tears of gratitude and smiles of admiration." Rather, Congress "tramples upon rights, disdains your cries, and insults your distresses."[49] After years of privations, the army was tired of peaceful petitions to Congress.

Since Congress had not listened to its pleas, the army would take more radical action. Additionally, the army would not obey the likes of a General Washington who endured years of privation at the hands of Congress yet continued to tolerate that body, and the officers would no longer do the same.

Washington spent the previous eight years staking his honor and reputation on defending republican government. He would tolerate no disloyalty from the army. On March 11, shocked by the address, he issued general orders for an assembly of officers to meet on March 15. The meeting would be presided over by General Gates.

Writing to Hamilton on March 12, Washington explained that he had strong suspicions that some members of Congress in Philadelphia were artfully scheming to use the army to compel the Congress to pay the army. As their commander, he had an obligation "to arrest on the spot, the foot that stood wavering on a tremendous precipice; to prevent the officers from being taken by surprise while their passions were all inflamed, and to rescue them from plunging themselves into a gulf of civil horror from which there might be no receding." He continued to hope that the officers would act with moderation but urged Hamilton to convince Congress to pay them. Otherwise, disastrous consequences would result, and Congress "must be answerable to God and their country for the ineffable horrors which may be occasioned thereby." Unwilling to abide threats to Congress, he also refused to absolve it of its sacred duties of governance.[50]

A chill day dawned on March 15—the Ides of March. The Newburgh camp was abuzz with rumors and tension. The officers gathered at the new public meetinghouse for the army, the Temple of Virtue, and Gates called the officers to order at noon. To the great surprise of the assembled officers, an agitated Washington strode into the hall to address his men. With calculated drama, he commanded all of the public presence that he had carefully cultivated over many years.

Washington addressed his men and immediately berated the author of the Newburgh addresses. The general bemoaned, "How inconsistent with the rules of propriety! How unmilitary! And how subversive of all order and discipline, let the good sense of the Army decide." He attacked the Newburgh Address because it appealed "more to the feelings and passions, than to the reason and judgment of the Army," and he said that the author "had another plan in view, in which candor and liberality of sentiment, regard to justice, and love of country, have no part." Rather, the author had in mind "to effect the blackest designs" against the republic.

He then made a personal appeal to his men, the same men who shared the ravages of war and a miserly Congress with him. Anyone who had seen him rally troops in the midst of battle or saw his talk to the men at Valley Forge knew that truth. He said that the author of the addresses was an insidious foe who was an enemy of the army and the republic, since his proposals would lead to the "ruin of both, by sowing the seeds of discord and separation between the civil and military powers of the continent."

Continuing, Washington encouraged his men to the highest respect for the civilian authority of government in the fledgling republic. He promised his men that he had no doubts that Congress would "entertain exalted sentiments of the services of the army; and, from a full conviction of its merits and sufferings, will do it complete justice." He explained that the Congress was a large, deliberative body that needed to reconcile differing interests in formulating sound laws. He counseled his officers to have patience and trust that Congress would make good on its promises.

Washington made one last patriotic entreaty to his men to uphold the American republic for which they had spilled their blood for the last eight years. The men had the opportunity to display their patriotism and virtue for all of posterity and achieve lasting fame. With a belief in American exceptionalism, he told them that their actions would determine the fate of republics everywhere. It was America's opportunity to defy the base instincts of human nature and historical failure of republics—such as Rome—to prove that a virtuous people were capable of self-government.

After reading the prepared speech to his men, many of whom were still unmoved by his words, Washington won the allegiance of his officers in one of the most dramatic moments of the American Revolution. In a carefully scripted gesture, he paused and fumbled around in his vest pocket. Pulling out a pair of spectacles, he put them on and apologized: "Gentlemen, you will permit me to put on my spectacles, for I have not only grown gray, but almost blind, in the service of my country."[51] With Washington's unusually open admission of his declining vigor, the officers wept openly. The cabal collapsed on the spot, and the officers unanimously pledged their support for Congress.

A few days after the conspiracy was defeated, Hamilton all but admitted his role in the affair. He explained to Washington, "If no excesses take place I shall not be sorry that ill-humors have appeared. I shall not regret importunity, if temperate, from the army." He thought that the localism of the states would continue to render the Congress impotent, threatening the stability and prosperity of the Union. Because he saw internal weaknesses as the greatest threat to the survival of the young republic, he was willing to take certain calculated risks. Incredibly, considering Washington's words and actions from a few days before, Hamilton actually confessed his belief that "I thought the discontents of the army might be turned to a good account. I am still of opinion that their earnest, but respectful applications for redress will have a good effect."[52]

Hamilton explained the importance of assuming greater federal power for American national honor and sovereignty. If America could erect a perpetual union, it could then "prevent being a ball in the hands of European powers bandied against each other at their pleasure." The American republic would survive in a world of contending powerful empires.[53]

Hamilton continued to believe that he had acted correctly and offered no apologies to Washington. He even praised the congressmen who were implicated in the affair as the "most sensible, the most liberal, the most independent and the most respectable characters in our body."[54] In short, they were acting in the best interests of creating an enduring republic rather standing idly by and allowing the edifice to crumble.

Washington responded to Hamilton that he agreed with much of his political philosophy, but he refused to countenance his actions. Washington concurred that the sovereignty of the states threatened disunion and opened America to domination by the European powers. Moreover, he advocated a revised constitution and a national character. He stated, "No man in the United States is, or can be more deeply impressed with the necessity of a reform in our present Confederation than myself." However, he excoriated Hamilton for deeming the threat of force an appropriate solution. Washington explained that "the idea of redress by force is too chimerical to have had a place in the imagination of any serious mind." He cautioned Hamilton that "the army is a dangerous instrument to play with." It would set a dangerous precedent at the birth of the republic. For Washington, statesmen such as himself must provide moderate leadership.

His last word to Hamilton on the matter ended with an expression of hope that the Congress would pay the army before its neglect caused real disorder. In Washington's view, the army and Congress had sacred obligations to meet regarding the army's pay. Republican government would only work if everyone performed their public duties.[55]

Congress never met its obligations to the army. Later that spring, it passed a weak impost that Hamilton himself voted against, and the states never ratified it. Robert Morris struggled to find the money to pay the army but failed. Most of the army melted away without pay when the final peace was announced.[56]

Hamilton's motivations in the Newburgh Conspiracy have been deeply scrutinized by historians who continue to come to different conclusions. One scholar has argued that Hamilton was acting prudentially during the Newburgh Affair, since all legal means to strengthen the national government seemed to have been exhausted.[57] He probably did not intend to launch a coup d'état. Rather, he wanted to use the questionable means of the threat of force to achieve his version of an energetic government. Regardless, Washington's virtue had saved the republic from a misguided conspiracy that at best utilized military force to gain political ends, and at worst might possibly have led to the destruction of the republic.

Through his towering presence as a symbol of republican disinterestedness, Washington thwarted the Newburgh conspirators. Thomas Jefferson claimed, with little hyperbole, that "the moderation and virtue of a single character has probably prevented this revolution from being closed as most others have been by a subversion of that liberty it was intended to establish."[58] Hamilton escaped with his reputation intact, largely because the conspiracy remained shrouded in mystery. Regardless, the problems of a weak national government continued. Both Washington and Hamilton remained at the vanguard of the nationalists in favor of a more powerful central government.

In June 1783, after a preliminary peace treaty was signed and the Newburgh conspiracy deflated, Washington had greater time and calm for reflection about the future at his headquarters in Newburgh. He composed a "Circular Letter to the States" in which he laid out his thoughts on the national union.

The means to achieve success for the new republic were clear. The national government must be strengthened in order to govern a continental union: "This is the favorable moment to give such a tone to our federal government, as will enable it to answer the ends of its institution; or this may be the ill-fated moment for relaxing the powers of the Union, annihilating the cement of the Confederation." Their decision would determine, with dramatic effects, "whether the Revolution must ultimately be considered as a blessing or a curse: a blessing or a curse, not to the present alone, for with our fate will the destiny of unborn Millions be involved." His view of American exceptionalism was not simply a celebration of the greatness of America but rather a grave burden that would determine the freedom of all peoples. This would not be an easy struggle, nor was success predetermined.[59]

In July 1783, Hamilton quit the Congress in disgust. On September 30, he wrote Washington, praising the "Circular Letter to the States." Hamilton wrote, "I trust it will not be without effect" but expressed some disappointment because it would have been more effective had it contained more of his ideas about the Union. Besides lecturing the commander in chief, Hamilton pressed Washington for a brevet, or honorary commission.[60] He thought it might be a boon for his legal practice. Washington granted Hamilton his wish, but perhaps tellingly, no record exists of the latter offering any thanks.[61]

After eight years of war away from his home, Washington looked forward to the repose of retirement "free from the load of public cares."[62] When the word came of the definitive treaty and British preparations to evacuate, Washington said farewell to his army. The great victory in the war for independence was "little short of a standing miracle." He called them "one patriotic band of brothers" and professed his "inviolable attachment and friendship." He encouraged them to be at the center of the movement for a national allegiance to the Union and virtuous national character.[63]

He made his way to New York with an embarrassingly small contingent of officers and soldiers, since the army was officially disbanded on November 15. The last British troops were disembarking when

Washington entered New York on November 25, 1783. Most of the Tories and Hessian mercenaries had already left. He arrived to the jubilation of the populace, who flew flags with thirteen stars and stripes.[64]

Washington even met with Hamilton's old friend, Hercules Mulligan, as part of a series of actions to rescue the reputations of suspected Tories who were actually in Washington's pay during the war as spies. Mulligan's relationship with the British was actually part of a ruse to cull information from them. Washington breakfasted at Mulligan's house on November 26, a sure sign that Mulligan was no Tory.[65]

As the British evacuated New York in late November, Hamilton moved his wife and infant son to Wall Street. He bought a home and set up his law practice. Despite his proximity to Washington's formal activities in reoccupying the city, no evidence exists that he took part in any of the festivities. Hamilton was conspicuously absent during the emotional good-byes that Washington said to his officer corps. His personal honor was still wounded by their split, and with this snub, it seemed irrecoverable at the time.

At Fraunces Tavern, Washington lunched with the rest of his beloved officers, including Henry Knox and Baron von Steuben, for the last time. One officer described the scene and remembered Washington's last words to them. After dining, the general raised his glass and tearfully choked out, "With a heart filled with love and gratitude, I now take leave of you. I most devoutly wish that your later days may be as prosperous and happy as your former ones have been glorious and honorable." He struggled to finish and fought to compose himself. He finally said, "I cannot come to each of you, but shall feel obliged if each of you will come and take me by the hand." He warmly embraced all of them in turn, each weeping, and then made his way off.[66]

After stops in Philadelphia and Baltimore with more patriotic celebrations, Washington arrived in Annapolis to surrender his military commission to the civilian authority of Congress. With carefully staged theatrics by Thomas Jefferson, Washington entered the state house with great dignity, dressed in his blue military uniform. At the appointed moment, he arose and addressed the Congress solemnly. The room was silent. "Happy in the confirmation of our independence and sovereignty, and pleased with the opportunity afforded the United States of becoming a respectable nation," he resigned his position as commander in chief. He humbly argued that victory was won because of the "rectitude of our cause, the support of the supreme power of the Union, and the patronage of Heaven." He thanked his countrymen and officers for their aid during the war. He finished his speech with faltering words to a weeping audience: "I consider it an indispensable duty to close this last solemn act of my official life, by commending the interests of our dearest country to the protection of almighty God, and those who have the superintendence of them, to his holy keeping. Having now finished the work assigned me, I retire from the great theatre of action."[67]

Like Cincinnatus, the Roman general who surrendered his dictatorial powers to the Senate and returned to his plow, Washington voluntarily gave up his powers to the republic. He presented the yellowed parchment of his 1775 commission to Congress and left for Mount Vernon to spend Christmas with his family. With his public retirement, he helped to create the American republic by setting the precedent of civil supremacy over the military. King George III correctly predicted that "if he does that [retires], he will be the greatest man in the world."[68]

Washington and Hamilton's paths diverged at the end of the Revolutionary War. Washington resumed his life as a Virginia planter and attended to his plantation after years of neglect. He looked forward to spending the rest of his years enjoying his idyllic farm. Hamilton, on the other hand, was still a young man on the make. He started a prosperous legal practice in a growing commercial city with seemingly unlimited opportunities. Their friendship and collaboration were seemingly over.

CHAPTER SIX

TWO ROADS TO PHILADELPHIA

THE AMERICANS HAD WON the Revolutionary War and their independence, but their leaders could not have been more divided. The great fruit of the alliance of George Washington and Alexander Hamilton had been born with the penultimate victory at Yorktown, but their collaboration, however, had been severed by their dramatic falling out, despite the great victory and their mutual work for a stronger national government.

The differences in their ages and stations further eroded any possibility that their relationship would continue after the war, because peace meant very different things to Washington and Hamilton. Washington was the great hero of the American Revolution, and when he retired from public life to his Virginia plantation, he thought it would be permanent and he would only be burdened by the cares of his land and a steady stream of visitors coming to pay homage. Hamilton was not yet thirty and had a growing family to support. He set up shop for his legal practice at 57 Wall Street, in the heart of one of America's busiest ports, and was anxious to begin his new career as soon as the British troops and their Loyalist allies departed. Washington had achieved the glory and fame he had sought, while Hamilton was still a young man with boundless ambition and energy.

While Washington went to great lengths to remain in close contact with other officers from the war, such as the beloved Henry Knox and Marquis de Lafayette, no comparable effort was made to reach out to Hamilton. Over the next few years, Washington and Hamilton exchanged only a handful of impersonal letters. They both continued to work for a stronger national government in their respective spheres but no longer together. Their relationship might never have been renewed but for the course of larger events that threatened the survival of the new nation.

★★★

IN NOVEMBER 1783, WHEN the British had sailed off from New York, the transports had carried almost thirty thousand Tories from the city. Hamilton thought that the exodus of Tories from New York and America would have significant negative consequences on New York. "Our state will feel for twenty years at least the effects of the popular frenzy," he wrote, thinking particularly of the commercial damage done when thousands of entrepreneurs left.[1] Singling out a class of citizens by violating property rights was a gross infringement of the principles of natural justice and a constitutional rule of law. Moreover, it broke the Paris peace treaty that had been signed only months before. America was an independent nation and must act "in a manner consistent with the dignity of that station."[2] Hamilton told his friend Gouverneur Morris: "I will in the lump, tell you that we are doing those things which we ought not to do. Instead of wholesome regulations for the improvement of our polity and commerce, we are laboring to contrive methods to mortify and punish Tories and to explain away treaties."[3]

In January 1784, Hamilton published a *Letter from Phocion* in which he fired a salvo in the public debate over the treatment of Tories. According to Hamilton, the Trespass Act was rooted in momentary, dark passions and a spirit of "revenge, cruelty, persecution, and perfidy," rather than fundamental principles of reason and justice. If the legislature could disfranchise and banish groups of citizens, it would "furnish precedents for future usurpations on the rights of the community" and make a mockery of a free government. Hamilton was particularly fearful that violating the "solemn engagements" of the peace treaty of 1783 would cause America to become "the scorn of nations" and ruin its international reputation at its beginning. Finally, Hamilton was alarmed that New York was blatantly disregarding the power of Congress to make treaties for the confederation that were binding on the states. If this were allowed to continue, Hamilton wondered, "Would not all the powers of the confederation be annihilated and the union dissolved?"[4]

Hamilton may have been aghast that the continuing violation of Tories' rights would mar the national honor and reputation of the new nation, but the dispute would certainly bear fruit for his burgeoning law practice. He confided to Morris that "legislative folly has afforded so plentiful a harvest to us lawyers that we have scarcely a moment to spare from…reaping."[5]

During the spring of 1784, Hamilton came out from under the cover of his classical pseudonym and publicly represented a Tory in a case that was as much a risk to his reputation as John Adams defending the redcoats in the Boston Massacre.[6] Elizabeth Rutgers was an eighty-year-old widow who had fled the British occupation in 1776 and abandoned her brewery and alehouse. A couple of British merchants, including Benjamin Waddington, had taken over the brewery at the instigation of the British army and operated it for the duration of the war. Waddington and his partner did not pay rent from 1778 until 1780. They made improvements to the property and paid rent after 1780 to the British army according to the law of nations. Two days before Washington and his army reoccupied New York, a fire destroyed the property. Mrs. Rutgers sued Waddington for £8,000 under the Trespass Act.[7]

On June 29, 1784, Hamilton, representing Waddington, appeared before the Mayor's Court of New York City and presented his arguments in the case. Hamilton argued that the Trespass Act was invalid because it violated the laws of war. New York incorporated common law, which included the law of nations, which in turn included the laws of war and permitted Waddington's actions. Secondly, under the Articles of Confederation, only Congress had the authority to make treaties, which the states were bound by the confederation to follow. New York, therefore, had to respect the rights of Tories. The new attorney also made the first of his many arguments for judicial review of legislative acts. He quoted Cicero to say that when two laws conflict, the fundamental law trumps the ordinary law. The court could also invalidate a legislative act if the majority were acting tyrannically by violating the rights of a minority group.[8]

In mid-August, the court rendered its decision and split the difference. Although it did not invalidate the Trespass Act, the court also did not award the sympathetic, elderly widow full damages. The decision accepted Hamilton's reasoning about the law of nations. Mrs. Rutgers won damages for the use of her property for two years when the rent went unpaid and settled the case for £800.[9]

The New York press and legislature harshly criticized the decision, with the assembly stating that the court had "subverted all law and good order." Hamilton was excoriated for arguing on behalf of Tories. Nevertheless, he would continue representing them in some seventy cases over the next few years. George Washington received a copy of the decision involving his former protégé (though not from him) and was pleased with its result. Washington noted that "reason seems very much in favor of it."[10] Common sense and reason, which he thought were notably absent from the Confederation Congress, were the "foundation of all law and government."[11] But while he agreed with the political sentiments Hamilton defended, Washington did not write to congratulate him on the outcome.

Washington spent the winter after his retirement free from the toils of war and with much time to contemplate the future. Although he and Martha would host hundreds of visitors to Mount Vernon over the next few years, the plantation was generally isolated that winter by almost constant snowstorms and ice. He kept abreast of national events through the newspapers and letters that filtered in. The hope for his country that he expressed at the outset of his retirement was tempered by the nearly constant failures of the Articles of Confederation to govern the country effectively.

In early January 1784, Washington conveyed a faint confidence that the "good sense of the people will ultimately [prevail]."[12] But underlying this tepid optimism was a suspicion that the country was "now sinking faster in esteem than we rose." The remedy was not patience that the government would do better in peace than in war but revision of the Articles of Confederation. Without giving Congress "competent powers for all federal purposes," Washington thought, the new nation faced probable collapse. Unlike those who continued to articulate the principles of 1776, he was more concerned that tyranny would result from a weak government rather than a powerful one. He predicted the "worst consequences from a half-starved, limping government that appears to be always moving upon crutches, and tottering at every step."[13] Washington's circle of correspondents included many who had been engaged in national politics or officers from the Continental army, and they shared a continental vision for America. Washington and Hamilton were at the core of this group of nationalists who saw events over the next few years through this lens and independently took steps to strengthen the national government.

One of the main weaknesses of the Articles of Confederation was the inability to regulate interstate commerce. The states set tariffs on each other's trade and tolls on their traffic. Disputes erupted several times throughout the 1780s and almost resulted in the states going to war. Hamilton's New York passed a tariff on trade from New Jersey as if "from any other foreign port."[14] Washington's Virginia competed with Maryland for trade and the navigation of the Potomac, involving the retired general in interstate relations and permitting him the opportunity to pursue a dream of opening up the West to trade. The plan would clearly benefit the master of Mount Vernon and his neighbors as a rich flow of river traffic floated past. Alexandria would become one of the country's major ports and the Chesapeake Bay a much larger center of trade. Investors in shares of Washington's proposed Potomac Company or Virginians who owned large tracts of land out west (such as Washington) would become fabulously wealthy. Yet the public good—not just private gain—would be served by the development of the Potomac. The eastern states would develop much closer commercial and political ties to those settling on the western frontier.

In December 1784, Washington and other Virginia commissioners met with their counterparts from Maryland and drafted a bill for both state legislatures for a Potomac River Company (which both soon passed). Washington was dismayed when the Virginia General Assembly voted him fifty shares in the company and another hundred in the James River Company, because he wanted to preserve his reputation for serving the republic in a disinterested manner. After debating the issue with confidants, he decided to donate the shares to a college (later Washington and Lee).[15]

Representatives from the two state assemblies, Maryland and Virginia, later met at the Mount Vernon Conference, which resulted in an agreement not to pass tolls on each other's vessels and share the cost of lighthouses.[16] More importantly, it was the basis for subsequent interstate meetings to settle disputes and increase national power.

The success of the Mount Vernon Conference may have resolved some navigation problems between two states amicably, but Washington was still worried about the state of national affairs and the weak central government. If localism continued to frustrate the designs of the nationalists, he thought it must "sap the constitution of these states (already too weak)—destroy our national character—and render us contemptible in the eyes of Europe."[17] The refusal of the states to pass the national impost was all the evidence he needed to prove the deficiencies of the Articles of Confederation.

Alexander Hamilton was arguably the most committed politician in America to the idea of revising the Articles. The problems of the Articles had commanded his attention since before the end of the American Revolution, and he had led the fight for a general convention to remedy them. "We have now happily concluded the great work of independence," he wrote, "but much remains to be done to reach the fruits of it. Our prospects are not flattering. Every day proves the inefficacy of the present confederation."[18] He had composed a resolution calling for a convention to amend the Articles in 1783 but never submitted it to Congress for a want of support.[19] His sense of urgency would only grow over the next four years. Rather than looking for support from his former mentor, he sought to work with active politicians who could push for reform in their states or Congress. In this, Hamilton could find no better collaborator than James Madison. In late 1785, based upon the positive outcome of the Mount Vernon Conference, Madison pushed for a "general meeting of Commissioners from the states to consider and recommend a federal plan for regulating commerce." Early the next year, the Virginia legislature finally resolved to call for a meeting to "examine the relative situations and trade of the said states [and] to consider how far a uniform system in their commercial regulations may be necessary to their common interest and their permanent harmony."[20]

Hamilton and Madison were chosen that spring by their state legislatures as delegates to the Annapolis Convention. Hamilton and the other delegates were authorized to examine "the trade and commerce of the United States; to consider how far a uniform system in their commercial intercourse and regulations may be necessary to their common interest and permanent harmony."[21] The site was chosen because of its distance from the Congress in New York "in order to disarm the adversaries to the object."[22] Several states, however, chose not to send delegates, including, ironically, Maryland, which was the host of the conference. Madison confided his fears to Thomas Jefferson that nothing would be accomplished: "I almost despair of success. It is necessary however that something should be tried and it is the best that could possibly be carried through the legislature here."[23] Hamilton and Madison arrived in Annapolis in early September, committed to a goal that Washington strongly endorsed.

Madison came to the meeting well prepared to address the flaws in the national government. He had pored over a shelf full of books on history and politics that Jefferson shipped from Paris. The resulting study, "Notes on Ancient and Modern Confederacies," revealed Madison's thinking that the decline of confederacies in the past was generally rooted in weak central control and stronger constituent parts. The inevitable result was impotency, leading to dissolution and collapse. Madison and Hamilton concurred that this historic problem now plagued the weak central government under the Articles and threatened disintegration in the near future. Their practical experience in Congress and in the state assemblies during the 1780s was confirmed by their intellectual study. When they met at Mann's Tavern, the site of Washington's retirement dinner in early September, the pair had much to discuss.[24]

Madison was anxious that so few delegates had arrived from so few states. On Friday, September 8, he glumly wrote, "The prospect of a sufficient number to make the meeting respectable is not flattering."[25] On Monday, twelve commissioners met at the Old Senate Chamber of the Maryland State House with their weak quorum and elected John Dickinson chairman. Stating that it was "inexpedient for this convention in which so few states are represented to proceed in the business committed to them," they appointed a committee to draft a report to the states.[26] Virginian Edmund Randolph began preparing a draft, but the audacious Alexander Hamilton stepped in and assumed control over the task, because he wanted to ensure that the statement was sufficiently bold and did not equivocate on the question of enhancing the powers of the national government.

The convention had been developing a consensus that more radical nationalist reform was necessary. Hamilton was emboldened by this consensus and penned a resolution that was too extreme even for the assembled group of nationalists. The more prudent Madison pulled Hamilton aside and privately advised him to tone down the language. "You had better yield...for otherwise all Virginia will be against you," Madison explained. Hamilton followed the advice, perhaps grudgingly, and amended the report.[27]

On September 14, the committee unanimously agreed to the final report, which was still quite radical. "That there are important defects in the system of the federal government is acknowledged by the acts of all those states, which have concurred in the present meeting," it began. The defects were "greater and more numerous" than previously imagined and caused the "embarrassments which characterize the present state of our national affairs—foreign and domestic." They endorsed a "deliberate and candid discussion" at another convention to explore possible solutions. The commissioners called on the states to meet "at Philadelphia on the second Monday in May next, to take into consideration the situations of the United States, to devise such further provisions as shall appear to them necessary to render the constitution of the federal government adequate to the exigencies of the Union."[28] Congress received the report and submitted it to a committee, where it lay for months until a rebellion in Massachusetts confirmed all the fears of the nationalists and stirred Congress to action.

Washington was already deeply concerned about the state of the Union before Shays's Rebellion erupted in western Massachusetts. He had informed Lafayette that "a general convention is talked of by many for the purpose of revising and correcting the defects of the federal government, but whilst this is the wish of some, it is the dread of others from an opinion that matters are not yet sufficiently ripe for such an event."[29] Washington was even more emotional when he told John Jay, "Something must be done, or the fabric will fall. It certainly is tottering!... I think often of our situation and view it with concern. From the high ground on which we stood—from the plain path which invited our footsteps, to be so fallen! So lost! [It] is really mortifying."[30]

Farmers in Massachusetts were just as frustrated with their own local and state governments. After fighting for their liberties in the Revolutionary War, the proud, independent yeomen were mired in debt because British trade markets had been closed, specie was in short supply, paper money was worthless, and crop prices were depressed. When eastern merchants and shopkeepers asked for payment of debts owed to them, the farmers simply could not pay them. They lost their farms to foreclosure and were thrown into debtors' prison.[31]

During the summer and fall, the farmers assembled in democratic local meetings at taverns and petitioned the Massachusetts General Court, begging for help in the form of fairer taxes, debt relief, an inflated paper currency, and, most importantly, the suspension of debtor courts to save their property.[32]

While Hamilton attended the Annapolis Convention, bayonet- and rifle-wielding farmers in Massachusetts angrily marched on county courthouses and shut them down as symbols of oppression. They rested their actions on Revolutionary principles that recalled the ideals of resisting tyranny in the previous decade. In late September, a massive crowd of fifteen hundred demonstrators blocked the Massachusetts Supreme Court from convening.

The response of the national government was predictably weak, while the reaction of the state government was draconian. The Continental Congress resolved to raise troops, but none ever appeared. The General Court passed a Militia Act, making it a penalty to join in "any mutiny or sedition," and a Riot Act, prohibiting twelve or more armed persons from meeting, under the threat of death. The government suspended the writ of habeas corpus and threatened rioters with the loss of their property, whippings of thirty-nine lashes, and lengthy jail time. Some farmers were intimidated, but most retired to their homes to bring in the harvest. The lull would prove to be only temporary.[33]

News filtered to Washington from some of his former Continental army officers, who sent messages that terrified their retired general. He heard exaggerated rumors of fifteen thousand licentious insurgents who ran amok, flaunted all law, and sought to destroy private property. Events were spiraling out of control, and the crisis meant that "the wheels of the great political machine can scarcely continue to move much longer."[34]

Influenced by these views coming from trusted correspondents, Washington replied with the same near-hysterical outrage at the rebellion. He wondered whether the people were "getting mad."[35] He wailed, "What, gracious God, is man!"[36] He was shocked that he and his soldiers fought for independence and republican government for eight years only to see that effort being squandered: "It is but the other day we were shedding our blood to obtain the constitutions under which we now live...and now we are unsheathing the sword to overturn them!"[37] Nothing solidified the need for greater national authority in Washington's mind than Shays's Rebellion.

Governor James Bowdoin agreed with Washington's overwrought view of the rebels and raised a private subscription army of forty-four hundred soldiers with the support of one hundred fifty wealthy individuals from the eastern counties who contributed funds. General Benjamin Lincoln agreed to lead the army to reestablish "system and order" in the Massachusetts countryside.[38] The rebellious farmers were in turn organized under the leadership of Daniel Shays, a Revolutionary War captain. Announcing their intention to overthrow the "tyrannical government of Massachusetts" and guided by Revolutionary principles, the Shaysites organized an attack on the federal arsenal in Springfield to seize the muskets and cannon housed there. In late January 1787, more than two thousand rebels marched through several feet of snow and assaulted the arsenal, which was defended by twelve hundred militiamen who repulsed the farmers with grapeshot that left four dead and dozens wounded. The insurgency largely ended with this skirmish, and while the General Court sought to punish the rebels for their "unprovoked, and wicked rebellion," the governor more prudently pardoned them.[39]

The profound impact of Shays's Rebellion on the thinking of Washington, Hamilton, and other nationalist leaders cannot be overestimated. Madison believed that the insurrection gave "new proofs of the necessity of such a vigor in the general government as will be able to restore health to any diseased part of the federal constitution."[40] Washington made the most direct link of the rebellion to the weakness of government. "The disturbances in New England, the declining state of our commerce, and the general languor which seems to pervade the union are in a great measure (if not entirely) owing to the want of proper authority," he wrote.[41] Nevertheless, in late February 1787, when Congress did finally approve the Annapolis call for another convention to revise the Articles, Washington was anguished over the decision whether to attend.

Washington's friends bombarded him with letters imploring him to join the planned Philadelphia Convention to revise the Articles. The onslaught started once the Virginia General Assembly unanimously resolved to send delegates to the convention in November. Madison, Randolph, and other Virginians put Washington's name forward and lobbied him intensely to attend. They played on his fears that the nation was crumbling and appealed to his strong sense of public duty. He exchanged letters with them for months and pulled out every excuse not to attend the convention, because he was greatly torn over his lasting reputation and fame. The one person with whom he did not confer was Alexander Hamilton in New York.

Washington was the president of the Society of the Cincinnati, a

fraternal order of Continental army officers with hereditary membership that had become an embarrassment to him, because it struck
many observers as an antidemocratic fraternity that at best appeared
to be aristocratic and at worst had the potential to be the beginnings
of a standing army. Thomas Jefferson had exaggerated fears about the
society becoming a "hereditary aristocracy which will change the form
of our governments from the best to the worst in the world," and his
concerns were shared by Benjamin Franklin, John Adams, and others.[42]
Washington was sensitive to the criticisms because of his public reputation and love of republican liberty and was irritated by the contention.
The Cincinnati was responsible for one of the few exchanges between
Washington and Hamilton during this period.

Washington thought the suspicion and attacks on the society
were "carried to an unwarrantable length" and that the officers were
motivated by a strong patriotism and "nobler and more generous sentiments than were apprehended." However, he was fearful of fostering
disunity and ultimately urged the revocation of the society's hereditary
membership clause. He wrote to Hamilton, who was heavily involved
in the New York chapter, and besought him to strike out the provision.
"If the Society of the Cincinnati mean to live in peace with the rest of
their fellow citizens, they must subscribe to the alterations," he wrote.[43]
Hamilton signed his name to a report of the New York members who
balked at the proposed changes but adopted them "in deference to the
sense of many of our fellow citizens, as in conformity to the true spirit
of the institution itself." They supported the principle of merit rather
than the aristocratic idea that was "inconsistent with the genius of a
society founded on friendship and patriotism."[44]

Washington had tried to distance himself from the public dispute
over the society by missing the society's annual meeting—which, coinci-
dentally, was being held in Philadelphia that spring—complaining of a
rheumatism flare-up.[45] Now, he could also not attend the Philadelphia
Convention, because he would offend the members of the Cincinnati.

But the most significant reason he gave for declining the invitation was related to his public retirement, when he dramatically laid down his sword and returned to his plow. He dreaded the consequences to his reputation for republican virtue if he returned from retirement and appeared to overthrow the existing regime, especially if there was dubious legality about the venture. Contrarily, a failed attempt to strengthen the Articles would be mortifying for any participants, but it would be "a disagreeable predicament...more particularly so for a person in my situation."[46] Interestingly, his attendance would only be predicated on whether "the delegates come with such powers as will enable the convention to probe the defects of the constitution to the bottom, and point out radical errors."[47]

From yet another perspective, Washington was troubled that his absence from the convention to set the government on a proper foundation would be perceived by the American people as a "dereliction to republicanism."[48] The "Father of His Country" could not watch the new nation crumble around him, all the while sitting on his porch as the Potomac rolled by. If Cincinnatus was his role model, then Caesar was the antithesis to be avoided. But the charge of Caesarism could be leveled not only against someone who marched his army against Congress but also against a leader who let it fall and then walked in to pick up the pieces.

Others vehemently disagreed with Washington's decision. His friends sent purposefully dire warnings about the fate of the republic to induce Washington to attend. Edmund Randolph, for example, stated, "I doubt whether the existence of [Congress] even through this year may not be questionable."[49] Washington was still deliberating over whether to attend only a month before the Constitutional Convention was supposed to meet. On April 9, he finally caved into the pressure from his friends across Virginia and the country. Announcing to Randolph his intention to attend the convention, he complained, "I declare to you that my assent is given contrary to my judgment."[50]

Hamilton faced his own set of problems regarding his appointment to the convention. First, in February, New York defeated the impost and Congress's ability to collect taxes. After learning of Congress's approval of the resolution for the Philadelphia Convention, Hamilton offered a proposal for five delegates to attend from New York. The Clintonite forces reduced this to three and transparently appointed Robert Yates and John Lansing to foil Hamilton's designs of strengthening the government. Washington even heard from Madison that the two were "pretty much linked to the antifederal party here, and are likely of course to be a clog on their colleague."[51] Neither Washington nor Hamilton had much hope that the Philadelphia Convention would achieve anything meaningful and save the nation from impending ruin.

On May 9, George Washington left Mount Vernon for what he expected to be a long trip to the Philadelphia Convention. As he traveled, he was still deeply conflicted about attending. He was not very sanguine that the delegates would be able to create an adequate government but was determined not to see the achievements of the American Revolution squandered. He had already heard from friends that he could expect to be elected president of the convention and that his name had "great influence to induce the states" to accept the result.[52] Thinking about such things was a source of even greater anxiety. On the other hand, he had recently read an early version of Madison's Virginia Plan and may have been encouraged by Madison's proposal.[53] A few days before he departed, Washington politely refused an invitation to stay at the home of Robert Morris, because he feared "there is great reason to apprehend that the business of the Convention (from the tardiness of some states, and the discordant opinions of others) will not be brought to a speedy conclusion."[54]

Washington arrived in Philadelphia on May 13, escorted by the light horse cavalry unit, which processed past saluting artillery officers. Joyous crowds, led by the president of the Supreme Council, Benjamin

Franklin, warmly and enthusiastically welcomed "the coming of this great and good man," while church bells rang.[55]

The convention was supposed to assemble the next day, but only the Virginia and Pennsylvania delegations were represented. Washington was annoyed by the delay, noting that it was "highly vexatious to those who are idly and expensively spending their time here."[56] The Virginia delegation, led unofficially by Madison, productively spent the time planning to control the early course of the convention with his plan for a stronger national government. The delegates met every day at three o'clock and conferred with each other for "two or three hours…in order to form a proper correspondence of sentiments."[57] The result was the nationalist-leaning Virginia Plan.

On May 18, Alexander Hamilton arrived in Philadelphia with Yates and lodged at the Indian Queen Tavern on Fourth Street. The New York delegation made their way over to the state house to join some of the preliminary deliberations. Although Yates may have been apprehensive about the talk of consolidating national power, Washington and Hamilton approved and, more importantly, had an opportunity to reestablish their relationship after four years.[58] The crisis in public affairs had brought the pair back together, and they would share their common vision of a stronger national government on the floor of the convention. They would also be able to cement personal ties through informal conversations over dinner and toasts in the taverns the delegates frequented.

Relatively few delegates arrived over the course of the week, souring Washington's mood because the delay was wasting his time but more importantly "greatly impeding public measures."[59] All the delegates respected General Washington as the great hero of the Revolutionary War, and like Massachusetts representative Rufus King, predicted that Washington would be "placed in the chair."[60] Finally, on May 24, enough states had assembled to form a quorum, and the convention convened the following day.

Octogenarian Franklin wanted to nominate Washington to be the president of the convention but was laid up by illness, so Washington's friend Robert Morris nominated him in Franklin's stead. Washington was unanimously elected, as expected. His very presence gave legitimacy to the entire convention, and Americans could trust that he would pursue the public good.[61]

Washington understood the gravity of the moment and the significance of dramatic gestures: "In a very emphatic manner he thanked the convention for the honor they had conferred on him, reminded them of the novelty of the scene of business in which he was about to act, lamented his want of better qualifications, and claimed the indulgence of the house towards the involuntary errors which his inexperience might occasion."[62]

Hamilton rose and nominated Major William Jackson, who had served on Washington's staff during the war, to be the secretary of the convention, though Madison would prove to be the most faithful record keeper of the proceedings. The delegates appointed a committee to establish rules that would govern debate. Hamilton, George Wythe, Jefferson's law professor at William and Mary, and Charles Pinckney were chosen to serve on the Rules Committee.[63] With that, "the Convention adjourned till Monday, to give time to the Committee to report the matters referred to them."[64]

George Washington was not known for his sense of humor, nor did the Philadelphia Convention generate a lot of lighthearted moments. But Hamilton was involved in an incident with Washington that was probably apocryphal but demonstrates the reserve he cultivated and perhaps reveals a mischievous side to Hamilton. Gouverneur Morris said that he "could be as familiar with Washington as with any of his other friends." Hamilton bet Morris a dinner and flight of wines for him and a dozen of his friends if he greeted Washington in an overly friendly manner. Morris supposedly accepted the challenge, and after bowing and shaking hands with the general, he laid a hand on Washington's shoulder and said, "My dear General, I am very happy to see you look so well!" Washington "withdrew his hand, stepped suddenly back, fixed his eye on Morris for several minutes with an angry frown, until the latter retreated abashed, and sought refuge in the crowd. The company looked on in silence. At the supper, which was provided by Hamilton, Morris said, 'I have won the bet, but paid dearly for it, and nothing could induce me to repeat it.'"[65]

On Monday, May 28, Franklin joined the convention after being carried aloft on a sedan chair by four prisoners from the city jail. The other members of the convention arrived in a more prosaic manner and agreed to the proposals of Hamilton and the Rules Committee. The delegates would treat each other according to the rules of civility as they debated. Each state delegation would have only one vote, following the precedent established by the Continental Congress and the Confederation Congress. Hamilton wanted to have individual voting, because he knew on the second day of the convention that his fellow New York delegates would negate his vote and thus his ability to achieve his objectives.[66] Finally, the proceedings of the convention would be conducted in secret. This would allow for greater candor in debate and allow the delegates to alter their minds freely in the course of deliberation. The delegates would also be free of public pressure. Hamilton later commented on the significance of this rule: "Had the deliberations been open while going on, the clamors of faction would have prevented any satisfactory result. Had they been afterwards disclosed, much food would have been afforded to inflammatory declamation."[67]

A vignette from the convention demonstrates how seriously Washington took this rule as the chairman of the meeting and how profoundly respected he was. One of the members dropped some notes on the floor that might have been discovered and compromised the secrecy of the convention. He supposedly dressed down his fellow delegates: "Gentlemen, I am sorry to find that some one member of this body has been so neglectful of the secrets of the convention as to drop in the State House a copy of their proceedings, which by accident was picked up and delivered to me this morning. I must entreat gentlemen to be more careful, lest our transactions get into the newspapers and disturb the public repose by premature speculations. I do not know whose paper it is, but there it is—let him who owns it take it." Georgian William Pierce reported that he nervously checked his pockets but was relieved to discover they were not his notes when he checked the handwriting.[68]

Pierce also left penetrating portraits of the characters of the members of the convention. He thought Hamilton was a brilliant thinker and persuasive speaker, if a bit arrogant because he knew he was the smartest man in the room and let everyone know it: "Col. Hamilton is deservedly celebrated for his talents. He is a practitioner of the law, and reputed to be a fine scholar. To a clear and strong judgment he unites the ornaments of fancy...he enquires into every part of his subject with the searchings of philosophy, and when he comes forward he comes highly charged with interesting matter, there is no skimming over the surface of a subject with him. He must sink to the bottom to see what foundation it rests on... His manners are tinctured with stiffness and sometimes with a degree of vanity that is highly disagreeable."[69]

Pierce's description of Washington was equally incisive about his character and fame: "General Washington is well known as the Commander in chief of the late American Army. Having conducted these states to independence and peace, he now appears to assist in framing a government to make the people happy. Like Gustavus Vasa, he may be said to be the deliverer of his country. Like Peter the Great, he appears as the politician and the statesman. Like Cincinnatus he returned to his farm perfectly contented with being only a plain citizen, after enjoying the highest honor of the Confederacy. Now only seeks for the approbation of his countrymen by being virtuous and useful."[70]

In the early days of the convention, Virginian William Grayson correctly noted that "the weight of General Washington…is very great in America" and would certainly be a strong factor in popular support of any measures that emerged from Philadelphia. Madison also recognized the salutary effect that Washington's presence had on the convention. He told Jefferson that "the attendance of General Washington is a proof of the light in which he regards it."[71]

Madison thought that the delegates concurred "in viewing our situation as peculiarly critical and in being averse to temporizing expedients."[72] To that end, on Tuesday, May 29, Virginian Edmund Randolph arose and presented the Virginia Plan for consideration. The plan was a remedy for the weakness of the Articles of Confederation and greatly strengthened the national government at the expense of the states. One of the keys to the plan in Madison's eyes was that the national government would enjoy a national veto over state laws, because he believed that the root of majority tyranny and violation of liberties in the 1780s occurred within the states.[73]

Representatives of small states were not pleased by what they heard. Yates, who scribbled a few notes while he remained in the convention, angrily noted that the Virginia Plan promised to create "a strong consolidated union in which the idea of states should be nearly annihilated."[74] That was exactly what Yates, and eventually his fellow New Yorker Robert Lansing, had come to prevent. On the other hand, Hamilton thought that the inquiry struck the right chord, because it addressed the central question of "whether the United States were susceptible of one government, or required a separate existence connected only by leagues offensive and defensive and treaties of commerce."[75] Washington would have quietly assented. When the vote was taken the following day on whether the national government "ought to be established consisting of a supreme legislature, executive, and judiciary," Hamilton voted yes, and Yates voted no.[76] This predictable turn of events soured Hamilton, for he knew that when Lansing arrived in Philadelphia, his vote would be completely negated.

On June 1, Washington took his seat in the chair as usual. That day would see the opening remarks on the creation of the executive branch, and every delegate who was present had Washington at least in the back of his mind as he thought and spoke on the presidency. There was no executive branch under the Articles, while the state constitutions had generally made state governors weak because of the American experience under the British monarchy. Although no one was quite sure how to empower yet restrain executive power, or what the office would look like, the example of General George Washington provided evidence that one could man could be trusted with power—as long as that power was checked.

Pennsylvanian James Wilson, who was one of the main proponents of a stronger national government, stood that day and expressed his support for an executive who would "consist of a single person," who could act with the requisite "energy, dispatch, and responsibility."[77] Based upon their Revolutionary War experience and ideals, Randolph warned that it would create "the fetus of monarchy."[78] When Franklin addressed the question of executive power, he made explicit reference to Washington. He suggested that perhaps the executive should not receive a salary but instead be guided by pure motives and devote himself to the classical ideal of selfless public service. Whether or not his idea was very realistic, he brought the model of Washington's wartime service to bear: "To bring the matter nearer home, have we not seen the great and most important of our officers, that of General of our armies executed for eight years together without the smallest salary, by a patriot whom I will not now offend by any other praise; and this through fatigues and distresses in common with the other brave men his military friends and companions, and the constant anxieties peculiar to his station?"[79]

Franklin's motion was not even debated by his fellow delegates, who summarily dropped the matter. Nevertheless, the one person who seconded the motion was Hamilton, who had witnessed Washington's virtuous conduct for several years. Hamilton supported "so respectable

TWO ROADS TO PHILADELPHIA * 149

a proposition," because he thought it was enforced by arguments that had a certain degree of weight.[80] No one else agreed, and while it was treated with respect because they venerated Franklin, the delegates did not think it was very practical and abandoned the idea.

During the discussion of the executive branch over the next few days, most of the members were more favorably disposed to accept a single executive instead of a council. The glaring exception was Yates, who again frustrated Hamilton's design for a stronger executive. Even worse, Lansing arrived during the first week of June and further dampened Hamilton's hopes. On June 4, New York voted no on creating a single executive. Hamilton supported a motion "to give the executive an absolute negative on the laws" and defended the proposal with an unfortunate example: "The King of Great Britain had not exerted his negative since the Revolution."[81] It was not the last time that Hamilton would use the example of the British in a favorable light during the summer.

That evening, the people of Philadelphia demonstrated their veneration for Washington. At the urging of General Thomas Mifflin and others, Washington agreed to review the troops of the light infantry, cavalry, and artillery.[82] One awestruck observer noted, "My wife and I went to Market Street gate, to see that great and good man, General Washington. We had a full view of him, and Major Jackson, who walked with him, but the number of people who followed him on all sides was astonishing."[83] In successive evenings, Washington was the celebrated guest at dinners hosted by Robert Morris and Benjamin Franklin as well as with luminaries at the Indian Queen Tavern and City Tavern.[84] Washington and Hamilton had many such opportunities to converse informally outside of the sessions of the convention. What they said can never be known, but they restored at least some of the former warmth of their wartime relationship in Philadelphia.

As Washington was feted and acted as the president of the convention and Hamilton fumed over his impotence within the New York delegation, the convention continued debating the Virginia Plan. The conflict grew worse as a result of William Paterson offering the New Jersey Plan for the consideration of the delegates. This plan sought to comply with the mandate of the convention by simply revising the Articles of Confederation. The New Jersey Plan would keep a one-house legislature with equal suffrage and the locus of power in the sovereign states. It would grant additional powers to the Congress to regulate trade and to tax but would not consolidate authority in the national government.[85] Lansing and Yates readily agreed with the New Jersey Plan and offered their full support.

During the weekend, Washington attended Episcopal services at Christ Church, after which he went riding several miles into the country.[86] Rather than seeking a respite from the convention, Hamilton spent the weekend frenetically drawing up his own plan of government. The Virginia Plan and the resulting debate did not go as far in producing a strong national government as Hamilton wanted. The New Jersey Plan would be simply a disastrous continuation of the failed Confederation government. Moreover, Lansing and Yates negated the value of his vote in the New York delegation. Hamilton decided his voice would be heard on the floor of the convention on Monday.

On June 18, Hamilton had his notes before him as he rose to deliver his declamation. The delegates had no idea what would hit them for the next six hours. He began deferentially, stating that he had not spoken very often out of deference to those of "superior abilities, age, and experience," though his wartime leadership and service in the New York legislature and Congress certainly equaled that of many in the room. He also revealed the frustration he felt as part of the New York delegation when he said he had been quiet due to the "delicate situation with respect to his own state." The crisis in public affairs, however, was too serious for him to hold his tongue any longer. He had a duty to "contribute his efforts for the public safety and happiness."[87]

Hamilton continued by expressing his dissatisfaction with both the Virginia and New Jersey Plans, since neither would "answer the purpose." The principles that guided his plan included a stronger national government with coercive power over the states and direct authority over the people, along with sufficient checks on potential abuses of power. The national government must have a "complete sovereignty" that "must swallow up the state powers." He also praised the British government as the "best in the world" and "doubted much whether anything short of it would do in America." It was the only government in the world that united the requisite "public strength with individual security."[88] If the other delegates looked askance at such praise of the British, they were doubly concerned when they heard the plan of government Hamilton now offered the convention.

The national congress in Hamilton's plan had a senate modeled after the "most noble institution" of the House of Lords, but in the American version, the members were to be elected for life (and good behavior). The British monarch received similarly high praise as the "only good one on the subject." Hamilton averred that no good executive "could be established on republican principles" and proposed that the executive serve for life and good behavior. The executive and senators would thus be free of corruption since they did not continually seek office and favors, although these would be elective offices. Abuses of power would be prevented through the separation of powers among three branches of government and a system of checks and balances. These key institutions would provide for the "stability and permanence" that Hamilton sought in the national government after the disastrous experience under the Articles. While Hamilton was seen then and now as a proponent of aristocracy, if not monarchy, his goal was to create a constitution that would contain as many elements of permanence and stability as republican principles would permit. Interestingly, Hamilton's proposal for the House of Representatives was actually more democratic than many of the convention delegates preferred.[89]

Hamilton was smart enough to anticipate the reaction to his

speech, and many of his comments were devoted to heading them off. He asked rhetorically, "Is this a republican government?" The answer was yes, in his belief, if "all the magistrates are appointed, and vacancies are filled, by the people, or a process of election originating with the people." Popular elections were a predominant characteristic of republican governments, but simply basing lifetime offices on an election was not something most delegates were willing to accept. Hamilton also sought to deflect the objection that "such an executive will be an elective monarch," since he was not proposing a king with unlimited power.[90]

Almost wistfully, Hamilton confessed that he was "aware that it [his proposal] went beyond the ideas of most members," but he was optimistic that the crisis in government would cause the American people to "be ready to go as far at least as he proposes." When the choice was put to the people of a stronger government or dissolution, they would see the inadequacy of either plan before the convention, should one be adopted.[91] After listening to the marathon speech for roughly six hours, the members of the convention were quite shocked by what they heard and adjourned without comment.[92]

Hamilton's speech was coolly received and ignored the following day as the convention got back to its former debate. The speech appeared to damage any influence that Hamilton had on the floor of the convention and would come back to haunt him for over a decade as his enemies would label him a monarchist and warn of his ambitious designs. It seemed to be remarkably unwise and obtuse. On the other hand, Hamilton was a brilliant political thinker and strategist. The plan he proposed was a sincerely designed government that he thought would solve the political crisis of the 1780s and was an expression of his honest thoughts about the other plans before the convention, but it was probably more than that. Hamilton may have thought that proposing a plan that was so radical was a prudential and strategic way to break the standstill in the convention and steer the members toward supporting the Virginia Plan.[93] George Washington never offered any thoughts about the speech.

Whether the speech had its intended effect, Hamilton did receive an opportunity to circle back around the speech and explain himself when James Wilson stated that when he spoke about national government, he "did not mean one that would swallow up the state governments as seemed to be wished by some gentlemen," and he thought, "contrary to the opinion of Col. Hamilton that they might not only subsist but subsist on friendly terms with the former."[94] Hamilton retorted that he had not been understood the previous day. He clarified that the national legislature "must...have indefinite authority... As states, he thought they ought to be abolished. But he admitted the necessity of leaving in them, subordinate jurisdictions." Much like Madison, Hamilton used historical examples such as the Persian Empire and the Roman Empire to demonstrate the problems of decentralized power.[95] He attempted to appease the smaller states by stating, "The more close the Union of the states, and the more complete the authority of the whole; the less opportunity will be allowed the stronger states to injure the weaker."[96]

Hamilton engaged in the debate over the shape of the national Congress over the next few days. He was manifestly against the state legislatures electing the representatives, because it would increase state influence "which could not be too watchfully guarded against."[97] Fear of state control over the representatives also made him argue in favor of the national government, not the states, paying them.[98] He was also against elections that occurred too frequently because of what many nationalists considered to be excessive democracy in the states, and he made the argument by appealing to the British system of elections for the House of Commons.[99]

By June 28, the convention was completely deadlocked. The chances that the delegates would successfully create a new government seemed in doubt. Benjamin Franklin intervened and played the magnanimous role of the aged mediator between the blocs at the convention. He told the delegates of a two-headed snake that encountered a stick that left it immobilized, because the heads pulled in different directions and refused to compromise.[100] Franklin proposed that the members stop for prayer to remind them of the trust and responsibility placed in them with their appointed task and to appeal for a higher source of wisdom to moderate their councils. "In this situation of this assembly, groping as it were in the dark to find political truth, and scarce able to distinguish it when presented to us, how has it happened, Sir, that we have not hitherto once thought of humbly applying to the Father of lights to illuminate our understandings?" he wondered.[101]

Hamilton actually opposed the proposal by Franklin, not from any antipathy to religion but because he feared that word might leak that they had suddenly invited a minister into the convention and alarm the public that they were experiencing difficulties, which, of course, they were. He stated that it would have been proper had such a resolution been offered "at the beginning of the convention," but now it was too late. According to legend surrounding the convention, he might have joked with Franklin that the convention did not need "foreign aid."[102]

Edmund Randolph tried to break the impasse by suggesting that "a sermon be preached at the request of the convention on the Fourth of July, the anniversary of independence—and thenceforward prayers be used in the convention every morning."[103] Dr. Franklin himself seconded this motion, but after several unsuccessful attempts, the matter was postponed without a vote. Franklin did not get prayers said at the Constitutional Convention, but the discussion—and the Fourth of July break—might have played a key role in moderating the contention and leading to a compromise.

On June 30, Hamilton, following the example of several other delegates throughout the summer of 1787, returned home to attend to personal business. He was absent for nearly six weeks and did not take part in some of the most important decisions of the Constitutional Convention. While he was gone, Hamilton and Washington exchanged letters that reveal that their broken friendship was mended by their time together in Philadelphia. While Washington wrote several letters to different correspondents, his letter to Hamilton is the most personal and reveals the great depth of Washington's despair at the impasse that the convention had reached and his willingness to share those feelings with his trusted confidant. Similarly, Hamilton divulged his own frustrations in an intimate manner. From this point until their deaths, the pair would continue to maintain the highest level of trust and amity.

On July 3, Hamilton wrote that on the way to New York, he had "taken particular pains to discover the public sentiment and I am more and more convinced that this is the critical opportunity for establishing the prosperity of this country on a solid foundation." He learned that there was "an astonishing revolution for the better in the minds of the people...that a strong well-mounted government will better suit the popular palate than one of a different complexion." He admitted that although "the people are yet ripe for such a plan as I advocate," they might consider "adopting one equally energetic." Hamilton shared his anxiety that the convention might fail: "I own to you sir that I am seriously and deeply distressed at the aspect of the councils which prevailed when I left Philadelphia. I fear that we shall let slip the golden opportunity of rescuing the American empire from disunion, anarchy, and misery." He promised to return, but only "if I have reason to believe that my attendance at Philadelphia will not be mere waste of time."[104]

After Washington spent the brief recess listening to a Fourth of July oration and attended the divided convention again for a week, he received Hamilton's letter and immediately responded.[105] He was equally despondent and pessimistic that the convention would turn out well. He informed Hamilton of "the state of the councils which prevailed at the period you left this city and add, that they are now, if possible, in a worse train than ever. You will find but little ground on which the hope of a good establishment can be formed." Thinking that all of his fears from the previous months were coming true, Washington wrote, "In a word, I almost despair of seeing a favorable issue to the proceedings of the convention, and do therefore repent having had any agency in the business." Finally, he told his former protégé that he needed his company: "I am sorry you went away—I wish you were back. The crisis is equally important and alarming, and no opposition under such circumstances should discourage exertions till the signature is fixed."[106]

On July 6, the New York delegation collapsed. Hamilton was gone, and Yates and Lansing left the convention for good and never returned. Before a compromise had been reached, they believed that the convention was inevitably going to strengthen the central government vis-à-vis the states, and they refused to participate.[107] Their departure did not bode well for ratification of the document in New York, should one ever be produced.

George Mason wrote to Jefferson, explaining that "Yates and Lansing never voted in one single instance with Hamilton, who was so much mortified at it that he went home." Hamilton was a model of civility toward the two men, telling them that "for the sake of propriety and public opinion," he would agree to accompany them back to Philadelphia, but they refused. Hamilton thought that New York's Governor Clinton had "clearly betrayed an intention to excite prejudices beforehand against whatever plan should be proposed by the Convention."[108]

The combative Hamilton did not take a break from politics surrounding the convention while he was in New York. He wrote to the *New York Daily Advertiser* and publicly accused Governor Clinton of attempting to thwart the work of the delegates in Philadelphia: "It is currently reported and believed, that his Excellency Governor Clinton has, in public company, without reserve, reprobated the appointment of the Convention, and predicted a mischievous issue of that measure.

His observations are said to be to this effect—That the present confederation is, in itself, equal to the purposes of the union." Hamilton then went on to defend the work of the convention, even though he was silent about what was happening behind closed doors. He also called Governor Clinton's motivations into question: "That such conduct in a man high in office, argues greater attachment to his own power than to the public good, and furnishes strong reason to suspect a dangerous predetermination to oppose whatever may tend to diminish the former, however it may promote the latter."[109]

Washington's despair at losing his trusted colleague matched the gloom felt by many of the delegates in the sweltering early days of July. After the Fourth of July break, the Committee of Eleven offered their plan for reconciliation, which was debated for over a week. On July 16, the delegates narrowly voted for the Great Compromise, creating a House of Representatives with representation based upon population and a Senate with state equality. As a compromise between the North and the South, slaves were counted as three-fifths of a person for apportioning representatives and taxes, as they were under the Articles of Confederation. With the compromise, the convention could begin deliberating on the shape and powers of the executive branch.[110]

For the next ten days, the delegates tried to hammer out various contentious issues related to the presidency. In the course of the debate, they were still split over whether they wanted a plural or single executive, whether the people or electors would vote on the president, how long the president's term would be, and the question of reelection. They tried to balance greater energy in the executive, longer duration in office for experience, and reeligibility with the need to protect the liberty of the people against abuses of executive power. The lessons of the past decade were not very instructive to resolving this dilemma: they had suffered tyranny under a powerful monarch and chaos under weak national and state executives. As they looked ahead, the delegates knew they could trust George Washington with power, but they could not necessarily trust his successors. They talked endlessly but came to no firm conclusions.[111]

Unlike Hamilton, who remained absent from the proceedings, Washington faithfully attended every day the convention was in session. On July 27, the Constitutional Convention appointed a committee of detail, made up of five members including Edmund Randolph, James Wilson, and John Rutledge, to reconcile and arrange the convention's work to date. The convention then adjourned for several days until Monday, August 6, when it would meet again to discuss the committee's handiwork.[112]

Washington took advantage of this break to relax by riding over to Valley Forge with Gouverneur Morris to fish for trout. Over the next few days, Washington enjoyed the idyllic setting and release from the stress of the convention, punctuated only by a nostalgic visit to the remains of the Valley Forge winter quarters.

On August 6, the Committee of Detail offered its report to the convention, which went through the document over the next month.[113] The convention agreed to a single president who would be selected by an electoral college and serve for four years with no constitutional limitations on eligibility for reelection. A national judiciary was also created. Pierce Butler noted Washington's influence on the creation of the presidency. He said that the executive powers would have been weaker "had not many members cast their eyes toward General Washington as president and shaped their ideas of the powers to a president by their opinion of his virtue."[114]

Hamilton finally arrived back in Philadelphia to attend the convention sessions by August 13, when he entered a debate that hit close to home. He joined with Scotsman James Wilson to oppose an attempt to restrict congressional offices to native-born Americans, or at the least to impose a residency requirement before immigrants could qualify to run for office. "The advantage of encouraging foreigners is obvious," Hamilton commented. "Persons in Europe of moderate fortunes will be fond of coming here, where they will be on a level with the first citizens. I move that the section be so altered as to require merely citizenship and inhabitancy."[115]

Curiously, after a brief stay, Hamilton disappeared back to New York as fast as he had come. He returned to attend to personal business and a meeting of the New York Manumission Society. The society sent a petition to the convention to "promote the attainment of the objects of this society," the liberation of African slaves.[116] Since his attendance at the convention was not sufficient to create a quorum for his home state and his vote would not count anyway, Hamilton determined that his participation in the deliberations was not worth his time.

Even Washington was confounded by the slow progress of the convention, and in mid-August, he was uncertain that the work of the convention would result in a good constitution. He confided to Henry Knox the hope that the states and people would accept the document, "because I am fully persuaded it is the best than can be obtained at the present moment under such diversity of ideas that prevail."[117] Washington was again reminded of the gravity of the purpose of the convention when he rode twelve miles to White Marsh, the last camp for the army before the move to Valley Forge, and toured the Germantown battlefield. "Traversed my old encampment, and contemplated on the dangers which threatened the American Army at that place," he wrote in his diary.[118]

In late August, the convention was, if anything, more split than ever. A few dissidents, Virginians Edmund Randolph and George Mason and Elbridge Gerry of Massachusetts, expressed strong reservations about the direction the convention had taken and were opposed to the shape of the final product that was emerging. Eleven members were appointed to a committee of unresolved issues to attempt to reconcile the disputed parts.[119] On August 31, the convention wrapped up its debate over the report of the Committee of Detail, but the members still disagreed over how the president would be elected. Gouverneur

Morris and Charles Pinckney moved that the Constitution should be submitted to the people through their representatives in popular ratifying conventions rather than state legislatures, which would "prevent enemies to the plan, from giving it the go by." Besides supporting the idea of popular sovereignty, the example of New York was instructive that the state legislatures might be the center of "intrigue" and reject the Constitution to keep their own power.[120]

Hamilton traveled back to Philadelphia for the final days of the convention. On September 6, he related to his fellow delegates that he "had been restrained from entering into the discussions by his dislike of the scheme of government in general; but as he meant to support the plan to be recommended, as better than nothing, he wished in this place to offer a few remarks."[121] Hamilton thought that the executive would prove to be an engine for corruption, but the convention ignored him and agreed on the final shape of the presidency. The president would serve four-year terms, be elected by an electoral college, and be eligible for reelection.

On September 8, the convention appointed a committee of style to "revise the style and arrange the articles" in drafting the Constitution, which was largely the work of Morris.[122] Although Hamilton had been absent for the lion's share of the convention and despite his reservations about the new plan of government, he joined the committee and showed himself to be a friend of a broad, democratic representation in the House of Representatives. Since he feared the possibility of a cabal forming between a corrupt president and Senate, "it was the more necessary on this account that a numerous representation in the other branch of the legislature should be established."[123] A week later, on the last day of the convention, Washington supported this idea, and it passed unanimously out of respect for the president who had hitherto remained silent.[124]

Washington, meanwhile, looked forward to the end of the convention: "God grant I may not be disappointed in this expectation, as I am quite homesick."[125] All the other delegates agreed with this sentiment. On September 12, the Committee of Style distributed copies of a draft of the Constitution to each of the members for their review and final comments.[126] A few days later, the delegates agreed to submit it to the Congress and the sovereign people for their acceptance or rejection.[127]

Finally, on September 17, the last day of the convention, Franklin opened the day's proceedings with an appeal to moderation and expressed a wish that all would sign the document out of a sense of humility.[128] Hamilton, who was not exactly known for his moderation, echoed Franklin's sentiments and made his own appeal. He feared that "a few characters of consequence, by opposing or even refusing to sign the Constitution, might do infinite mischief." He reminded them that "no man's ideas were more remote from the plan than his were known to be; but it is possible to deliberate between anarchy and convulsion on the one side, and the chance of good to be expected from the plan on the other."[129] Hamilton joined the others signing the document, but his vote did not count since New York did not officially have a delegation.[130] Washington, on the other hand, did not need to give a speech calling on the recalcitrant to sign the document; all he needed to do was to affix his signature. Thirty-nine of the remaining delegates (out of fifty-five who had attended) signed the new Constitution—Gerry, Mason, and Randolph refused.

As the last of the delegates was signing the document, Franklin mused to a few delegates seated near him that he had frequently looked at the sun on the back of Washington's chair "without being able to tell whether it was rising or setting. But now at length I have the happiness to know that it is a rising and not a setting sun."[131] Franklin revealed that even he had been initially pessimistic about the convention but now believed it had produced a worthy framework of government. Still, he had lingering doubts as to whether that government would endure.

When the delegates walked outside, a woman allegedly asked

Franklin, "Well, Doctor, what have we got, a republic or a monarchy?" "A republic," replied the doctor, "if you can keep it."[132] Washington reported that after the Constitutional Convention closed, "The members adjourned to the City Tavern, dined together and took a cordial leave of each other."[133]

Washington departed Philadelphia the next day in awe of the results of the convention and traveled home. He understood the magnitude of what had transpired. It was a great deliberative moment unprecedented in world history. The delegates had proven, as Hamilton would later note, that men were not forever destined to depend for their political constitutions on accident and force. Washington was also profoundly aware of his own indispensable role in the creation of the republic. Though he had said very little during the Constitutional Convention, he knew the legitimizing effect that his mere presence had and would continue to have in the ratification of the document. His signature expressed to all the American people that he supported the new Constitution, and he already decided that he would stay above the fray of the ratification debate. "It is now a child of fortune, to be fostered by some and buffeted by others. What will be the general opinion, or reception of it, is not for me to decide, nor shall I say anything for or against it—if it be good I suppose it will work its way good—if bad it will recoil on the Framers," he wrote.[134]

Martha welcomed her husband home after sunset four days later.[135] The only burden he felt was the likelihood that his countrymen would call on his service again to be the country's first president.

Conversely, Hamilton was divided about the Constitution. He did not like its final shape but was ironically deeply committed to expending a great deal of energy in advocating its ratification. He was a clever political strategist who knew that he could not simply sit on the sidelines and trust others to fight for the document. He knew as he traveled back to New York that the Constitution would face some of its greatest opposition in his native state from Governor Clinton.

Hamilton was already considering the means by which he would ensure that the Constitution would be ratified, especially in his own state. He understood the impact Washington's name would have in the popular mind. When he jotted down some notes about the Constitution that were never published, the first thing on his mind was the "very great weight of influence of the persons who framed it, particularly in the universal popularity of General Washington… If the government be adopted, it is probable General Washington will be the President of the United States. This will insure a wise choice of men to administer the government and a good administration. A good administration will conciliate the confidence and affection of the people."[136] Unsure of any specific office that he himself might gain in the new government, he was still in his early thirties and knew he would serve in some capacity.

More importantly for the future of the nation, the relationship between Washington and Hamilton was renewed by the crisis of public affairs that brought them to Philadelphia. This reenergized collaboration would ensure that the vision for the new nation that emerged during that long, hot summer of 1787 would come to pass. Washington and Hamilton would lead the fight to guarantee that the people ratified the instrument and would then collaborate to breathe life into the institutions of a lasting constitutional republic.

CHAPTER SEVEN

WINNING RATIFICATION

THOUGH WASHINGTON AND HAMILTON had accepted each other as friends again, there was no guarantee that the proposed constitution would be accepted by the people. There was passionate opposition from many Americans who believed that one tyranny was about to be replaced by another. The battle to secure ratification would be especially fierce in Alexander Hamilton's home state of New York, and without New York, the whole ratification effort would likely collapse. The irony was not lost on Hamilton that such a lukewarm supporter of the Constitution would now have its fate in his hands.

Washington and Hamilton would play different roles in securing ratification that reflected their different stations. Washington stood aloof at Mount Vernon and supported the Constitution with his reputation, while Hamilton openly battled the Anti-Federalists who opposed the Constitution. Washington and Hamilton even formed a triumvirate with the brilliant thinker and statesman, James Madison, as they concentrated their efforts in the key states of New York and Virginia and made their unique contributions to the ratification of the Constitution.

★★★

THE CONSTITUTION FIRST HAD to be approved by Congress before it could be sent for ratification by the people of the states. Congress quickly received copies of the Constitution, and the document was read there—only the Rhode Island delegation was absent. Debate on what to do with the document was delayed until those who were also members of the Constitutional Convention could arrive in New York to participate. Meanwhile, George Mason, Richard Henry Lee, and Edmund Randolph were already circulating their objections.[1] Mason was bold enough to send a copy to Mount Vernon, where they were ignored except in critical letters to others, while Mason went unanswered in a sign of disapproval.[2] James Madison rushed from Philadelphia to New York to counter Lee's machinations and guide the debate there. Less than two weeks after the Constitution first appeared in Congress, that body called upon each of the states to hold ratification conventions.

The battleground then shifted to the states. In New York, Hamilton came under personal attack as Governor Clinton's supporters went on the offensive. He was the victim of a biting piece of doggerel that accused him of personal ambition:

> Smit with the love of honor, or the pence,
> O'er-run with wit, and destitute of sense,
> Legions of factious authors throng at once;
> Fool beckons fool, and dunce awakens dunce.
> To Hamilton's the ready lies repair;
> Ne'er was lie made which was not welcome there.
> Thence, on mature judgment's anvil wrought,
> The polish'd falsehoods into public brought;
> Quick circulating slanders mirth afford,
> And reputation bleed in ev'ry word.[3]

This ditty was followed by another Anti-Federalist writer accusing Washington of being Hamilton's "immaculate daddy," which fed the rumor (which persists in some quarters to this day) that Hamilton was actually Washington's son.[4] Hamilton's enemies then tried to drive a wedge between Hamilton and Washington in order to isolate Hamilton in New York and damage the ratification cause. "I have also known an upstart attorney palm himself upon a great and good man for a youth of extraordinary genius under the shadow of such patronage make himself at once known and respected," Hamilton's enemies charged. "He was at length found to be a superficial, self-conceited coxcomb and was of course turned off and disregarded by his patron."[5]

Defensive to a fault about his honor, Hamilton sought to protect his character and his relationship with Washington by appealing to the general to disprove the unfair—and untrue—accusation. Washington was torn: he felt genuine affection for both Hamilton and Clinton and was thus somewhat reluctant to get involved in their public dispute. Nevertheless, he relented and told Hamilton that "both charges are entirely unfounded." Washington answered the charge with words he knew would be made public: "With respect to the first, I have no cause to believe that you took a single step to accomplish, or had the most distant idea of receiving, an appointment in my family, till you were invited thereto. And with respect to the second, that your quitting it was altogether the effect of your own choice." Washington could not help lamenting that this childish bickering was occurring when the public good called for unity, but he intervened anyway.[6] Hamilton thanked Washington "for the explicit manner in which you contradict the insinuations mentioned in my last letter. The only use I shall make of your answer will be to put it into the hands of a few friends."[7]

As the people digested the import of the Constitution, supporters and opponents began organizing themselves and plotting strategy to persuade the people of their states. Both sides wrote hundreds of essays under pseudonyms to contribute to the public deliberation in this highly literate, democratic society, where essays were read aloud and debated in taverns, coffeehouses, and other public spaces. Those who opposed the Constitution were labeled as Anti-Federalists, even though they argued they were the ones who defended a balanced federal system contrary to the proposed consolidated government, but the name stuck. In early October, some of the first Anti-Federalist essays appeared under the byline "Centinel," claiming that the new Constitution would destroy the states and create an aristocracy and that Washington was a dupe of those who took advantage of his "unsuspecting goodness and zeal."[8]

In mid-October, Madison informed Washington that "the newspapers here [in New York] begin to teem with vehement and virulent calumniations of the proposed government."[9] Madison need not have worried, for his ally Hamilton was then traveling down the river from Albany to his home on Wall Street and conceiving a plan to combat the Anti-Federalists. Hamilton, operating as the de facto spokesman for the Federalists, outlined an idea for a series of essays defending the Constitution. He solicited essays from several able friends and eventually persuaded Madison and John Jay to contribute to the series.

On October 27, Hamilton's first Federalist essay as "Publius" appeared in the *New York Independent Journal*. It asserted that Americans were facing a momentous choice that would affect the future of republican government in America and the world: "It has been frequently remarked, that it seems to have been reserved to the people of this country, by their conduct and example, to decide the important question, whether societies of men are really capable or not, of establishing good government from reflection and choice, or whether they are forever destined to depend, for their political constitutions, on accident and force."[10]

Hamilton and Madison immediately circulated the essays to Washington, who offered high praise for their defense of the Constitution and articulation of political principles. This correspondence was at the core of a strong Federalist network coordinating ratification activities. Hamilton sent Washington "the first number of a series of papers to be written in its defense" only three days after its initial publication.[11] Although he would not write any essays, Washington predicted that the ratification of the Constitution would depend upon "literary abilities, and the recommendation of it by good pens."[12] Washington did take up his pen and sought to shape the outcome in his neighboring state of Maryland. The many recipients of letters from Washington included his former aide James McHenry and former Maryland governor Thomas Johnson.

Madison followed up by transmitting the first seven essays from the *Federalist* and admitting to being one of the authors. He told Washington, "If the whole plan should be executed, [the *Federalist*] will present to the public a full discussion of the merits of the proposed Constitution in all its relations…I will not conceal *from you* that I am likely to have such a degree of connection with the publication here." He conspired with Washington to put the essays into the hands of some of his friends to publish them.[13] Washington complied and forwarded them with a caveat: "Although I am acquainted with some of the writers who are concerned in this work, I am not at liberty to disclose their names, nor would I have it known that they are sent by me to you for promulgation." Washington thought the essays "place matters in a true point of light."[14] He told Hamilton that he expected "the subject will be well handled" in the "remaining numbers of Publius."[15]

In the coming weeks and months, Washington might have regretted participating in the subterfuge, since he was nearly buried in a pile of posts from his two friends in New York. Madison sent an additional seven *Federalist* essays soon after the first seven. Nevertheless, Washington was very thankful, since he thought that there were "many, and some powerful" Anti-Federalists and that "their assiduity stands unrivaled." Meanwhile, the timid friends of the Constitution contented themselves "with barely avowing their approbation of it." He wanted a more vigorous effort in solving the public crisis with the new government and read letters and newspapers voraciously for the latest news regarding its fate.[16]

From his vantage point, Washington informed Hamilton that "I can give but little information with respect to the general reception of the new Constitution in this state. In Alexandria, however, and some of the adjacent counties, it has been embraced with an enthusiastic warmth of which I had no conception. I expect notwithstanding, violent opposition will be given to it by some characters of weight and influence in the state." The letter ended on a tone that was emblematic of their newfound warmth: "Mrs. Washington unites me in best wishes for Mrs. Hamilton and yourself. I am—Dear Sir Yr. most obedient and affectionate humble servant."[17]

In late October, both houses of the Virginia Assembly agreed to call a popular ratifying convention in the state.[18] Washington was pleased to inform Hamilton that the legislature had advanced the Constitution a step closer to ratification: "The new Constitution has, as the public prints will have informed you, been handed to the people of this state by a unanimous vote of the assembly."[19] Washington, however, was still fearful of Mason, Henry, Lee, and other respected Virginia Anti-Federalists who "leave no stone unturned to increase the opposition."[20]

Hamilton faced a more significant challenge in New York, though he tried to be optimistic. Governor Clinton and his allies were organizing a massive campaign that Hamilton would have to counter at the convention, while Washington had the luxury of staying above the fray. Hamilton told Washington, "The new Constitution is as popular in this city as it is possible for anything to be—and the prospect thus far is favorable to it throughout the state. But there is no saying what turn things may take when the full flood of official influence is let loose against it."[21] A few weeks later, he wrote to Mount Vernon again: "The Constitution proposed has in this state warm friends and warm enemies. The first impressions everywhere are in its favor; but the artillery of its opponents makes some impression. The event cannot yet be foreseen."[22] Washington and Madison were hardly the only recipients of materials from Hamilton's lobbying effort. He sent Philadelphia physician Benjamin Rush copies of the *Federalist*: "They do good here [in New York] and it is imagined some of the last numbers might have a good effect upon some of your Quaker members of convention."[23]

As Federalists and Anti-Federalists flooded the papers with essays and fought to sway public opinion, the first ratifying conventions assembled in several states.[24] Delaware became the first state to ratify the Constitution (unanimously) on December 7, 1787, followed by Pennsylvania, New Jersey, Georgia, Connecticut, Massachusetts, Maryland, South Carolina, and New Hampshire. The latter state made the ratification official, but without the critical states of New York and Virginia, the Federalists would have won a hollow victory.

Washington was aware that his home state's assent was critical to secure a truly legitimate ratification of the Constitution. He gathered information about the relative strength of Federalist and Anti-Federalist sentiment across the state and concluded that his own northern part of the state was pretty secure on the Federalist side while the southern part was weighted in favor of the Anti-Federalists. The middle of Virginia was generally divided, it appeared. The greatest opposition, almost everyone told him, was centered on the frontier. Composed of people who were fearful of centralized power and averse to taxes, the citizens moving to what he called the Kentucky district were terribly frightened at the prospect that the new government would "barter away the right of navigation to the Mississippi River," as John Jay had nearly done recently.[25] Washington knew months before the convention that the Federalists faced an uphill battle and any victory would be narrowly won.

In New York, Hamilton was writing the final *Federalist* essays. He had worked at a feverish pace for the last six months, only taking a break to attend to his legal practice. There was seldom time for a quick perusal of each other's work (or even to do their own edits) before they were demanded at the press.[26] In late March, Hamilton had the first thirty-six essays handsomely bound into book form after reorganizing their order for logical sequence. He intended to distribute them to his opponents in New York to change their minds. Madison also distributed hundreds of copies around Virginia, especially to the delegates preparing to attend that state's ratifying convention.[27]

On April 2, the last of the *Federalist* essays written in newspaper form was published. Hamilton had written extensively on the need for a stronger executive before finishing with an essay calling for an independent judiciary with the power of judicial review and an essay arguing against a Bill of Rights.[28] "I send you the *Federalist* from the beginning to the conclusion of the commentary on the executive branch," Hamilton told Madison.[29] Washington would laud the *Federalist* to Hamilton:

The political papers under the signature of Publius has afforded me great satisfaction. I shall certainly consider them as claiming a most distinguished place in my library...I have read every performance which has been printed on one side and the other of the great question lately agitated... When the transient circumstances...which attend the crisis shall have disappeared, that work will merit the notice of posterity, because in it are candidly discussed the principles of freedom and the topics of government, which will be always interesting to mankind so long as they shall be connected in civil society.[30]

Hamilton might win great praise for his elucidation of political principles, but he still faced the daunting practical task of winning ratification in New York. He was uncertain as to which side would win. He told Madison, "In this state our prospects are much as you left them—a moot point which side will prevail."[31]

New York held elections for delegates to the ratifying convention during the last week of April, but the results were not known for a couple of weeks. Then, when the results came in, they were hardly encouraging. Hamilton complained, "I fear much that the issue has been against us." The Anti-Federalists won large majorities and were under the control of Governor Clinton, who had proved himself time and again "inflexibly obstinate" against the Constitution. Hamilton thought the only hope the Federalists had was in cultivating a "favorable disposition in the citizens at large" and applying the pressure of public opinion or capitalizing on the fact that nine states had already ratified. Virginia would carry the greatest individual influence on New York and would be "of critical importance."[32] Even then, Hamilton learned that the Anti-Federalists might hold out even if all the other states had ratified. Still, he persevered and determined to fight with every ounce of will until the Federalists had won.

Hamilton strategized with Madison to keep each other abreast of the course of ratification in their respective states, since a favorable outcome in either would have an influence on the other. They agreed to keep in constant communication, and Hamilton requested Madison to "dispatch an express to me with pointed orders to make all possible diligence, by changing horses, etc.," when any question was decided with the promise that "all expenses shall be thankfully and liberally paid."[33]

With the two conventions scheduled to meet so soon, Hamilton and Madison worked on publishing the second volume of the *Federalist* with a few final essays that did not appear in newspapers. It was published on May 28, and copies were dispatched to convention delegates in both states. In the last essay, Hamilton wrote of the opposition the Constitution faced in his home state: "I dread the more the consequences of new attempts because I know the POWERFUL INDIVIDUALS, in this [New York] and in other states, are enemies to a general national government in every possible shape."[34]

With his work on the *Federalist* and events coming to a head in New York, Hamilton did not have the leisure to write to Washington or anyone else, except to plan with Madison. Washington, however, received mixed news from friends and newspapers that caused him concern. The possible defeat of the Constitution after such a favorable course of events over the previous eight months led Washington to reflect philosophically. "The plot thickens fast," he told Lafayette. "A few short weeks will determine the political fate of America for the present generation and…the happiness of society through a long succession of ages." The progress in framing a constitution and watching the people deliberate over it was a historic moment. "It will," Washington thought, "demonstrate as visibly the finger of Providence as any possible event in the course of human affairs."[35]

In the end, Washington's concerns were misplaced. His home state ratified the Constitution on June 25, 1788, by a vote of 89–79, but only after rebuffing spirited opposition led by George Mason, James Monroe, and Patrick Henry. The latter believed that the proposed Constitution leaned in the direction of monarchy, and pressed for amending the new charter to include a Bill of Rights, a concession that many Federalists were willing to make.[36]

In New York, Alexander Hamilton faced the fight of his life, even though the Constitution was already the law of the land. He confronted tenacious Anti-Federalist adversaries controlled by Governor Clinton, who, to make matters worse, was elected president of the New York ratifying convention. Hamilton arrived at the Poughkeepsie convention believing he would be outvoted by a margin of more than two to one.

The Anti-Federalists were so confident they nonchalantly brushed aside the impact of ratification in other states, whatever the diligent efforts of riders traveling day and night. Clinton shrugged off the news of New Hampshire and Virginia's ratification and stated that they would not have the "least effect." One observer thought they took it as a "trifling occurrence."[37]

Hamilton's genius was handicapped by the odds against him at the convention. However, he adeptly defended the Constitution and articulated arguments that were just as brilliant as those found in the pages of the *Federalist*. His arguments neatly summarized the basis of republican government and the principled architecture of liberty found in the Constitution.[38]

In mid-July, the opposing sides at the convention stopped dancing around each other and finally started debating the amendments that the Anti-Federalists sought. Hamilton called upon the names of Hancock, Adams, Dickinson, Franklin, and, of course, Washington, in support of the Constitution. Hamilton said Washington "proved himself a patriot. This man came forward again and hazarded his harvest of glory. In this case he saw the work he had been engaged in was but half finished. He came forward and approved this Constitution."[39] Although the Anti-Federalists had plenty of votes, their state did not have as much clout as they thought, and their obdurate stance began to weaken. During the month that had passed since the delegates convened, the feeling that New York could not stand alone superseded the sense of power as a solitary bastion fending off the forces of consolidation.

The Anti-Federalists lamely began working on recommended amendments, and Hamilton forcefully reminded them that ratification was binding. Surprisingly, Hamilton felt compelled to join Lansing and Smith in drafting a circular letter to the states calling for a second convention. He may have decided prudentially that it was a necessary step to win ratification but that he was giving nothing away. Moreover, it was the only way he would achieve ratification against such great odds in New York. Madison viewed this concession with great alarm: "The circumstances involved in the ratification of New York will prove more injurious than a rejection would have done."[40] The concession would have "a most pestilent tendency."[41] Washington later agreed with Madison that it might have "pernicious consequences."[42] But on July 26, it proved a winning strategy when the New York convention narrowly accepted the Constitution by the razor-thin margin of 30–27.[43]

News of the ratification set off exultant celebrations in New York City. Artisans paraded and displayed their wares with patriotic and allegorical symbols of the national union. A nearly thirty-foot ship, dubbed the *Hamilton*, seemed to "float" down Broadway. As it passed the Battery, the guns fired in salute of the Constitution, which was now truly the law of the land.[44]

After the celebrations had ended, Washington and Hamilton did not dwell on the Federalist victory. Instead, they looked forward to the step of setting the machinery of government into motion. Hamilton immediately pressed Washington to "comply with what will no doubt be the general call of your country in relation to the new government. You will permit me to say that it is indispensable you should lend yourself to its first operations." Hamilton brooked as little argument as he did when he was a teenager directing ship captains in the West Indies: "It is to little purpose to have *introduced* a system, if the weightiest influence is not given to its firm *establishment*, in the outset."[45] As a trusted advisor and friend, Hamilton could be presumptuous with such advice.

The alliance of George Washington and Alexander Hamilton that had helped to achieve victory in the Revolutionary War had now built a "more perfect Union." Their work at the Constitutional Convention and on the ratification of that instrument in two key states created a stronger national government. Hamilton may have played a stinted role at the Constitutional Convention, but he was a leading figure in securing ratification, writing the *Federalist* and fighting at the ratifying convention in a state with the strongest group of Anti-Federalists. Washington's presence at the Constitutional Convention and his known support for the document was perhaps more decisive than any other factor. A couple of contemporaries noted this, including William Grayson, who said, "I think that were it not for one great character in

America, so many men would not be for this government… We do not fear while he lives: But we can only expect his fame to be immortal."[46] James Monroe more pithily asserted, "Be assured, his influence carried this government."[47]

Most importantly, their collaboration (with the assistance of James Madison) was essential to the creation of the new government. Now their continued alliance would be crucial for successfully implementing that government and keeping the nation alive.

CHAPTER EIGHT

THE INDISPENSABLE PRESIDENT

WHAT WAS TRUE OF the founding of America as a country was especially true of the American presidency—George Washington was the "indispensable man." The revolutionary generation, the nation's greatest generation, had defeated the superpower of their time and overcome parochial interests and powerful passions to prove that, as Alexander Hamilton put it, "societies of men are really capable...of establishing good government from reflection and choice."[1]

Perhaps no aspect of the new Constitution generated as much passionate opposition from these parochial interests as the office of the presidency. Washington's reputation for integrity legitimated an office that was viewed with apprehension by many of his fellow citizens. Washington was the only national figure who was known to his fellow citizens (other than Benjamin Franklin, who was eighty-three when Washington was elected) and trusted by them to safely wield the powers the president was granted in article two of the new Constitution. Suffice it to say that these powers were unlikely to have been granted without the assumption by the delegates at the Constitutional Convention and by those who attended the state ratifying conventions that George Washington would be the first president. Washington's indispensability was succinctly noted by historian Forrest McDonald, who argued that "the office…could scarcely have been created had George Washington not been available to become its first occupant."[2]

No one understood Washington's indispensability better than Alexander Hamilton. The possibility of Washington becoming the nation's first president was initially suggested by David Humphreys, a former wartime aide-de-camp. But it was Alexander Hamilton's persistent lobbying that carried the day.[3] Hamilton wrote the retired general on August 13, 1788, sending a copy of the *Federalist Papers* and urging Washington to return to his nation's service, this time in a civilian capacity as the nation's first president. Washington responded that he was waiting to ensure that it was the will of the electors to elevate him to the presidency but noted that his preference was to remain at Mount Vernon, unless his service became "indispensable":

You know me well enough, my good Sir, to be persuaded that I am not guilty of affectation, when I tell you, it is my great and sole desire to live and die, in peace and retirement, on my own farm. Were it ever indispensable, a different line of conduct should be adopted; while you and some others who are acquainted with my heart would *acquit*, the world and Posterity might probably *accuse* me of *inconsistency* and *ambition*. Still I hope I shall always possess firmness and virtue enough to maintain (what I consider the most enviable of all titles) the character of *an honest man*.[4]

Hamilton, as was his wont, would not take no for an answer. He urged Washington to become the nation's first chief executive, noting the risks involved but appealing to Washington's sense of duty to complete the unfinished work of the American Revolution:

I should be deeply pained my Dear Sir if your scruples in regard to a certain station should be matured into a resolution to decline it... I have...come to a conclusion, (in which I feel no hesitation) that every public and personal consideration will demand from you an acquiescence in what will *certainly* be the unanimous wish of your country. The absolute retreat which you meditated at the close of the late war was natural and proper. Had the government produced by the revolution gone on in a *tolerable* train, it would have been most advisable to have persisted in that retreat. But I am clearly of opinion that the crisis which brought you again into public view left you no alternative but to comply—and I am equally clear in the opinion that you are by that act *pledged* to take a part in the execution of the government... In a matter so essential to the well being of society as the prosperity of a newly instituted government a citizen of so much consequence as yourself to its success has no option but to lend his services if called for. Permit me to say it would be inglorious in such a situation not to hazard the glory however great, which he might have previously acquired.[5]

In the end, Washington acquiesced to Hamilton's plea and returned to the public arena. When the members of the Electoral College convened in the nation's state capitals on February 4, 1789, they unanimously elected George Washington as president.[6]

The president-elect devoted a remarkable amount of time ruminating over matters of presidential protocol appropriate for a republican chief executive. One of the first issues to be raised was the question of the president's title, and the manner in which this was handled rankled the incoming president. Vice President John Adams had proposed a high-toned title at odds with republican simplicity, forever reinforcing his reputation as something of a pompous New Englander. Washington avoided that debate but was nonetheless disturbed that the politically tone-deaf Adams had pressed a proposal that was "contrary to my opinion" and had provided ammunition to "adversaries of the government."[7] Adams's misstep was the beginning of a strained relationship between the new president and his vice president.

Beyond the question of how to address the president, other fundamental issues needed to be settled as well, and Washington turned to longtime acquaintances, including Alexander Hamilton. These issues concerned "the etiquette proper to be observed by the President." Hamilton responded that "dignity" was the primary object to be desired, but that great care must be taken to avoid going too far with this notion in a society devoted to equality. Some elements of a "high tone" in the demeanor of the president would be accepted by the public, but it would be vital to avoid any "extremes" in carrying this out. Hamilton proposed a weekly "levee" during which the president would greet citizens and exchange pleasantries for thirty minutes, and he proposed formal dinners including members of Congress, cabinet officers, and foreign ministers, to mark major anniversaries of the new nation, including Independence Day, inauguration day, and perhaps the anniversary of the Franco-American Treaty and the treaty with Great Britain that brought the Revolution to a close. Hamilton also proposed more informal "family dinners" of six to eight persons that would also include "members of the legislature and other official characters." The purpose of these more informal dinners would be to "remove the idea of too immense an inequality," which would "excite dissatisfaction and cabal."[8] Hamilton's hopes that his recommendations would not incite a populist backlash were quickly dashed by the emerging faction that celebrated hardscrabble frontiersmen and republican simplicity and would later rally behind Thomas Jefferson. One member of that coalition, Pennsylvania senator William Maclay, was particularly offended by the whiff of elitism that he detected around the chief executive.

But all of this lay in the future as George Washington was inaugurated in New York City on April 30, 1789, taking the helm of an
executive branch with a mandate to execute and define the nebulous
powers of article two. Washington understood that the precedents he set
would shape the presidency and the nation for as long as the American
experiment survived. Writing to a British historian less than a year after
assuming the office, he noted that "my station is new; and, if I may use
the expression, I walk on untrodden ground. There is scarcely any part
of my conduct [which] may not hereafter be drawn into precedent."[9]

Washington's inaugural ceremony began at approximately 2:00
p.m. on the second floor of Federal Hall, with a nervous president
taking his oath from Chancellor Robert Livingston. According to a
contemporaneous newspaper account, the president kissed the Bible
after completing the oath. Whether Washington added the words "so
help me God" at the end of his oath is a matter of intense controversy to this day, although historian Gordon Wood believes it is likely
that Washington did add this phrase, since it quickly became standard
practice for members of the newly created judicial branch to do so.
Washington was overcome with emotion upon completing his oath
and had a difficult time reading his inaugural address; while some of the
emotion was the result of his understanding the historical importance of
the occasion, the president also approached his new, uncharted assign-
ment with a sense of dread. He wrote his old wartime ally Henry Knox
that his elevation to the presidency was "accompanied with feelings not
unlike those of a culprit who is going to the place of his execution."[10]

The new president had little to guide him, although along with
most prominent Americans of the time, he had read the series of essays
that came to be known as the *Federalist Papers*. Washington believed
that the essays shed "new light upon the science of government" and
were likely to make a "lasting impression" on those who read Publius's
"clear and forcible" arguments.[11] He may have found some guidance
in these essays, as two of the authors, Alexander Hamilton and James

Madison, were his political allies. The third author, John Jay, had drafted the Constitution for the State of New York, which created a strong chief executive. Hamilton was the primary author of the essays dealing with the presidency, and while he would never serve as president, his influence on President Washington and on the long-term health of the office was significant.

In his *Federalist* essays, Hamilton had argued that an "energetic executive" was a crucial ingredient for the preservation of the nation and the protection of liberty. He contended that the president needed to be equipped with "competent powers" and be given incentives to resist congressional incursions on his power through a fixed salary, and a lengthy term of office, with no restrictions on reeligibility, would allow him to implement his plans. Hamilton also argued that "unity" in the executive, meaning one person, not a committee, was a vital element for presidential success. He noted in *Federalist* No. 74 that "of all the cares or concerns of government, the direction of war most peculiarly demands those qualities which distinguish the exercise of power by a single hand."[12] The president brings to the conduct of war and foreign policy the essential qualities of "decision, activity, secrecy and dispatch."[13] The ability of the nation to coherently conduct war and foreign affairs was deeply felt by both Hamilton and Washington, for they had seen, up close and personal, the near-disastrous results of conducting war by committee. The nation's first president would set innumerable precedents that would be cited by his successors to justify presidential leadership in matters of war and national security.

Washington's distaste for conducting war and foreign policy by committee was evident in his failed attempt in August 1789 to solicit the Senate's advice on treaty negotiations with the Creek Indians. The new president believed that his constitutional power to negotiate treaties was shared with the Senate, and he met in person with the entire body. As Washington looked on, members of the Senate pontificated for hours and then deferred action on a proposed treaty, leaving

Washington in a "violent fret" and grousing that "this defeats every purpose of my coming here."[14] Washington had genuinely sought the advice of the upper chamber, but he quickly abandoned the practice after this dismal experience.

Washington went on to shape so many aspects of the presidency that are taken for granted today. He created the president's cabinet, and his first appointee was Alexander Hamilton, aged thirty-four, for the position of secretary of the treasury. It should be noted that Hamilton was not Washington's first choice. That honor belonged to Robert Morris, who had served as a financier of the American Revolution but whose personal financial situation was in considerable disorder. Thankfully for the new nation, Morris declined the offer, recommending instead "Colonel Hamilton," a suggestion that caught Washington off guard, so the story goes, for he was unfamiliar with Hamilton's mastery of the intricacies of finance.[15] Joining Hamilton in the cabinet were Washington's faithful subordinate from the war, General Henry Knox, as secretary of war (General Nathaniel Greene, perhaps the most brilliant American general of the war, would likely have been Washington's choice for this position, but he had died at the age of forty-three in 1786), and for a time, John Jay, who was the de facto secretary of state until Thomas Jefferson returned from France in March 1790.[16] Rounding out the cabinet was the president's lawyer, Edmund Randolph, as attorney general.

It took some time for the idea of a cabinet to take hold; Washington did not convene his first cabinet meeting until February 25, 1793, and he did not use the term in any written correspondence until April of that year. He took care to ensure that his cabinet was geographically balanced so that no region of the nation would feel slighted. In addition to appointing high-ranking cabinet officers and members of the federal judiciary, Washington had close to a thousand lesser offices to fill, including customs officials, lighthouse tenders, and postal officials, and he ensured that only those Americans who were "of known attachment" to the new Constitution received these posts. He personally supervised the selection of these officials, focusing on their integrity and character rather than on any subject matter expertise, although prior public service was a plus, as was the good standing of the individual within his community. All of this was designed to further bind the citizenry to the idea of a U.S. government and to a nation rather than a locality.[17]

Both Washington and Hamilton sought to convince their fellow Americans, as Hamilton had put it in a letter to Washington in April 1783, of the virtues of "men who think continentally"—all this at a time when most Americans seldom journeyed beyond the confines of their birthplace.[18] As an immigrant, Hamilton never considered himself a citizen of a particular state; he was an American. Washington, however, considered himself a Virginian, and his transformation from parochial Virginian to champion of American nationalism is one of the more dramatic facets of his life. He was determined that his fellow citizens follow the same path. Part of this effort involved the seemingly innocuous issuance of a Thanksgiving Proclamation on October 3, 1789. Many members of Congress assumed that this proclamation would be issued by the various state governors, but Washington, sensing an opportunity to bind the citizenry to the national government and to the presidency, issued the proclamation himself. The proclamation was filled with references to the new nation and was addressed to the "People" of the United States:

Whereas it is the duty of all Nations to acknowledge the providence of Almighty God...[Congress] requested me to recommend to the People of the United States a day of public thanksgiving and prayer to be observed by acknowledging with grateful hearts...an opportunity peaceably to establish a form of government for their safety and happiness. Now therefore I do

recommend and assign Thursday the 26th day of November
next to be devoted by the People of these States to the service
of that great and glorious Being... That we may then all unite
in rendering unto him our sincere and humble thanks—for his
kind care and protection of the People of this Country previous
to their becoming a Nation.

Washington then requested that the state governors circulate his
proclamation in a manner that was agreeable to them.[19] As a result, he
seemed to distance himself from those who envisioned a high wall of
separation between the federal government and semireligious observances.

In addition to taking steps to ensure that Americans thought of
themselves as one people, Washington left the American presidency in
a strong position within the federal government. He breathed life into
the veto power, and in concert with Congressman James Madison, he
set the precedent that the president alone possessed the power to remove
executive branch appointees, a power that was not at all clear even to
those who drafted the Constitution. Many members of the founding
generation believed that this was a shared power between the Senate and
the president. Hamilton contributed to the confusion over the president's
removal power when he wrote in *Federalist* No. 77 that "the consent of
that body would be necessary to displace as well as to appoint" executive
branch officers. According to Seth Barrett Tillman, in Hamilton's view,
"displace" equaled "replace," which would certainly be more consistent
with Hamilton's endorsement of what today is known as the unitary
executive.[20] Nonetheless, both then and now, no one is quite certain
what Hamilton meant by his pronouncement in *Federalist* No. 77.
Despite this, the "decision of 1789" stands as one of the most momentous in terms of presidential power, and once again the outcome was
unlikely without the stature of Washington to ease the concerns of those
who wanted the Senate to share in the removal power.

As historian Gordon Wood has noted, had Washington and Madison failed to carry the day, the United States would have moved dramatically in the direction of adopting a parliamentary system. Madison had not yet developed suspicions over Washington's intentions or of the executive branch in general, and in fact he believed the legislature was "the stronger branch of the system," most prone to "abuse."[21] Madison corralled the votes needed in the House to sustain the president's removal power, but many members of the Senate, for obvious reasons, balked. A deeply divided Senate ultimately upheld Washington and Madison's position, but only due to Vice President John Adams casting one of his many tie-breaking votes.

Once again, Washington set a lasting precedent, a role that he was comfortable in and well aware of. In May of 1789, he wrote Madison that "many things which appear of little importance in themselves and at the beginning, may have great and durable consequences for their having been established at the commencement of a new…government."[22] A few days after writing to Madison, Washington wrote to Adams that it was important to correctly settle matters at the start, for it was far more difficult to change things "after they shall have been confirmed by habit."[23]

While the Constitution clearly outlined the veto power of the president, Washington seemed hesitant to exercise it. Nevertheless, he cast the first vetoes in the history of the presidency, issuing two vetoes in his eight years in office, one in each term. Washington's first-term veto involved the question of congressional reapportionment, which Secretary of State Jefferson had strongly urged the president to reject on constitutional grounds but also due to its favoritism toward larger northern states over the southern states. Jefferson also urged the president to veto the bill on the grounds that "non-use of his negative begins already to excite a belief that no President will ever venture to use it." Washington's second-term veto was cast as the president was packing to return to Mount Vernon for the final time, on March 1, 1797, when he struck down a bill that would have reduced the size of the American army. The House was unable to override the veto and later returned the same bill with the alterations Washington had proposed.[24] There is a popularly accepted myth that Andrew Jackson cast the first vetoes based on policy grounds rather than on constitutional grounds, but that honor in fact belongs to George Washington, as his second veto reveals.

Washington set other precedents as well and left a legacy of respect for the new office through his deft blend of accessibility and detachment. His frequent presidential tours of the nation allowed the people to see their president, although always at a distance. This was not a glad-handing president who pandered to the people and tried to win their affection by presenting himself as a "regular guy." Washington believed that the people wanted to look up to their president and that a certain amount of awe toward the office, even in a republic, was an attribute that contributed to a respectable government. A visit from President Washington was the biggest event to happen in some remote American towns, even to this day. Traveling over nearly impassable roads in a resplendent "coach and six," the president would inevitability be greeted by a welcoming committee of the respectable citizens of the town, and he would utter a few inconsequential pieties about the destiny of the new republic. All of this served to bind the nation together (a nation in which the citizens of South Carolina had about as much in common with the citizens of Massachusetts as they did with residents of Tasmania) and garner respect for the office of the chief executive. Washington's tours had the added benefit of clarifying the relationship between the states and the federal government, another relationship left somewhat ambiguous under the new constitution.

His first presidential tour was "of the Eastern states" [New England], although Washington pointedly excluded Rhode Island, which had yet to ratify the Constitution. The tour lasted from October 15 to November 13, 1789, and included stops in New Haven, Hartford, Springfield, Worcester, Cambridge (where Washington had taken command of the Continental army fourteen years earlier), and Boston, where he received a somewhat chilly reception from the governor of the commonwealth, the pompous John Hancock. The latter would be a mere footnote in American history were it not for the presence of his oversized signature on the Declaration of Independence. Hancock believed that as he was the governor of the Bay State, he outranked Washington on Massachusetts soil, and it was up to Washington to pay a courtesy call on him. Feigning gout, Hancock made it clear that he could not greet the president upon his arrival in Boston but left open the door for the president to visit him. After seeing the tumultuous reception that Washington received in Boston, Hancock suddenly recovered from his case of gout, strategically applied some bandages, and managed to greet the president.[25] Washington, whose life was characterized by repeated examples of magnanimity, accepted Hancock's cover story with grace, knowing full well that this was one more small victory on the path of getting Americans to look beyond the parochial. Washington was greeted, as he noted in his diary, by a "vast concourse of people" who accepted the legitimacy of the new Constitution and the authority of that most controversial office, the American presidency.[26]

Early on in Washington's administration, contentious issues on the domestic front threatened to tear the nation apart. Hamilton's proposals as treasury secretary for a diversified American economy were seen as part of a northern conspiracy to undermine the southern slave states, and while there are elements of truth to this, national security considerations also compelled him to urge the United States to adopt policies that would encourage manufacturing. Hamilton wanted to remake the economy so that the United States would be independent of the old world powers for the necessities of war. In fact, he hoped to create an integrated economy capable of surpassing the European powers. In order for this to happen, he first had to stabilize the perilous fiscal situation that confronted the new nation, something that was of great concern to President Washington. Hamilton proposed that the U.S. government assume all the debts contracted by the states during the American Revolution, and while Congress passed this assumption plan, it did so only after negotiations between Hamilton, Jefferson, and Madison to move the nation's capital to the banks of the Potomac River in exchange for southern support for the plan. The deal would later prompt Jefferson to observe that he believed Hamilton had hoodwinked him into accepting a plan that enhanced the power of the central government: "I was duped into it by the Secretary of the Treasury, and made a tool for forwarding his schemes...and of all the errors of my political life this has occasioned me the deepest regret."[27]

Next, Hamilton proposed that a national bank be established to facilitate the economic policies of the federal government and to serve as a catalyst for national growth. The national bank would be a "nursery of national wealth" and would serve to bind the nation's wealthy to the new government. It would allow the federal government to conduct four constitutionally specified powers: to collect taxes, borrow money, regulate trade among the states, and raise and support fleets and armies.[28] Hamilton viewed the power to create a national bank as part of the federal government's "implied powers," an argument that would be adopted years later by Chief Justice John Marshall in his famous decision of McCulloch v. Maryland (1819).[29]

Interestingly, one of the most ardent opponents of the national bank, James Madison, had endorsed the doctrine of implied powers in Federalist No. 44 in 1788 but then reversed his position during the debate over the bank in January 1791. Both Hamilton and Jefferson, along with Attorney General Edmund Randolph, wrote lengthy treatises for Washington, with Jefferson and Randolph arguing against the constitutionality of the bank; in the end, Washington accepted Hamilton's argument regarding the constitutionality of the bank. Hamilton's argument focused in part on history, on the "practice of mankind," and in a clear rebuke to Jefferson, the treasury secretary noted that in disputes over issues like the national bank, practice and experience should have greater weight than "theories of individuals." Hamilton's massive treatise in defense of the constitutionality of the bank and the doctrine of implied powers was read by the president on February 24, 1791. The next day, Washington signed the bill creating the first bank of the United States—a significant measure of their aligned political and economic thinking.[30]

It should be noted that Jefferson's hatred of banks—and of the national bank in particular—was so impassioned that he wrote Madison in October 1792, recommending that any banker in Virginia who cooperated with the newly established national bank should be charged with treason and executed. This is one of many aspects of Jefferson's thinking that tends to be downplayed by historians and biographers who continue to describe Jefferson as a champion of the rights of man and conceal the many examples of his zealotry and immoderation. Jefferson was increasingly frustrated that President Washington and his secretary of the treasury were so closely allied and that his political opinions (and those of his ally Madison) were seemingly ignored. The fears that Federalists later felt upon Jefferson's election in 1800 were based in part on taking the man's words seriously—Jefferson's own declarations led many rational men to believe, then and now, that he was an extremist.[31]

With the national bank in place, Hamilton proposed that the federal government pursue policies, including protective tariffs and government bounties, that would assist in the development of an American manufacturing capability. Hamilton submitted his "Report on the Subject of Manufactures" to Congress on December 5, 1791, in compliance with a request from the House of Representatives, which acted on a recommendation from President Washington. In his report, Hamilton linked political independence to economic independence; as he put it in *Federalist* No. 79, "in the general course of human nature, a power over a man's subsistence amounts to a power over his will."[32]

Almost all of the manufactured goods essential for national defense and for the nation's overall economic security were made in Europe, a situation that put the United States in a vulnerable position. True American independence required the creation of domestic sources of manufactured goods. Two decades later, Jefferson and Madison belatedly acknowledged this after the near-calamitous experience in the War of 1812 (Madison also reversed his position on the necessity of a national bank as a result of the war), but at the time, Hamilton's manufacturing proposals were seen as part of his broader conspiracy to destroy the South. Hamilton wanted to "multiply the objects of enterprise" and "stimulate the activity of the human mind"; in other words, he wanted to unleash the entrepreneurial talents of the American people. Although Hamilton's recommendations were ignored due to "the money panic of March 1792," on this, as with many issues, Hamilton was ahead of his time.[33] His vision would come to pass after the founding generation had left the scene. As in most cases, Hamilton's economic vision was also George Washington's vision; as Joseph Ellis has noted, Washington "was just as much an economic nationalist as Hamilton, a fact that Hamilton's virtuoso leadership" tended to obscure during the great debates of the 1790s.[34]

The Washington administration's fiscal and economic policies and its response to the political events in France put Secretary of State Jefferson in an awkward spot, for he belonged to an administration whose policies he found inimical to his revolutionary ardor. Jefferson had adopted radical political principles in France during the 1780s and saw Hamilton's policies as an attempt to introduce European-style corruption and perhaps even monarchism into the United States, to the detriment of the virtuous yeoman farmer. Sensing that he had little influence with the president compared to Hamilton, Jefferson turned to creating a political opposition and the first party, even though parties were seen as contrary to the public good and consequently hated by the Founders.

In response to what he saw as dangerous centralizing tendencies, Jefferson hired a newspaper editor and placed him on his State Department payroll to write editorials critical of the administration. The editor, Philip Freneau, published scathing editorials outlining Hamilton's plans to overturn the republic and establish a hereditary monarchy. Washington was, at this time, exempt from the accusations, but as the president observed to Jefferson, the implications of Freneau's accusations were clear: either the president was "too careless" to halt the conspiracy or "too stupid to understand" Hamilton's evil intentions. Hamilton's policies were his policies, the president told a frustrated Jefferson, but he also reminded his secretary of state that "there were so many instances within [Jefferson's] own knowledge" of Washington siding with Jefferson against Hamilton.[35]

As the Washington administration began to slowly break apart over the economic policies, the debate became even more rancorous over the Neutrality Proclamation of 1793. While this was primarily a constitutional dispute over the war and foreign policy powers granted in articles one and two of the Constitution, underlying it was a conflict of world views, as could be seen in the differing attitudes of Hamilton, Washington, and Jefferson toward the French Revolution. In the proclamation, Washington announced that the United States would remain neutral in the war between Britain and France. He made it clear that while Congress had the power to declare war, the president had the authority to declare American neutrality in the absence of such a declaration. President Washington's Neutrality Proclamation divided the government and the nation along partisan lines, with the Hamiltonians arguing that Washington's decision was constitutional and was good policy for the new nation. For Hamilton, the fact that article two vested the president with executive power was grounds enough to sustain Washington's unilateral issuance of the proclamation. Hamilton believed that the power of the Congress to declare war and the power of the Senate to ratify treaties were the exceptions to a general grant of power given to the president over foreign affairs and national security. It was simply impossible, Hamilton argued, for any constitution to include a "complete and perfect specification of all cases of executive authority." In other words, the "vesting" clause was an open-ended clause that permitted the president to deal with contingencies as they arose. Congress could change the nation from a "state of peace" to a "state of war," but the president could "do whatever else the laws of nations...enjoin in the intercourse of the United States with foreign powers."[36]

James Madison, on the other hand, speaking for the Jeffersonian advocates of a strict interpretation of the Constitution, argued that Washington's position represented a dangerous move in the direction of monarchical government. By removing the "landmarks" or limitations on presidential power, Washington was violating the spirit of separation of powers and checks and balances by blurring the line between declaring and conducting war. Executives were prone to war, Madison argued, for war strengthened their power, provided them with opportunities for patronage, and raised them to a position of preeminence that was inimical to republican government. According to Madison, Washington's actions and Hamilton's defense of those actions in the neutrality crisis made it more likely that future chief executives would be tempted to absorb the power to both declare and conduct war. It was a dangerous step to ignore the wisdom of the framers of the Constitution, who "separated the power of declaring war from that of conducting it." Madison warned that Washington and Hamilton had heightened the prospect of "the danger of [war] being declared for the sake of its being conducted."[37]

The foreign policy debate over how to respond to the French Revolutionary Wars was one of ideology as well as constitutional power. When the Reign of Terror began, Jefferson remained content with the progress of the movement, as churches were converted into "Temples of Reason" and priests, nuns, and aristocrats, along with

VI, were beheaded. The latter's execution was condoned by
a and Jefferson, with Madison calmly observing that if the king
was a traitor, "he ought to be punished as well as another man," and
Jefferson noting that monarchs should be "amenable to punishment
like other criminals." Monroe summed up the prevailing attitude of the
Jeffersonians: the guillotining of the king was a relatively routine event
in the service of "a much greater cause." The French Revolution,
Jefferson believed, was a sign that the principles of 1776 were beginning to take hold in Europe, and it had the added benefit of sparking a
rebirth in the United States of a passion for liberty, especially among the
various "Democratic Societies" forming around the nation, all of which
offered a healthy corrective to the growing influence of "monocrats,"
"fashionable people," "paper men," and "Anglomen."[38]

Jefferson was far more comfortable with the notion of revolutionary violence than either Hamilton or Washington, to the point
of endorsing the idea that if French revolutionaries killed every man
and woman in France, save one each, it would be worth it. A little
revolution now and then was a good thing, he believed, and served in
the political world to refresh the order of things, just as storms served
a positive function in the natural world. In fact, Jefferson believed that
the American Constitution should be revised every generation, as it was
unjust for the dead to govern the living. Washington and Hamilton,
who had personally experienced the impact of violence, were far less
taken with juvenile notions of the positive effects of bloodshed and
upheaval. Hamilton had come from a Caribbean environment rife with
lawlessness and simmering violence, and his family upbringing was
marked by instability and dislocation. In contrast, Jefferson's earliest
childhood memory was a recollection of being carried on a pillow by
a slave. One was shaped by fragility of life and the constant struggle
for mere survival, the other by the infinite possibilities of a carefree life
built on the toil of others. In no way were these differing world views
more pronounced than in their attitude toward the French Revolution.

Hamilton was also repulsed by the ease with which the French revolutionaries and their American supporters countenanced violence as a means of purging elements of the old order. In Hamilton's view, there was nothing in common between the American and French Revolutions; the former was characterized by a devotion to liberty, the latter by a passion for licentiousness. The American Revolution was a revolution of sober expectations, to borrow a term coined two centuries later, while the French Revolution presaged the totalitarian upheavals of the twentieth cemetery, with their mass executions and their propensity to turn on themselves with unbridled ferocity.

Hamilton, like Washington and almost all Americans, had initially welcomed the events in France, and in fact, the president and his treasury secretary had been granted the title of honorary French citizenship by the revolutionary government. But by the fall of 1792, after the murder of fourteen hundred "counterrevolutionaries," many Americans began to turn against the Revolution, including Washington and Hamilton. There was nothing comparable, Hamilton correctly observed in May 1793, between the bloodletting in France and what had occurred in the United States.[39] Hamilton was particularly appalled at Jefferson's support for the French Revolution even when it deteriorated into a bloodbath; however, he took solace in the fact that if "virtue" had any meaning in the affairs of men, the day would come when advocacy of "the Revolution of France in its late stages" would be seen as a "disgrace."[40]

Washington feared that the French Revolution would veer into the dark side almost from the start, warning the Marquis de Lafayette, or simply Lafayette as he was known in the new revolutionary order, "against running into extremes and prejudicing your cause." He was, as Ron Chernow observes, "astonishingly prophetic" about the descent into violence that the Revolution would follow although remaining publicly supportive for as long as possible.[41] Jefferson remained committed to the French Republic even after it turned into a "Napoleonic dictatorship," and he continued to believe that the bloodletting in France was a necessity, despite the fact that 85 percent of the well over seventeen thousand victims of the regime's liquidation policies were commoners.[42]

With his administration split over domestic and foreign policy, Washington pleaded with Hamilton and Jefferson to halt the combat that was taking place openly on the pages of the newspapers in the capital city, Philadelphia, but to no avail. Hamilton's own pieces were written under pseudonyms, while Jefferson, true to form, relied on surrogates, including James Madison and James Monroe, to attack Hamilton. Madison claimed in one piece that Hamilton and his supporters wanted to conduct government by "the terror of military force." Matters came to a head in October 1793, at a breakfast Washington hosted at Mount Vernon for Jefferson. When Jefferson began outlining Hamilton's plot to transform "this government into a monarchy," Washington dismissed the accusations out of hand, claiming that there were not "ten men in the United States whose opinions were worth attention who entertained such a thought."[43]

In the aftermath of their contentious breakfast, Jefferson concluded that Washington, whose "mind has been so long used to unlimited applause," was incapable of accepting information of a challenging nature. In Jefferson's view, Washington was an aging president with a closed mind who was being manipulated by Hamilton and was showing "a willingness to let others act and even think for him."[44] This notion of a somewhat slow-witted president being manipulated by a Svengali-like advisor is ludicrous. While no one, Hamilton included, would ever describe Washington as an avid reader or a closet philosophe, the former respected his judgment and never condescended to the president as Jefferson now did.[45] Meanwhile, the constant combat that dogged his administration did not abate.

At the conclusion of his first term in office, Washington could look back with satisfaction at all that he had accomplished and look forward to a peaceful retirement at Mount Vernon. Much to his despair, however, his retirement was put on hold, for once again, there was no one who could replace him. Only Washington could hold the fragile Union together and keep the warring factions led by Jefferson and Hamilton from tearing the country apart. Jefferson and Hamilton hated each other by the end of the president's first term, but they were both in agreement that there was no substitute for George Washington.

As he had demonstrated four years earlier in appealing to Washington to accept the presidency, Hamilton knew how to craft a message that would move Washington. He hit all the right notes by tapping into the president's deep sense of patriotism as well as his personal pride. Hamilton noted that if Washington "quit," much was "to be dreaded"; the use of the loaded word "quit" was guaranteed to cause the dogged Washington to do the "right thing." "The clear path to be pursued by you," Hamilton added, "will be again to obey the voice of your country; which it is not doubted will be as earnest and as unanimous as ever."[46] Washington stayed in the arena and was unanimously reelected by the Electoral College, which provided something of a lift to the beleaguered president, who nonetheless still yearned to return to Mount Vernon. He wrote to one of his old wartime commanders, "Light-Horse Harry" Lee, "to say I feel pleasure from the prospect of commencing another tour of duty would be a departure from truth."[47] Nevertheless, his fellow citizens did not want to let him go, and they dreaded the thought that the day would come when nature insisted that they say good-bye. Until that day came, he was the bond that held the nation together.

CHAPTER NINE

A TIME OF "FOLLY AND MADNESS"

THE PARTISANSHIP THAT PLAGUED Washington's first term continued to bedevil him in his second. Divisions over domestic and foreign policy only grew worse as his supporters and opponents saw every presidential decision through their partisan lenses. Although Hamilton resigned from his cabinet position, he continued to serve as Washington's confidant and adviser. Jefferson meanwhile persisted in guiding the forces of political opposition to Washington's policies.

President Washington, for his part, had a successful second term, although he was greatly fatigued by the divisions in the new government. Whether in the army or political life, he had always believed in national unity as a source of strength. The nation was not yet a decade old and suffered divisions of the kind that weakened the confederation. Washington's second term was an attempt to institute policies that would hold the nation together and strengthen it into an enduring republic. All the while, Hamilton would remain at his side as this indispensable relationship continued to forge the new American nation.

★★★

ONE OF THE MORE controversial actions of George Washington's presidency and one that continues to excite critics of the Federalists was Washington's suppression of the Whiskey Rebellion of 1794. Thousands of rebels in western Pennsylvania defied a federal excise tax on alcohol, armed themselves, and at one point threatened to burn Pittsburgh to the ground. Washington considered the repression of this insurrection as fulfilling his constitutional obligation to "take care that the laws be faithfully executed," but that view tends to be dismissed in lore and legend. Instead, this episode of lawlessness on the part of whiskey distillers and their sympathizers is frequently celebrated by progressive historians as an example of early American democracy in action. The whiskey distillers are portrayed as well-intentioned countryfolk who stood up to the East Coast establishment; legend has it that these good old boys simply wanted to drink their moonshine in peace and sing folksy songs while whittling around the cracker barrel. Washington and Hamilton and the "moneyed interests" are the bad guys in this caricatured account of what was in fact one of the earliest tests of the rule of law. Hamilton is often described as itching for a chance to crush this populist uprising, but here again, a thorough, unbiased examination of this event reveals that this is Jeffersonian-inspired propaganda masquerading as history.

The same principles at stake in the Whiskey Rebellion would be tested some eighty years later during the American Civil War—does an armed minority have the right to defy laws enacted through constitutionally approved procedures through the use of violence? Hamilton's Treasury Department had made concessions to the rebels in the period leading up to the worst outbreak of violence, but this did not appease the distillers. In order to offset the impact of the whiskey excise, Hamilton had directed that the United States Army purchase whiskey from distillers who had obeyed the law and paid the tax. As historian Darren Staloff has noted, "westerners contributed almost nothing to the federal Treasury while draining it through costly military actions that were taken to protect frontiersmen from the [Native Americans] whose land they continually encroached upon."[1] Additionally, violence against federal agents attempting to collect the tax was commonplace. In one instance, a "revenuer" was held in a distillery for three days without food and told that he could secure his freedom by submitting to "the mild punishment of having his nose ground off at the Grindstone."[2]

While Hamilton tends to be the villain in various progressive portrayals of the rebellion, it was President Washington who authorized the use of force against the rebels, and even led, for a time, the fifteen-thousand-man force (which Washington cunningly named "the Army of the Constitution") that marched into western Pennsylvania. But as is frequently the case in accounts of Washington's presidency, Hamilton serves as the "heavy" for a policy that was in fact George Washington's. The president celebrated the demise of the Whiskey Rebels in his sixth State of the Union message to Congress, noting that the uprising's suppression "demonstrated that our prosperity rests on solid foundations," for the American people were "ready to maintain the authority of laws against licentious invasions."[3]

Thomas Jefferson and James Madison viewed this as an instance of high-handed Federalists attempting to crush the spirit of democratic frontiersmen, but for Washington and Hamilton, the rebellion was a serious challenge to the legitimacy and viability of a new and fragile government. In the end, the rebellion was crushed, and the instigators were treated with magnanimity, as President Washington exercised his pardon power over those convicted of the most serious offenses. For Jefferson, Washington's response to the Whiskey Rebellion, or "Hamilton's insurrection" as Jefferson called it, was further evidence of the great man's decline; the president had become a captive of a dictatorially inclined Hamilton, which was fiction. Washington believed it to be his duty to uphold the Constitution—especially only a few years after its inception—against dangerous threats such as Shays's Rebellion had presented to the old confederation.

Alexander Hamilton resigned from President Washington's cabinet on January 31, 1795. Having sacrificed his financial well-being as a public servant, the father of what would soon be a family of eight children looked forward to putting his finances on a sound footing. Despite his departure from Washington's cabinet, Hamilton remained in an unofficial capacity as the president's closest advisor. As Forrest McDonald has noted, this was the phase of Hamilton's career where he served as "Minister in Absentia."[4] Hamilton's views, even in retirement, predominated during Washington's second term in office. In fact, during the final years of Washington's presidency and what turned out to be the final years of his life, the two men drew closer together than ever. This was due in part to the ferocity of the criticism that was directed against both of them throughout Washington's second term. This criticism exacted a bitter toll, particularly on Washington, who continued to be accused in the Jeffersonian press of betraying the nation that he, more than any other man, had created.

Hamilton had informed the president of his intention to resign as treasury secretary on December 1, 1794, upon returning to Philadelphia after successfully quashing the Whiskey Rebellion. Hamilton's wife, Elizabeth "Eliza" Schuyler, seems to have had a hand in Hamilton's decision to resign, for she was deeply upset by the unceasing attacks on her husband, more so than he was. But in many ways, the worst was yet to come. The looming battle over the Jay Treaty was to become far more than just a battle over the limits of executive power; the remarkably unpopular treaty settled some of the lingering disputes between the United States and Great Britain, but as Gordon Wood has noted, the Jeffersonians were "opposed to the treaty even before they learned of its terms. The very idea of the United States arranging any sort of friendly connection with Great Britain was detestable."[5]

The Jeffersonians were also horrified by the prospect that John Jay might negotiate a treaty that would benefit the United States and damage their party's electoral prospects. One of Jefferson's key lieutenants, James Monroe, wrote to Madison expressing his fears that a treaty beneficial to the United States would present a dilemma for the party. The secrecy that is essential to all successful diplomatic endeavors was seen as prima facie evidence that Jay was engaged in illicit activities, having been co-opted by corrupt royal courtiers.[6] This was populist parochialism at its worst, but it was at the core of the attitude of those who composed Jefferson and Madison's base.

In the eyes of many Americans, John Jay, who had been dispatched by President Washington to Great Britain in 1794, had made far too many concessions to the British. Indeed, Washington and Hamilton would have preferred more concessions *from* the British, particularly on the question of guaranteeing the neutrality of American ships on the high seas. But these ships were routinely supplying Britain's wartime opponent, France, which made the idea of a British concession on this point unlikely. On this question, the British did not yield, but they agreed to abandon their posts in the American Northwest and send a boundary dispute between what is now the state of Maine and Canada to an arbitration commission. Most importantly, the United States was awarded most-favored-nation status with Great Britain, which contributed to the tripling of exports from the United States between 1792 and 1796 and generated a dramatic economic expansion at home. As diplomatic historian George Herring has noted, "Britain recognized U.S. independence in a way it had not in 1783," and most importantly, the Jay Treaty "bought for a new and still weak nation that most priceless commodity—time."[7]

While most diplomatic historians view the Jay Treaty as a positive step for the new nation, at the time, hatred of all things British ran deep, as did suspicions of New York Federalists such as John Jay. James Madison considered the treaty to be "unworthy [of] the voluntary acceptance of an Independent people," while Jefferson saw it as an "infamous act" and a "monument of folly and venality." Southerners were particularly irate that the issue of reparations for the British seizure of their slaves remained unresolved and suspected that Jay, an opponent of slavery, had intentionally dismissed the slaveholders' clams. So ferocious was the opposition to the treaty that Jay allegedly joked that he could travel the length of the Atlantic seaboard at night and find his way illuminated by the fires of those burning him in effigy.[8]

Hamilton, only weeks into his retirement, was immediately called back into service to assist with the campaign to ratify the Jay Treaty. Washington, apparently harboring some doubts about the treaty, requested Hamilton's advice, considering him to be a "dispassionate" man who had the requisite knowledge of the subject and the "abilities to judge" each of the articles in the treaty and "the result of it in the aggregate."[9] Hamilton complied in his usual thorough, lawyerly manner. First, he urged the president to lift the veil of secrecy surrounding the treaty, arguing that "all further mystery" was "unnecessary & ought to be waived for the satisfaction of the public mind."[10] While Hamilton objected to some of the treaty's provisions, he endorsed the treaty as a reasonable accord that helped the young nation avoid war and settled most of the disputes with Great Britain in an equitable manner.

Washington responded to Hamilton by noting that "the cry against the Treaty is like that against a mad-dog" and that the treaty had been subjected to "tortured interpretation" and "the most abominable mis-representations," although on a trip to Mount Vernon, he had also heard of concerns expressed by "many well-disposed men." Hamilton also contributed a series of brilliantly reasoned public essays under the pseudonym of "Camillus" that built on his memo to the president. It was this Hamiltonian barrage that prompted Jefferson to utter his famous backhanded compliment regarding Hamilton's skills as a debater and as a defender of Federalist policies: "Hamilton really is a colossus to the anti-republican party. Without numbers, he is an host within himself."[11]

Hamilton not only engaged in newspaper debates over the merits of the Jay Treaty, he also ventured into the public square to build support for the treaty in New York City. He organized business owners who would benefit from enhanced trade with Britain and called for a rally as a counterdemonstration to treaty opponents, who were led by Vice President Adams's son-in-law. At this rally, Hamilton was met with rock-throwing demonstrators as he called for, according to one newspaper account, "the necessity of a full discussion before the citizens could form their opinions." One rock found its mark, either grazing or connecting with Hamilton's head. This prompted one Federalist wag to opine that the "Jacobins" were attempting to knock Hamilton's brains out in order to "reduce him to an equality with themselves." When informed of the actions of the mob, Thomas Jefferson was delighted, telling Madison that the treaty's New York City opponents "appealed to stones and clubs and beat him [Hamilton] and his party off the ground."[12] In the end, Jefferson and his allies overplayed their hand, and their vituperative attacks on Washington, Hamilton, and Jay probably did as much as any well-reasoned argument to change the tide in favor of ratifying the treaty.

During the ratification battle over the Jay Treaty, the politics of personal destruction became the norm, and whatever slim hope Washington held of a government of national unity was forever lost. Republicans accused Jay and other Federalists, especially Hamilton, of being covert British agents. Jefferson, as was his wont, accused Jay and President Washington of treason, for the treaty was an "alliance between England & the Anglomen of this country against the legislature & people of the United States."[13] Jefferson's Federalist opponents were engaged in a conspiracy so immense that it reached to the very top of the U.S. government; Jefferson claimed that the president, who had once been a Samson "in the field" and Solomon "in the council," had his head "shorn by the harlot England."[14]

From this point on, George Washington, understandably so, would have nothing to do with Jefferson. Having repeatedly put his life on the line during the American Revolution, he had little tolerance for armchair revolutionaries who questioned his patriotism. How ironic that Washington and Hamilton, who had fought in combat against Great Britain, were now being accused of treason by a man whose closest brush with combat occurred when he fled from a British raiding party that targeted his plantation on June 4, 1781.[15]

Jefferson tried in July 1796 to make amends with Washington, disingenuously telling him that he had nothing to do with the attacks on Washington appearing in his party's press. Washington, who had been warned repeatedly of Jefferson's duplicity, had for years rejected accusations that his fellow Virginian, whom he had appointed to one of the highest offices in the new government, was engaged in such treachery. But by the summer of 1796, he acknowledged what was known by others all along: that Jefferson considered him to be senile and a dupe of Hamilton, if not of the British government.[16]

While Washington's schism with Jefferson and Madison intensified, his reliance on Hamilton after the battle over the Jay Treaty only deepened. For a period of three months in 1795, Hamilton served as the de facto secretary of state, as an overwhelmed Timothy Pickering attempted to deal with all of the ramifications associated with the Jay Treaty. Washington wrote to Hamilton on August 31, pleading for his help: "Altho' you are not in the Administration—a thing I sincerely regret—I must, nevertheless, (knowing how intimately acquainted you are with all the concerns of this country) request the favor of you to note down such occurrences as, in your opinion are proper subjects for communication to Congress at their next Session; and particularly as to the manner in which this treaty should be brought forward to that body." For the remainder of Washington's presidency, the actual secretary of state, Pickering, turned repeatedly to Hamilton for guidance in directing the foreign relations of the United States, as did Oliver Wolcott, Hamilton's protégé and successor at the Treasury Department, who turned to him for his economic and financial expertise.[17]

Washington's appeal to Hamilton for assistance was followed by an even more extraordinary letter on October 29, 1795, in which the president complained to Hamilton about the dearth of talent that was available for him to fill positions in his administration. He asked for his advice on a litany of issues, ranging from diplomatic relations with Morocco to depredations committed by white settlers toward the Creek Indians in Georgia. "What am I to do for a Secretary of State?" the beleaguered president wrote Hamilton. "I find the selection of proper characters an arduous duty."[18]

Historian Forrest McDonald correctly notes that public service had become so odious in the destructive atmosphere created by Jefferson and Madison that many Federalists, concerned for their reputations, were unwilling to subject themselves to vicious personal attacks. This led to a situation, as Hamilton noted to Washington, where "second rate [men] must be taken with good dispositions & barely decent qualifications... 'Tis a sad omen for the Government." Washington then requested that Hamilton compose his seventh annual message to Congress, which the latter drafted after receiving reams of documents sent from Philadelphia to New York City.[19]

The final months of Washington's presidency saw Hamilton deeply engaged with the president on matters of state. Washington and Hamilton were embroiled in rebuffing the efforts of the House to delay implementation of the Jay Treaty by demanding all correspondence related to the negotiations. Washington refused, and by so doing, he invoked for the first time what became known as the doctrine of executive privilege. While the Senate ratified the Jay Treaty with no votes to spare, the Jeffersonian-controlled House injected itself into the dispute, reversing Thomas Jefferson's earlier stance that the House should not be involved in treaty matters. The House demanded all of the documents related to Jay's negotiations with the British, in the hope of revealing embarrassing information about the negotiations, perhaps even evidence of treason. Madison and Congressman Albert Gallatin led the battle in the House to force the administration to turn over the correspondence, with the implied threat that the House would not provide the funding necessary for the treaty's implementation.

Hamilton advised Washington on how to approach this demand, urging the president to resist the request, noting that "while a too easy compliance will be mischievous, a too peremptory and unqualified refusal might be liable to just criticism." Hamilton argued that "a discretion in the Executive Department how far and where to comply in such cases is essential to the due conduct of foreign negotiations and is essential to preserve the limits between the Legislative and Executive." If the House wished to proceed with impeachment, then "the grounds for an impeachment must primarily be deduced from the nature of the Instrument itself and from nothing extrinsic."[20] In the end, Washington issued a statement produced by Secretary of State Pickering and Attorney General Charles Lee, due to Hamilton's advice not reaching him in time.

As noted, Washington refused to comply with the demands of the House, citing the fact that the Constitution vested the treaty power with the president and the Senate. He also suggested that only in cases of impeachment could the House rightfully demand access to such documents, a crafty move on the part of a president who was still widely respected by most Americans. Washington, though wounded, ultimately forced the House to back down, as Madison's forces began "melting" away under the pressure of public opinion that shifted in favor of the president. As they were frequently inclined to do, the Jeffersonian opposition attributed the collapse to conspiratorial forces of the rich and well born; Gallatin told Jefferson that "the banks" were to blame for their defeat, a charge echoed by the Jeffersonian press, which claimed that the Federalists were "armed with all the terrors of Banks" and "all the influence which wealth can give."[21]

Madison and Jefferson were convinced that once again Hamilton was manipulating the president. On April 4, 1796, Madison wrote to Jefferson, "there is little doubt in my mind that the [President's] message came from N.Y.," followed two weeks later with, "I have no doubt that the advice & even the message were contrived in New York."[22] While it had gone unused, Washington was grateful for the advice he had received from Hamilton, offering his "sincere thanks for the pains you have been at to investigate the subject, and to assure you, over & over, of the warmth of my friendship."[23] Hamilton was delighted that the president had rebuffed the House request.[24]

From the president's perspective, this was a time of "folly and madness," a characterization echoed by Hamilton in a letter to Washington on May 5, 1796, when the former treasury secretary noted that "in these wild times every thing is possible."[25] One event that contributed to this assessment was the actions of the American envoy in Paris, James Monroe, who many of the Federalists believed had "gone native" and was advancing the cause of the French government as opposed to his own. Monroe reassured the French that if they were patient, relief would soon arrive in the form of a new president, Thomas Jefferson.

To make matters worse, Monroe was leaking information to Benjamin Franklin Bache's newspaper, the *Aurora*, which was the mouthpiece of the Jeffersonian Republicans. Once again, a member of the Washington administration sought to undermine the policies of the president to whom he reported. Washington asked Hamilton's advice regarding what appeared to be a looming conflict with France, as well as how to handle the delicate situation of Monroe's duplicity. Hamilton wrote Washington on June 16, 1796, implying that Monroe was not a "faithful organ" of the administration.[26] Washington responded on June 26, asking "what should be done with Mr. M——?" According to Washington, the American envoy was the cause of "great embarrassment" and was "mis-represent[ing], and tortur[ing]" the administration's views in an attempt to "make it appear odious."[27] After discussing the pros and cons of removing Monroe, Hamilton recommended that he be recalled and suggested the appointment of Charles Cotesworth Pinckney to replace Monroe, a proposal that Washington adopted.[28]

For his part, Monroe considered both himself and the French to be blameless in the worsening state of affairs between the United States and France. The fault lay with an imperial president, George Washington, who lacked any sense of obligation to a nation that helped the United States win its independence. With his ingratitude toward France, a "monarch[ical]" Washington had surpassed the "little monarchs of the present day," all the while presiding over a government "of vain super-ficial blunderers" who had "never before been placed at the head of any respectable state."[29]

Monroe's recall further inflamed the French, whose anger at the perceived pro-British bias of the Jay Treaty was deep and abiding. They accelerated their intervention in American internal affairs, working through friendly newspapers such as the *Aurora*. The French attempted to influence the outcome of the election of 1796 in a manner that, as diplomatic historian George Herring noted, has not since been dupli-cated by a foreign government. The French minister to the United States, Pierre Adet, warned that war with France could only be averted by electing Thomas Jefferson. Washington was outraged at this viola-tion of American sovereignty, claiming Adet's conduct and that of the government he represented was "outrageous beyond conception."[30]

In the midst of the repercussions from the never-ending conflict between Britain and France, Washington enlisted Hamilton to assist with the drafting of his farewell address. In May 1796, Hamilton began to work on crafting the address, basically discarding the version that Madison had drafted in 1792 due to intervening events but also discard-ing much of Washington's draft, which as one historian has described, "was in many respects a product of the criticism Washington had received in his second term. His remarks were largely defensive in tone, occasionally verging on self-pity."[31]

This self-pity was understandable of course, since Washington was

enraged by the constant barrage of attacks that questioned his patriotism and his integrity. By 1796, an exhausted president was anxious to
return to Mount Vernon and escape from the daily slanders offered by
"a set of infamous scribblers."[32] These "scribblers" had written editorials praising the French seizure of American ships in the aftermath
of the Jay Treaty and accusing Washington of being on the British
payroll during the American Revolution. As Joseph Ellis has noted,
"what no British musket or cannon had been able to do on the military
battlefield, the Republican press had managed to accomplish on the
political one. Washington was wounded."[33] In his draft of the Farewell
Address, Washington mentioned his disgust with the "virulent abuse"
he had been subjected to in newspapers containing "all the invective
that disappointment, ignorance of facts, and malicious falsehoods could
invent to misrepresent my politics."[34]

Washington told Hamilton to feel free to abandon the previous
drafts of his address and to "throw the whole into a different form,"
prompting Hamilton to reply that "it is important that a thing of this
kind should be done with great care and much at leisure touched &
retouched."[35] Great care was applied as the two men worked closely
throughout the summer of 1796, with Washington concerned about
keeping the address focused and a manageable length. (Washington was
likely concerned about Hamilton's verbosity, which would be problem-
atic for publishing the address in a newspaper.) Hamilton served in a
sense as the wordsmith while Washington was the editor, but the two
men saw the world through the same lens, and as with many such
collaborative efforts, the final product contained the best that both had
to offer. Washington maintained strict control over the process, including asking Hamilton to ensure that all changes in the draft were clearly
marked, allowing him to monitor each specific change. It would take
years before the extent of Hamilton's participation was known to the
public at large or even to those who normally would have been in a
position to know. Hamilton's critics, who tend to see him as something

of an egomaniac, would do well to acknowledge the great lengths he went to to conceal his degree of involvement in drafting the address.

The address made its first public appearance in *Claypoole's American Daily Advertiser* on September 19, 1796. Readers that day were treated to a clarion call for realism in foreign policy and urged to reject what Hamilton had once referred to as "womanish attachment" to any foreign nation.[36] This was a shot across the bow of the Francophile Jeffersonians, for "there can be no greater error to expect, or calculate upon real favors from Nation to Nation. 'Tis an illusion which experience must cure, which a just pride ought to discard." And to further the point, the address warned against "the insidious wiles of foreign influence" and claimed that any nation "which indulges towards another a habitual hatred or a habitual fondness is in some degree a slave." "Passionate attachments" may be part of the life of individuals, but they were to be avoided at all costs by nations. Joseph Ellis has brilliantly summarized the gist of the Farewell Address as follows: "it was a vision of international relations formed from experience rather than reading, confirmed by early encounters with hardship and imminent death, rooted in a relentlessly realistic view of human nature."[37]

Addressing the domestic sphere, Washington returned to a theme that he and Hamilton had embraced since the days of the revolution, which was the need for Americans to "think continentally." All American citizens, whether by birth or choice, are part "of a common country," and "that country has a right to concentrate your affections. The name of American, which belongs to you in your national capacity, must always exalt the just pride of patriotism more than any appellation derived from local discriminations." He urged Americans to resist state or regional biases and to reject the emotional appeals of parties and factions, imploring them instead to embrace the common good of the nation. The lawlessness symbolized by the Whiskey Rebellion was at the forefront of Washington's concerns, leading him to urge fealty to the young Constitution, a document worthy of obedience changed by an explicit and authentic act of the whole people"; otherwise, it was "sacredly obligatory upon all."

Washington confronted directly the criticism of the new Anti-Federalists, Jefferson and his followers, reminding them that the Constitution was designed to rectify the defects of the Articles of Confederation and that true liberty required a government vigorous enough to defend it from foreign and domestic depredations. And in passages in which he again seemed to have his Republican opponents in mind, Washington warned of the dangers of party spirit and of demagoguery: "[Parties are] likely, in the course of time and things, to become potent engines, by which cunning, ambitious, and unprincipled men will be enabled to subvert the power of the people and to usurp for themselves the reins of government."

For those who see in the address a simplistic, perhaps even authoritarian, condemnation of opposing political views, it is important to remember that Washington sought to create a government of national unity and had done everything he could to do so, including offering key positions in this unity government to Jefferson, Madison, and Monroe. As Stanley Elkins and Eric McKitrick observed, Washington had exhausted himself in attempting to represent and reconcile conflicting views within his administration. "I was no party man," he wrote to Jefferson in July 1796, "and the first wish of my heart was, if parties did exist, to reconcile them." Elkins and McKitrick were certainly correct to note that there is hardly any instance where the new leader of a revolutionary government had displayed so much tolerance for the opposition.[38]

While most Americans celebrated Washington's address and paid homage to all of the sacrifices the retiring president had made on behalf of the "glorious cause," the Jeffersonian press was not impressed. The president was a "tyrannical monster," and the principles of the Farewell Address were "the loathings of a sick mind," according to various editorials. The *Aurora* published a letter from Thomas Paine, a genuinely disturbed mind, expressing the hope that Washington would soon die and arguing that "the world will be puzzled to decide whether you are an apostate or an imposter, whether you have abandoned good principles or whether you ever had any."[39]

After attending the inauguration of the new president, John Adams, in March 1797, Washington returned to his beloved Mount Vernon. Hoping to escape from the pathologies of politics, he tried his best to conceal the anger he felt toward Jefferson and his Republican "scribblers," but they would not let him go peacefully into the night. Remarkably, Jefferson's nephew attempted to entrap the former president by writing a letter under a pseudonym to which he hoped Washington would respond with expressions of anti-French sentiment, which could then be printed in the Republican press. Washington was warned by a source in Charlottesville that the letter writer was actually "a favorite nephew of your *very sincere friend* Mr. Jefferson." The scheme did not work, but it was indicative of the lengths to which members of the Republican inner circle were determined to destroy Washington's reputation. Whether Jefferson knew about his favorite nephew's scheme is uncertain, but it did lead to Washington endorsing the assessment of his source, who described Jefferson as "one of the most artful, intriguing, industrious and double-faced politicians in all America."[40]

Washington's belated realization that Jefferson and Madison, as Joseph Ellis put it, had been "orchestrating a concerted and often covert campaign against the Federalists since 1791" cut him to the core. For a man devoted to honor and possessed of great personal integrity, this treachery was difficult to fathom.[41]

Washington's Republican detractors persisted with their campaign against the former president and Alexander Hamilton long after the president left the political scene, with James Monroe leading the charge in both cases. In regard to President Washington, Monroe decided to go public with a defense of his at best duplicitous, and at worst treasonous actions during his tenure as the president's envoy to France.

Monroe's account, which was published in December 1797, was drafted with input from Jefferson and provided a spirited defense of his rogue diplomacy, and, consistent with the Republican practice at the time, it accused Washington of engaging in treason for removing him.

After receiving a copy of Monroe's account of his mistreatment, the retired president read the book and jotted down a series of impassioned responses in the margins that revealed the depth of his anger toward Monroe and other members of the "French Party" in the United States. Where Monroe observed that "the appearance of the [Jay] treaty excited the general disgust of France against the American government, which was now diminished by the opposition which the American public made to the treaty," Washington wrote in the margins of his copy, "who were the contrivers of this disgust and for what purpose was it excited. Let the French Party in the U.S. and the British debtors therein answer the question." ("British debtors" was a reference to the massive debts Jefferson and others owed to British merchants for the expenses related to running their plantations.) Washington bristled when Monroe mentioned that that he did not inform his own government regarding a development in France, charging Monroe with "neglect of duty." Monroe was "none but a party man, lost to all sense of propriety" and "a mere tool in the hands of the French government" who held that the "sufferings of our Citizens is always a secondary consideration when put in competition w[i]th the embarrassments of the French." To make matters worse, Monroe's secretary in France was a Frenchman who Monroe fully trusted and gave complete run of the embassy "for the sole purpose of communicating to the [French] Directory the Secrets of his Office."[42]

While Washington was wrestling with Monroe's revisionist history, Hamilton was confronted with a more serious challenge to his reputation. Republicans were determined to destroy Hamilton and whatever political aspirations he may have harbored, and in this instance, Hamilton provided his opponents with the ammunition they needed to accomplish that goal. Once again, Monroe served as the point man for Jefferson and Madison's efforts to neutralize their Federalist opponents. It was not enough to counter the policies of the Federalists with rational argument; reputations had to be destroyed to ensure that the nation returned to the spirit of 1776 and that the Federalist flirtation with authoritarianism was brought to a permanent end.

The ammunition that Hamilton gave the Republicans came in the form of an extramarital affair. In the summer of 1791, Hamilton had been visited by a woman named Maria Reynolds, who introduced herself to him as someone in an abusive marriage who was in dire financial straits; Hamilton decided to provide Mrs. Reynolds with money, and more. The affair lasted for almost a year and was accompanied by requests from Reynolds's husband, James, that Hamilton pay hush money to cover up the affair. It appears that the entire affair was likely a blackmail scheme concocted by the couple from the start, since James Reynolds acted more like a pimp than a spouse. Nonetheless, Hamilton demonstrated remarkably poor judgment for a sitting—and controversial—secretary of the treasury and caused, needless to say, considerable pain for his wife.

Hamilton's enemies in Congress quickly got wind of the blackmail payments, and it was assumed by them that these payments were somehow related to lawless activities involving Federalist speculators lining their own pockets (perhaps including Hamilton himself). The matter was investigated by three stalwart Republicans in late 1792, including the former Speaker of the House Frederick Muhlenberg, then Senator James Monroe, and Congressman Abraham Venable, the latter two from Virginia. Hamilton was able to convince the delegation that the matter was strictly a case of infidelity and did not involve corrupt activities at the Treasury Department. There was an understanding that the issue was put to rest, but in the heated environment of the politics of the 1790s, this was wishful thinking. Jefferson was fully apprised of the scandal within hours of the meeting, and despite

Hamilton's disclaimers, Jefferson remained convinced that this was a case involving public corruption. The visiting delegation had obtained copies of some of the letters between Hamilton and Maria Reynolds, and Monroe made sure that these were kept in a safe place (possibly with Thomas Jefferson, but most likely with Jefferson's factotum John Beckley) for use at a future date.[43]

That date arrived in June 1797, around the time Monroe was busily preparing his attack on Washington for his "treasonous" activities. One of Jefferson's "infamous scribblers," whom he covertly supported with financial aid, was James Callender. Jefferson considered Callender, an alcoholic gossipmonger, to be a "man of genius" and a "man of science [who] fled from persecution in his native Scotland." (Jefferson would later change his mind regarding Callender's virtues, when, as justice would have it, Callender broke the story of Jefferson's alleged affair with one of his slaves, Sally Hemings.) Callender accused the former treasury secretary of violating the public trust by engaging in official misconduct with James Reynolds. These accusations against Hamilton prompted the latter to publish a lengthy and somewhat overly detailed account of his affair with Maria Reynolds, in which he claimed that "my real crime is an amorous connection with his [James Reynolds's] wife." Jefferson was of course delighted with the exposure of Hamilton's extramarital affair, although he persisted in contending that the matter involved official misconduct. Hamilton's admission of an affair, he wrote a friend, "seems rather to have strengthened than weakened the suspicions that he was in truth guilty of the speculations."[44]

Two key individuals stood by Hamilton in the wake of the Reynolds affair—his wife, Eliza, and former president Washington. As with most matters of this sort, we can never be certain what transpired between Hamilton and Eliza when the affair was revealed, but it had to have been a horrible time in her life, with the *Aurora* taunting her in bold print with lines such as "Art thou a wife?... See him, whom thou has chosen for the partner of this life, lolling in the lap of a harlot!!"[45]

At the height of the scandal, George Washington embraced his longtime confidant in a subtle message to the same Virginia cabal that was determined to destroy him. Catching the Hamiltons completely by surprise, Washington sent the couple a wine cooler on August 21, 1797, with a note that did not mention the scandal but reassured his loyal lieutenant that he was standing by his side: "As a token of my sincere regard and friendship for you, and as a remembrance of me, I pray you to accept a wine cooler… [I] present my best wishes, in which Mrs. Washington joins me, to Mrs. Hamilton & the family; and that you would be persuaded, that with every sentiment of the highest regard, I remain your sincere friend, and affectionate H[um]ble Servant."[46]

As the scandal-mongering frenzy subsided, Hamilton turned his attention to the growing conflict with France, which would also draw Washington, however reluctantly, back into the public arena. With John Adams ensconced in the executive mansion, there was hope in some Federalist precincts that the new president would continue the policies of his illustrious predecessor. Adams had made an impressive gesture of continuity with the outgoing Washington administration by retaining Washington's cabinet, which included Secretary of State Timothy Pickering, Secretary of the Treasury Oliver Wolcott, and Secretary of War James McHenry. The first two were extremely loyal to Hamilton, the latter more so to Washington but also a confidant of Hamilton. It quickly became apparent that the new president was not the figure that Washington was.

John Adams despised Hamilton, partly out of a nativist sense that Hamilton was not quite "American" enough, having emigrated from the Caribbean. To make matters worse, this "foreigner" was illegitimate, which rendered him unacceptable to the "well-born" of the time, since, as Adams delicately put it, Hamilton was a "bastard brat of a Scotch pedlar." Jefferson shared Adams's native-born contempt for Hamilton, noting that he would not permit his retirement "to be clouded by the slanders of a man [Hamilton] whose history, from the moment at which history can stoop to notice him, is a tissue of machinations against the liberty of the country which has not only received and given him bread, but heaped it's honors on his head." Adams was so deranged when it came to his assessment of Hamilton that at one point he implied that Hamilton might have been a drug addict whose written and spoken work was the result of a "bit of opium in his mouth."

Adams was repulsed by the Caribbean immigrant's "superabundance of secretions" which led him into whoring, and he was also resentful of the close relationship Hamilton enjoyed with Washington, an overestimated figure whose "talents" were derived primarily from being tall and having a "handsome face" and an "elegant form." These were Washington's primary "talents," not "the faculties of the mind."[47] Adams also resented Washington for his tactic of allegedly marrying into a position of prominence: "Would Washington have ever been commander of the revolutionary army or president of the United States, if he had not married the rich widow of Mr. Custis?"[48] For once, Thomas Jefferson had the character of one of his fellow founders pegged; in a letter to Madison, he said of Adams, "He hates [Benjamin] Franklin, he hates [John] Jay, he hates the French, he hates the English."[49]

As tensions with France escalated during the first months of Adams's presidency, the new president dispatched a diplomatic mission in hope of avoiding a war. Adams's emissaries, John Marshall, Charles Cotesworth Pinckney, and Elbridge Gerry, were mistreated upon their arrival in France, and worst of all, they were extorted to pay a fee by operatives of the Foreign Minister, Charles-Maurice de Talleyrand-Périgord, for the mere pleasure of being allowed to meet with him. War fever gripped the United States in the wake of this affront to the nation's honor, and President John Adams basked in the glow of patriotic support for his administration, even parading around at times in uniform and with a sword at his side. Jefferson, whose mind tended toward conspiratorial interpretations of events, believed that the

problem lay not with his beloved French but with the corrupt machinations of the American delegates, especially his hated distant cousin
and well-known Federalist, John Marshall. The XYZ affair, according
to Vice President Jefferson, was "cooked up by [John] Marshall, where
the swindlers are made to appear as the French government." Jefferson's
scribblers followed suit, with some in fact blaming Hamilton, of all
people, for the affair. The *Aurora*, reaching another new low, accused
Hamilton of being an "intimate friend" of the corrupt Talleyrand, and
somehow this connection, coupled with Hamilton's known hostility
to France, led the French government to "consider us only as objects
of plunder."[50]

Throughout his life, Washington had never been able to resist the
siren call of service to his nation, and once again the aging general was
prepared to saddle up, at least figuratively speaking, in the defense of
the United States. When it appeared that war with France was inevitable, Hamilton's protégés in the cabinet, in concert with Hamilton
himself, began to lobby President Adams to appoint Washington to
take command of the American military, with Hamilton as his deputy.
Adams found himself in the uncomfortable spot of appointing the
one individual whose fame he resented and whose intellect he held in
contempt and one whom he positively despised as an authoritarian-
inclined serial adulterer.

The spring of 1798 is the point at which the Federalists, including
Hamilton, overreached in their attempt to quash once and for all what
they believed, with some justification, was the near-traitorous actions
on the part of the Jeffersonians toward France. This was all part of the
Federalist design to build a nation and has to be seen in that light, not
as an excuse for the excesses that occurred but as part of the historical
record. Some Federalists saw war with France as having the potential to
unify the nation, which is the tendency of most wars. It was an attempt
by one party, the party of neutrality whose sense of realism led them
to tilt toward Great Britain, against another party that included many

protagonists anxious to ally the United States with a nation that had no chance of winning the war. Nonetheless, as Joseph Ellis has observed, "the Federalists were exploiting the anti-French hysteria in the same partisan fashion that the Republicans had exploited the pro-French hysteria during the debate over the Jay Treaty."[51]

This starkly revealed itself with the passage in the summer of 1798 of the various Alien and Sedition Acts, which forever tarnished the reputations of Adams and all of the Federalists. Needless to say, the passage of these odious measures played right into the hands of the Republicans. One of the first targets of Federalist prosecutors was Congressman Matthew Lyon of Vermont, the publisher of a Republican newspaper and harsh critic of the Adams administration. Tried and convicted under the Sedition Act, Lyon was hailed as a martyr for the First Amendment and successfully ran a campaign for reelection to Congress from his prison cell.[52]

Both Washington and Hamilton supported the acts, but Hamilton urged caution and restraint in crafting and implementing these laws. Nonetheless, Hamilton's support for this destructive legislation represents one of the low points of his career and is indicative of the deep mistrust with which both sides viewed the other. In response to the outrages of the Alien and Sedition Acts, Jefferson and Madison covertly drafted the Kentucky and Virginia Resolutions, which defended the doctrine of states' rights, and in Jefferson's case, in a most extreme manner, advocated "nullification" and hinted at the prospect of "revolution and blood." The Kentucky legislature deleted these polemical passages, which reflected Jefferson's belief that the United States was in the grip of a "reign of witches."[53] Federalists and Republicans were locked in a destructive series of retaliatory exchanges with no end in sight and with a president constitutionally incapable of halting these reciprocal acts of vengeance.

In May 1798, Congress authorized a massive expansion of the American military, and Hamilton appealed to Washington to lead this army in the impending war with France. In Hamilton's view, the struggle with France could bring the partisan battles of the decade to a disastrous head, possibly leading to a civil war that split the nation in two. Hamilton then made his pitch, noting that this "extraordinary" situation may require another sacrifice from Washington and that "you ought to be aware, my Dear Sir, that in the event of an open rupture with France, the public voice will again call you to command the armies of your Country."[54] In a passage frequently ignored by historians who see Hamilton as plotting to make himself an American Napoleon, he also suggested that Washington travel through Virginia and North Carolina, urging the citizens of those states to remain loyal to the government. In addition, when the crisis first began, Hamilton suggested that the French be appeased instead of confronted, urging the Adams administration to leave "the door to accommodation open and not [proceed] to final rupture."[55] This, coupled with his proposal to Washington, suggests that Hamilton was looking for alternatives beyond a nefarious scheme to oppress Republican sentiment in the South.

Washington responded that he shared Hamilton's concerns, noting that he was "not a little agitated by the outrageous conduct of France towards the United States; and at the [ini]mical conduct of its partisans among ourselves, who aid & abet their measures." The former president dreaded the prospect of being called back into service. He was aware of the respect in which he was held as a result of his "former services" but suggested that preference be given to a man "more in his prime." But Washington did not entirely rule out the possibility of returning to command, inquiring as to "who would be my coadjutors, and whether you [Hamilton] would be disposed to take an active part, if arms are to be resorted to."[56]

Washington ultimately accepted the command but only after winning the assurance of a bitterly opposed John Adams that Hamilton would be his key "coadjutor" instead of Adams's choice, former secretary of war Henry Knox. The current secretary of war, James McHenry, along with Secretary of State Timothy Pickering, led the effort to persuade Adams to appoint his two foes, thereby permitting Adams's enemies to steal the limelight, a point that was not lost on this remarkably vain and somewhat unstable president. Adams had the last laugh, however, switching his position to the surprise of the entire American government. Washington was as astounded as Hamilton at Adams's relatively rapid transition from a sword-carrying cheerleader for war to a proponent of peace at any price. In October 1799, he wrote to Hamilton, "I was surprised at the *measure* [sending a peace delegation to France], how much more so at the manner of it? This business seems to have commenced in an evil hour, and under unfavourable auspices; and I wish mischief may not tread in all its steps, and be the final result of the measure."[57]

Adams's change of heart likely had as much to do with his desire to avoid giving Hamilton any opportunity to secure even greater fame than with any assessment that the strategic situation between the United States and France had changed. In June 1798, Adams was still engaged in saber rattling, but just days after receiving a terse letter from Washington on September 25, 1798, insisting on Hamilton's appointment as second in command of the army, Adams begin to reverse course and eventually dispatched a peace mission to France. This mission, as historian Forrest McDonald has noted, produced a lopsided agreement that led to "a cessation of hostilities that France had momentarily lost the capacity to sustain. Furthermore, in a secret agreement signed the same day…(though dated a day later), France obtained Florida and Louisiana from Spain. Finally, when it suited France's purposes to do so, the French resumed their piratical policies regarding American shipping."[58]

As with so many events from the founding era, the machinations involved in selecting Washington and Hamilton to lead the American army during what came to be called the Quasi-War led to more accusations that a doddering Washington was controlled by his conniving subordinate. According to this account, a Svengali-like Hamilton was able to do what no other mortal on the planet had done for over sixty years—manipulate or intimidate George Washington. This is fiction, of course, as a reading of Washington's correspondence from the time reveals a man in complete control of his faculties, who shared some but not all of Hamilton's concerns regarding the French and who agreed with his view that the Jeffersonian opposition verged on crossing— and at times crossed—the line when it came to loyalty to France over the United States. One can differ with Washington and Hamilton's positions on the issues of the day, but to attempt to portray this episode as a conspiracy to depose Adams and install an authoritarian government is to continue to propagate myths generated by Jefferson's political and journalistic allies.

This conspiracy-mongering grew out of the deep fears of a standing army that animated Republican thinking, a fear that was shared to some extent by President Adams. The First Lady, Abigail Adams, once said that she had "read his [Hamilton's] heart in his wicked eyes" and the "very devil is in them. They are lasciviousness itself." She considered Hamilton to be "a man as ambitious as Julius Caesar" and "a second Bonaparte" as a result of his actions in the Quasi-War.[59] Her husband agreed with this assessment, and was inclined to assume the worst when it came to this dangerous "foreigner" whose militaristic ambitions represented an unparalleled threat to the young republic. Adams's attitude toward the army that was ultimately his responsibility as commander in chief bordered on the irrational. This army, which he had a hand in creating, was "as unpopular as if it had been a ferocious wild beast let loose upon the nation to devour it."[60]

In some ways, the conflict between Adams and Hamilton was the result of the absentee president's propensity to consider everyone he knew to be a potential foe instead of a possible ally. Perhaps no president other than Richard Nixon was obsessed as much as Adams was with his "enemies." In Adams's mind, there could be no other motive on Hamilton's part except to acquire and abuse power. Adams had kept Hamilton distant from the start, frequently ignoring letters that he received from him, which was his passive-aggressive way of reminding Hamilton that he was no longer important. In fact, Adams kept himself distant from his own cabinet, leaving the capital for months on end and isolating himself at his Massachusetts farm. He then appointed, under duress no doubt, the man he hated most as the de facto commander of the American military, proceeded to have nothing to do with him, and then, without any consultation, dispatched a peace mission to France.

Adams repeatedly endorsed the concept of peace through strength, which was precisely Hamilton's thinking as well, and yet he attacked Hamilton for preparing the nation for war. Hamilton, a systematic thinker who believed in careful preparation, was horrified at the constantly shifting policies of a president who was guilty of negligently carrying out his constitutional duties. This erratic governing style, or "want of a system" as Hamilton and his allies viewed it, was damaging America's reputation abroad and ran the risk of inviting conflict. Hamilton is often accused of destroying the Federalist party with his notorious letter attacking John Adams during the election of 1800, but a strong case can be made that the Federalist party was destroyed in 1798 when a reclusive president balked at reaching out to potential allies, including Washington and Hamilton, out of pride and vanity.

Hamilton's actions in the Quasi-War, including the fact that he contemplated marching south in a show of force similar to the Whiskey Rebellion and into Spanish-held territory in the Southwest, has permanently tarnished his reputation. This can be seen in the work of military historian Richard H. Kohn, who characterized the Quasi-War as one of the most dangerous periods in American history, primarily due to the fact that Hamilton was "infected with dreams of lasting historical fame." Hamilton "lusted" for military command, and no one "posed a greater danger to the nation's emerging military traditions," according to Kohn. Thankfully for the republic, a heroic John Adams prevented this "Hamiltonian cancer" from consuming his administration.[61] As Forrest McDonald has noted, the claim that Hamilton itched for military glory is based in part on a letter that a fourteen-year-old Hamilton wrote to a friend that concluded with the line, "I wish there was a War," a somewhat common sentiment expressed by young teenage boys. "That he was similarly motivated as a mature, forty-one-year-old father of a large family is an idea unsupported by evidence," McDonald correctly notes, adding that "every extant document of Hamilton's for 1798 attests that he was reluctant to reenter military service."[62]

As the election of 1800 approached, the blood feud between Hamilton and Adams deepened, as Hamilton and much of the Federalist Party leadership concluded that Adams was temperamentally unsuited to be president. Adams's candidacy prompted Hamilton to write a fifty-four-page condemnation of Adams, focusing on his "eccentric tendencies" and "distempered jealousy" and his "ungovernable temper." The letter was apparently intended to be private but was leaked through the machinations of Aaron Burr and his cohorts. Hamilton's assessment of Adams was accurate, and it was the work of a political figure who believed that honesty was always the best policy. In other words, Hamilton had a tin ear for politics; while his great adversary Thomas Jefferson would have relied on surrogates to destroy a rival, Hamilton chose to do it himself and thereby drove another nail into his own coffin. Hamilton's close friend Robert Troup wrote of the letter, "The influence…of this letter upon Hamilton's character is extremely unfortunate. An opinion has grown out of it, which at present obtains almost universally, that his character *is radically deficient in discretion*, and therefore the federalists ask, what avail the most preeminent talents—the most distinguished patriotism—without the all important quality of discretion? Hence he is considered as an unfit head of the party."[63]

On another occasion, Troup added that "I find a much stronger disapprobation of it expressed every where. In point of imprudence, it is coupled with the [Reynolds] pamphlet."[64] Hamilton's ally George

Cabot of Massachusetts minced no words in telling his friend that the Adams letter had damaged its author more than its target: "I am *bound* to tell you that you are accused by respectable men of Egotism, & some very worthy & sensible men say you have exhibited the same *vanity* in your book [letter] which you charge as a dangerous quality & great weakness in Mr. Adams."[65]

A divided Federalist Party was no match for Thomas Jefferson, who in keeping with the manner of the time ran for president by disavowing any interest in the office. Unfortunately for the Republicans, they made the mistake of trusting Aaron Burr, who was supposed to finish second in the Electoral College and thereby become the vice president of the United States. This scheme almost ended up with a fiasco when Burr and Jefferson tied with the same number of electoral votes. Hamilton, in a genuine act of statesmanship for which he deserves more credit, tried to break the logjam when the election of 1800 was thrown into the House of Representatives. Hamilton wrote a Federalist member of Congress that the well-being of the nation required Jefferson's election, despite the fact that "if there be a man in the world I ought to hate it is Jefferson." Hamilton always put the national interest ahead of personal considerations, and the election of 1800 was no exception. "With Burr I have always been personally well," Hamilton acknowledged, "but the public good must be paramount to every private consideration."[66] Burr, despite many recent revisionist attempts to burnish his image as a man ahead of his time on matters of race and gender, was a man lacking in principle and distrusted by almost every key figure from the founding era, including Jefferson, Hamilton, Monroe, and Washington. These men agreed on very little except in their contempt for Burr.

It is not at all clear that Hamilton's efforts during the election of 1800, either to damage Adams's candidacy or urge Federalist members of Congress to vote for Jefferson, had much of an impact. Hamilton was damaged goods, as his former King's College classmate Troup had noted. At the age of forty-five, his best years were behind him, and he realized it. Writing to his friend Gouverneur Morris in the dark of winter in 1802, Hamilton seemed to be a man lost in the nation he helped to create:

> Mine is an odd destiny. Perhaps no man in the U[nited] States has sacrificed or done more for the present Constitution than myself...I am still labouring to prop the frail and worthless fabric. Yet I have the murmur of its friends no less than the curses of its foes for my rewards. What can I do better than withdraw from the scene? Every day proves to me more and more that this American world was not made for me.[67]

Hamilton's gloom regarding the long-term health of the republic was due to the elevation of his archrival to the seat of government. He was skeptical that the constitutional order could withstand the assaults of a party with an idealized version of an agrarian past, that was fearful of economic change and sympathetic to slavery, and that seemed determined to eviscerate the minuscule powers granted the federal government. Fortunately, Jefferson the president turned out to be more Hamiltonian than Hamilton could have imagined at the time, and the institutions and practices that Washington and Hamilton put in place were more resilient than expected.

Hamilton's sense of despair had been growing since the death of the man who for over two decades had restrained his worst impulses and who would likely have never approved of Hamilton's letter condemning the Adams presidency. Washington had recognized Hamilton's genius long before and had raised the unknown immigrant into a position of prominence almost unequaled in the entire history of the United States. With his passing, the one man whose endorsement was capable of resurrecting Hamilton's political career was gone. But more importantly, the nation had lost its first, and at the time its only, national hero, the central character who held the country together through repeated trials. Washington could no longer be called back to service as he had been time and again during the birth of the nation. The country was now on its own, and no one else had the stature to replace him. It was an open question in the minds of many whether the United States was sturdy enough to survive without him.

For all of his Herculean sacrifices in the cause of American nationhood, George Washington's end came in a rather pedestrian fashion. He was a man of ritual and routine, and on December 12, 1799, he had gone on his habitual lengthy horseback ride to inspect his property at Mount Vernon. It was a bitterly cold day, and a mix of snow and freezing rain soaked him to the bone as he spent five hours touring his property. After completing his ride, Washington took the time to write his last letters, including one to Alexander Hamilton, where he endorsed Hamilton's plan for the establishment of a military academy, although he refused to offer any detailed suggestions as to organizing it. This final contact epitomized the relationship between the two men, which was a respectful and affectionate one, with Washington acting as a sobering influence on Hamilton's creative and somewhat frenetic mind.

By the next day, Washington was complaining of a sore throat; by that night, he could barely breathe. He maintained his composure, as was his wont, to the bitter end, even expressing concern for one of his exhausted slave attendants as he slowly suffocated to death. His physicians, practicing the quack "medicine" of their day, hastened his demise through a combination of laxatives and bleeding techniques. Washington died on December 14 and was buried four days later.[68]

Some two hundred miles to the north, in Philadelphia, where it all began, Alexander Hamilton received the news of Washington's death. Washington's secretary, Tobias Lear, wrote him within hours of Washington's passing that "he died, as he had lived, a truly great man." Hamilton was moved by Washington's death, for the passing of his "beloved [C]ommander in Chief" left his "heart sad" and his "imagi-nation...gloomy."[69] Writing to Martha Washington, Hamilton noted the unique role he had played throughout the general's career: "no one better than myself knows the greatness of your loss or how much your excellent heart is formed to feel it in all its extent."[70]

Later generations of Hamilton's detractors would point to another comment of Hamilton's as evidence of his alleged manipulative, Machiavellian nature. Writing to Tobias Lear shortly after Washington's death, Hamilton noted that the late president was "an Aegis very essen-tial to me," and he went on to inquire into the status of Washington's papers, since "our very confidential situation" made the disposition of Washington's papers a matter of great interest to him.[71] Hamilton's use of the term "aegis" would later be interpreted by some as evidence that he viewed Washington as a mere instrument, a tool for his personal advancement. It was in fact an acknowledgment that Washington raised him to prominence, shielded him, and deflected attacks from those who viewed him as somewhat alien, somewhat un-American. Unlike Thomas Jefferson or the bitter and petty John Adams, Hamilton never dispar-aged Washington's greatness. It was simply a fact that without George Washington, Alexander Hamilton would likely have been a relatively unknown attorney practicing law in New York City. Hamilton grasped this fact and was magnanimous enough to acknowledge it.

Not everyone was as shattered by Washington's passing as Hamilton. President Adams attended Washington's memorial service in Philadelphia, but he would spend a considerable amount of his remaining life complaining about the tributes paid to his presidential predecessor. In one of his milder observations, Adams claimed that "the Federalists had done great damage to themselves and their country...by making Washington their military, political, religious, and even moral Pope and ascribing everything to him."[72] Vice President Jefferson, whom Washington had long since ostracized, did not bother to attend the memorial service. He seemed to welcome Washington's death, noting that it would allow for the reemergence of the "republican spirit" now that the surviving Federalists would be shorn of Washington's protection. Martha Washington would later say that the two worst days of her life were December 14, 1799, the day her husband died, and a day in January 1801, when Thomas Jefferson, whom she detested, paid her a courtesy call at Mount Vernon. A close friend of Mrs. Washington later recalled, "She assured a party of gentlemen, of which I was one…that next to the loss of her husband," Jefferson's visit was the "most painful occurrence of her life." Two months later, when Jefferson paid homage to Washington in his first inaugural address, Martha Washington dismissed his comments about her husband as "sarcastic" and asserted that Jefferson's ascension to the presidency was the "greatest misfortune our nation has ever experienced."[73]

In his capacity as a major general in the American army, Hamilton was responsible for organizing all of the state honors to be "paid to our departed Chief" in the capital, and he did so in his usual expedient fashion.[74] Hamilton wrote to Major General Charles Cotesworth Pinckney, a loyal Federalist from South Carolina, on December 22, 1799, including his instructions for what was in essence the nation's first state funeral. (Washington's private funeral service and internment had occurred at Mount Vernon on December 18, 1799.) Hamilton could not resist sharing his feelings with Pinckney before delving into the crisp formality of his "General Orders." He wrote, "I can be at no loss to anticipate what have been your feelings. I need not tell you what are mine. Perhaps no friend of his has more cause to lament, on personal account, than my self."[75]

On the day after Christmas, Hamilton participated in the memorial march he had planned, proceeding from the Congress building to the German Lutheran Church in Philadelphia, where he listened to one of his Revolutionary War comrades, "Light-Horse Harry" Lee, extol Washington as "first in war, first in peace, first in the hearts of his countrymen."[76]

CHAPTER TEN

"ENOUGH TO MELT A MONUMENT OF MARBLE"

WHEN GEORGE WASHINGTON DIED in December 1799, no one would have predicted that Hamilton would only outlive him by slightly less than five years. As he approached his forty-fifth birthday in January 1800, Hamilton knew that his political effectiveness had come to an end with Washington's passing. To compound matters, Hamilton feared the worst with the approaching inauguration of President Thomas Jefferson.

On March 4, 1801, in a final act of bitterness and pettiness, John Adams fled the capital at 4:00 a.m. to avoid having to attend Jefferson's inauguration, thereby further tarnishing an already tarnished presidency. The new president wasted little time issuing a directive to his treasury secretary to comb through the department's files and find the "smoking gun" to prove once and for all that Alexander Hamilton was corrupt. The treasury secretary, Albert Gallatin, had the onerous task of reporting back to Jefferson that he found no evidence of corruption and that the system that Hamilton created was quite impressive. "I think Mr. Jefferson was disappointed," Gallatin recounted years later to one of Hamilton's sons.[1]

Thomas Jefferson made what appeared to be a gracious gesture in his first inaugural address when he proclaimed that "every difference of opinion is not a difference of principle. We have called by different names brethren of the same principle. We are all Republicans, we are all Federalists."[2] Four days after delivering this conciliatory rhetoric, Jefferson wrote in a private letter of his desire to "obliterate" the Federalists by recruiting the "honest part" of that faction.[3] And by the fall of 1802, any notion of tolerating Federalism had entirely disappeared. In a letter to Attorney General Levi Lincoln, Jefferson referred to Federalist officeholders as "our enemies" and made it clear that he would cleanse his government of any Federalist taint, noting that he was "determined to remove officers who are active or open mouthed against the government." Jefferson vowed to "sink federalism into an abyss from which there shall be no resurrection for it."[4]

Back in New York City, Jefferson's nemesis occasionally mused about his desire to escape the public arena, but despite the fact that Alexander Hamilton was politically damaged, he could never fully remove himself from the public sphere. He was too concerned about the fate of the American experiment to remain indifferent to politics. Nevertheless, Hamilton had frequently proved that he was no match for Jefferson, and his belief that the "talents of low intrigue, and the little arts of popularity" would hold less sway at the national level proved to be one of his more inaccurate predictions.[5] In terms of exploiting these "little arts," the populist Jeffersonians were the masters of the field. When contesting an issue, Hamilton's favored approach was to marshal the facts and present point-by-point briefs rooted in reason, but in an increasingly democratized America, lawyerly briefs were proving ineffective.

Rational argumentation had its place, but it was a prescription for defeat in Jefferson's America. This was especially true for a party that was labeled as a traitorous cabal of monarchists, a highly incendiary charge designed to curtail debate and "sink" the party "into an abyss." Accusing a public figure of being a monarchist in the 1790s was the equivalent of accusing someone of being a communist in the 1950s. This charge was repeated incessantly after 1792; as with all lies, repetition was the key to its success.[6] This propaganda weapon, as Hamilton's biographer John C. Miller put it, was wielded with "consummate skill" by Jefferson, whose supporters in later years switched to the epithet "plutocrats" to describe the Federalists. As the Federalist leader Fisher Ames once observed, the charge of "monarchist" was "a substitute for argument, and its overmatch."[7]

The bulk of the Federalist Party's emotional appeal, to the extent that it had any, rested on the heroic reputation of the now deceased George Washington. In 1802, groping for a way to reverse the rapidly declining prospects of his party, Hamilton proposed that the Federalists create a Christian Constitutional Society to serve as a counterweight to Jeffersonian populism. In a letter written to Congressman James Bayard of Delaware in April 1802, Hamilton laid out a detailed proposal for the establishment of a society that would serve as a grassroots organization, building on the network of churches and churchgoers in the Northeast and mid-Atlantic states. The letter revealed that Hamilton grasped the fact that he and his party were outmaneuvered by their skillful opponents at the "street" level. Hamilton's preferred course of action was to avoid direct emotional appeals to the public, appealing to reason usually in the form of lengthy arguments in the hope of persuading Americans to "think continentally" in one form or another. This approach was simply not effective, especially in light of the successful Republican effort to portray the Federalists as the party of privilege.

A large portion of Hamilton's letter to James Bayard is worth quoting in light of what it reveals about Hamilton's approach to politics and the moral qualms he wrestled with in embracing some of the tactics of the Jeffersonians. Hamilton was reluctantly trying to find a way to appeal to reason, but a reason bolstered in part by an appeal to certain positive passions, such as religion:

Nothing is more fallacious than to expect to produce any valuable or permanent results, in political projects, by relying merely on the reason of men. Men are rather reasoning tha[n] reasonable animals for the most part governed by the impulse of passion. This is a truth well understood by our adversaries who have practiced upon it with no small benefit to their cause. For at the very moment they are eulogizing the reason of men & professing to appeal only to that faculty, they are courting the strongest & most active passion of the human heart—*VANITY!* It is no less true that the Federalists seem not to have attended to the fact sufficiently; and that they erred in relying so much on the rectitude & utility of their measures, as to have neglected the cultivation of popular favour by fair & justifiable expedients... In my opinion the present Constitution is the standard to which we are to cling. Under its banners, *bona fide* must we combat our political foes—rejecting all changes but through the channel itself provides for amendments.[8]

The Federalists needed a grassroots organization, just like the Democratic-Republican societies of the 1790s, and Hamilton believed the Christian Constitutional Society would be the place to start. The society would attempt to rally public support for the Christian religion, which was seen as a natural impediment to the agenda of the "atheistic" Jeffersonians, and also generate support for the Constitution itself, which was designed to check visionary schemes and passing impulses. The Federalist Party, which Hamilton saw as the party of fidelity to the Constitution, would of course benefit from the various educational and charitable initiatives undertaken by the society. Hamilton's hope, similar to that expressed by Abraham Lincoln only thirty-six years later, was that Americans would develop a type of "civil religion," venerating, in a sense, their constitutional order. As with Hamilton, Lincoln believed that "a reverence for the constitution and laws" should "become the political religion of the nation... Reason, cold, calculating, unimpassioned reason, must furnish all the materials for our future support and defense."[9] This American civil religion would not displace traditional religion, but each would buttress the other, indirectly, in that both traditional religion, based on faith, and the new American civil religion, based on reason, shared a common goal: resistance to utopian schemes rooted in the notion of creating a heaven on earth, as the French Revolutionaries had attempted.

Once again, for many of Hamilton's critics, his "scheme" is portrayed as yet another indicator of his "well known" contempt for civil liberties, for his society would have allegedly led to a dangerous blending of church and state.[10] Modern critics may find in it a troubled breach in Jefferson's "wall" between church and state, but Hamilton's proposal was closely aligned with Abraham Lincoln's later assessment of the requirements for a healthy American political order.

The extent to which Hamilton was a Christian has vexed generations of historians and biographers, although many have ultimately concluded that Hamilton was a nonbeliever who used religion solely to advance his political agenda, especially with his proposed Christian Constitutional Society. The evidence, however, does not support this conclusion, at least in regard to the last years of Hamilton's life. Hamilton was a changed man, buffeted by the loss of Washington, his own failings as a husband, and a sense that he lacked any high purpose in pursuing a career as an attorney in New York City. The savagery of the attacks against him by a movement whose leader was an avowed skeptic regarding Christianity (Jefferson, whose ego knew no bounds, considered himself worthy of editing the New Testament, taking a pair of scissors and excising all reference to Jesus's divinity) likely contributed to Hamilton's return to his faith as well. And it was a return, for his college roommate, Robert Troup, described Hamilton as a "devout" student at King's College, having observed Hamilton's "habit of praying upon his knees" every night and every morning.[11]

More than any other event, it was the death of his eldest son Philip in a duel in November 1801 that led Hamilton to renew his faith. A Republican lawyer named George Eaker had delivered a speech critical of Alexander Hamilton at a Fourth of July celebration in 1801, and Philip Hamilton later confronted Eaker at a theater in Manhattan. A duel ensued as a result of that confrontation, and while attempts were made to avoid the altercation, they were unsuccessful. Philip, who on his father's advice did not fire at Eaker, was shot and died approximately fourteen hours later. Philip's death crushed both Alexander and Eliza Hamilton and led to the breakdown of their daughter Angelica, whom Martha Washington had taken under her wing during Hamilton's tenure as treasury secretary. Angelica never recovered from the events of that day, and in a sense, neither did her father. Robert Troup observed Hamilton in the days after his son was killed and noted, "never did I see a man so completely overwhelmed with grief as Hamilton has been," adding that his face was "stamped with grief."[12] Writing four months after his son's death, Hamilton described it as an event "beyond comparison, the most afflicting of my life... The highest as well as the eldest hope of my family has been taken from me."[13]

Hamilton had less than three years to live before he too would die in a duel under circumstances somewhat similar to his son. Part of his remaining life was devoted to publishing the *New York Evening Post*, which Hamilton established shortly before Philip's death and which is today the nation's longest running daily newspaper. One of the first stories the *Post* covered was Philip Hamilton's duel with George Eaker. The *Post* provided Hamilton with a vehicle to continue his prodigious editorial output, which he utilized on issues such as the Louisiana Purchase.

Hamilton also continued practicing law and lent his services pro bono to the case of Harry Croswell, a Federalist newspaper editor who was under indictment for libel against President Jefferson. Jefferson, who was and is portrayed as a champion of freedom of the press, had encouraged such prosecutions at the state level in keeping with his commitment to states' rights. "A few prosecutions," Jefferson wrote the governor of Pennsylvania, "would have a wholesome effect in restoring the integrity of the presses."[14] The Croswell case concerned accusations that Jefferson had paid James Callender and considered him part of his stable of "infamous scribblers." Hamilton's efforts on behalf of Croswell earned him plaudits from both Federalists and Republicans, and his oral arguments before the New York Supreme Court moved some witnesses to tears. Hamilton claimed that a writing that was truthful was "a reason to infer that there was no design to injure another" and dramatically added, "I never did think the truth was a crime." Hamilton's argument that the truth of a claim was admissible on the part of a defendant and that a particular writing must be "false, defamatory, and malicious" in order to be held libelous has become a permanent feature of American law. Hamilton also pleaded for the use of jury trials in libel cases, so as to avoid the specter of judges appointed by the executive serving as the enforcement arm of an oppressive government.[15]

Personal attacks and malicious gossip lay behind the final act of Hamilton's life, his duel with Vice President Aaron Burr, which unfortunately holds the honor of being the only thing most Americans know about Hamilton. A long train of perceived abuses led to the incident at Weehawken, New Jersey, an event that removed two of Thomas Jefferson's formidable foes from the political scene. Hamilton and Burr were no strangers to one another, having contested each other in various New York courtrooms, and in a few instances, they represented the same clients. There was something inevitable about the duel in that both men were ambitious and sensitive to slights, and their two egos were too big even for the confines of New York City. The antagonism could be traced back to Burr defeating Hamilton's father-in-law for a U.S. Senate seat from New York in 1790, Burr publicizing Hamilton's letter critical of President John Adams in 1800, Hamilton's endorsement of Jefferson over Burr for president that same year, and Hamilton's opposition to Burr's quest to become governor of New York in 1804. As early as 1792, Hamilton had described Burr as "unprincipled, both as a public and private man," and as to the former, his "only political principle" was an ambition for the highest honors and offices in the land.[16]

The final straw, at least for Burr, was the allegedly malicious comments made by Hamilton in the aftermath of Burr's losing the race for governor of New York in 1804, which were reported to Burr by a Dr. Charles Cooper. Historian Joanne Freeman has written the most impressive account of the code of honor that "formed the very infrastructure of national politics, providing a governing logic and weapons of war" from an era that is completely unrecognizable to modern Americans. "In the blink of an eye," Freeman notes, a verbal altercation could be converted "into a regimented ritual of honor."[17] Political figures from this era frequently defended their honor using weapons that ranged from publishing a pamphlet, nose tweaking (grabbing and twisting a critic's nose), caning, or the nuclear option, a duel. Although it may seem odd to modern Americans, these options provided some element of restraint in a new system that lacked the discipline provided by organized political parties as the nineteenth century evolved. One would have to think twice before insulting a fellow public figure, or the consequences could be grave. In a way, the code surrounding these "affairs of honor" acted as an eighteenth-century form of deterrence. Should the situation clear the threshold of requiring a dual, the rules were understood by all the parties involved. Freeman observes, "a duel enabled an aggrieved politician to refute character slurs by acting in accordance with the most exacting standards of behavior. A true gentleman was always gracious and calm, even in the face of imminent death. Attitude was the key to proving oneself a man of honor."[18]

Burr and Hamilton rowed separately across the Hudson River and met in Weehawken early on the morning of July 11, 1804. The entire affair was conducted so as to minimize the potential legal repercussions, including selecting New Jersey as the site due to its more tolerant approach to dueling. Each man was accompanied by his "second," which in Hamilton's case was Nathaniel Pendleton, and in Burr's, William P. Van Ness, and the regulations for the duel required each party to leave Manhattan "about five o'clock." The duelists were instructed to march off ten paces, and once reaching their station, one of the seconds, chosen by lot, would "ask whether they are ready." An affirmative answer would be followed by the word "present" by the second, "after which the parties present & fire when they please."[19] The men fired, with Burr aiming at Hamilton and lodging a bullet that nicked his liver and embedded itself in his spine, while Hamilton fired his shot in the air.

Hamilton had announced his intention to throw away his shot in a letter to his wife that was delivered to her after the duel; his Christian scruples led him to "expose [his] own life" rather than subject himself to the "guilt of taking the life of another." A second letter, written on July 4, was also presented to Mrs. Hamilton, noting that if she were reading this letter, her husband had "terminated" his "earthly career." As with the Reynolds letter in which he exposed embarrassing personal information in order to defend his public reputation, Hamilton's reputation took precedence over his obligation to his family. He told Eliza that he wished his "love for you and my precious children would have been alone a decisive motive," but it was "not possible" for him to have "avoided the interview" without "sacrifices which would have rendered me unworthy of your esteem." Hamilton concluded by noting that the consolations of religion would sustain his wife and that he looked forward to "the sweet hope of meeting you in a better world. Adieu best of wives and best of Women. Embrace all my darling Children for me."[20]

In addition to writing Eliza on the day before he was shot, Hamilton drafted a letter to Theodore Sedgwick of Massachusetts, a former Speaker of the House, urging Federalists in the Bay State to reject the schemes of Burr and others who were engaged in a secessionist plot involving New York and the New England states. "Dismemberment of our Empire," he told Sedgwick, "will be a clear sacrifice of great positive advantage, without any counterbalancing good."[21] This was a fitting final statement from a man who consistently urged his fellow Americans to "think continentally." Unlike his great rival, Hamilton categorically rejected Jefferson's flirtation with nullification and secession, despite his distress at living in the latter's America. On more than one occasion, Hamilton discouraged those Federalists who wished to break away as a result of their disdain for slavery and their fears of the enhanced power that Jefferson's Louisiana Purchase would give to the slaveholding states. This was Hamilton's final act of statesmanship.

Alexander Hamilton died thirty-six hours after he was shot by Vice President Burr. In portions of New England and the Middle Atlantic states, the news was greeted with shock and genuine sadness. In parts of the South and the West, the news was greeted with delight. Jefferson was silent for the most part, although there had to be some sense of relief that two of his key rivals were dead, one literally, the other finished politically. Jefferson only made two references to Hamilton's passing in writing, including once in a letter to his daughter, in which he referred to the deceased as "Colonel" Hamilton, demoting him in death. The other was to his good friend Philip Mazzei, to whom he had written in the spring of 1796 accusing George Washington of being a whore for England, in which Jefferson reported the deaths of Samuel Adams, his own daughter Maria, and Alexander Hamilton.

Jefferson's two lieutenants, James Madison and James Monroe, along with other leading Republicans, were solely concerned about the political impact of Hamilton's death, fearing an emotional reaction that might redound to the advantage of the Federalists. Madison wrote Monroe that "you will easily understand the different uses to which the event is turned." The treasury secretary, Albert Gallatin, echoed these fears, noting that Hamilton's death had produced an "artificial sensation" shared by "a majority of both parties [who] seem disposed at this moment to deify Hamilton." Senator John Armstrong Jr., who would later oversee the burning of the nation's capital while serving as Madison's secretary of war, noted with disgust that "the English interest" was determined to erect a statue to Hamilton in the capital. Upon hearing the news of Hamilton's death, Jefferson's cousin, Congressman John Randolph of Roanoke, the de facto leader of the House Republicans, noted that "I feel for Hamilton's immediate connections real concern; for himself, nothing."[22]

The Adams family, ensconced in their bitterness at their ironically named home "Peacefield," did their best to conceal their relief that the "bastard brat" had been removed. But they failed for the most part, regurgitating their condemnation of Hamilton's alleged lust for power and women. Abigail Adams refused to wear black, and while she managed to offer some faint praise for Hamilton's talents, she could not get past her obsession with his sexual conduct. "Why then idolize a man," she asked, "who showed on many occasions that he was a frail, weak man subdued by his passions." Her husband was even more dyspeptic, noting that "vice, folly, and villainy are not to be forgotten, because the guilty wretch repented, in his dying moments." To clarify things, Adams added that he was unwilling to allow his moral or religious beliefs to lead him to forgive Hamilton even if the penitent author of that criticism died "with a pistol bullet through his spinal marrow." Louisa Adams, John Quincy's wife, urged her husband to attend a memorial service for Hamilton in Boston, but the latter refused, noting that he felt no regret in his heart and that "I had no respect for the man."[23]

Hamilton's funeral in New York City on Saturday, July 14, 1804, was a majestic affair, one that likely would have impressed him. Thousands turned out for the two-hour funeral procession, so many, in fact, that citizens were forced to climb trees and stand on the roofs of houses to get a glimpse of the mahogany coffin that was adorned with Hamilton's hat and sword. The coffin was followed by four of Hamilton's sons who walked behind his gray horse, the boots and spurs reversed. A death march performed by the Sixth Regiment of militia echoed through the streets, coming to a halt when the casket was taken into Trinity Church on Broadway. One reporter noted that "not a smile was visible, and hardly a whisper was to be heard, but tears were seen rolling down the cheeks of the affected multitude." The church was a familiar site to Hamilton's wife and children, as at least four of the children were baptized there, and their father had rented pew 92 since the family's return to New York City. Gouverneur Morris delivered the eulogy, leaving out, as he oddly took pains to note in his diary, any references to Hamilton's illegitimacy, adultery, or his "opinionated" nature. Following the service, Hamilton was interred in the Trinity Church graveyard near his son Philip. Three volleys were fired over the grave, while British and French warships anchored in New York harbor fired a salute. This final scene, according to another reporter at the funeral, was "enough to melt a monument of marble."[24]

Eliza Hamilton would outlive her husband by more than half a century and struggled to raise eight children by herself. Without the financial assistance provided by Gouverneur Morris, Rufus King, and other Federalist leaders, she might not have been able to keep her family intact. In addition to these private contributions, Eliza waited until Jefferson left the White House in March 1809 to appeal for help from President James Madison in the form of a bounty and some land that her husband had earned as a veteran of the Revolution; Hamilton had waived any right to this compensation so as to avoid any appearance of a conflict of interest. Madison was apparently unmoved by the request, as seven years would pass before Congress finally approved an act providing partial compensation to Hamilton's family in 1816.[25]

Eliza spent fifty years promoting and protecting her husband's memory, searching for an appropriate author of something akin to an authorized biography and ultimately settling on her son, John Church Hamilton. She visited Mount Vernon and combed through the correspondence between her husband and George Washington in hope of including these letters in her husband's biography. She approached this task with a sense of urgency as the years drifted by. "I have my fears I shall not obtain my object," she wrote to one of her daughters in 1832. "Most of the contemporaries of your father have also passed away."[26]

Hamilton's widow become a fixture in the nation's capital, attending dinners at the White House hosted by presidents James K. Polk and Millard Fillmore, all the while regaling her hosts with stories of dancing with George Washington, "with whom I was a great favorite." She would also recall his kindness in sending the wine cooler and a note of support at one of the low points in her husband's life. She "cherished her status," as Ron Chernow has put it, "as a relic of the American Revolution" and continued the family's tradition of opposing slavery.[27]

Mrs. Hamilton volunteered with Dolley Madison and Louisa Adams (John Quincy Adams's wife) to raise funds to build the Washington Monument in the nation's capital and attended the laying of the cornerstone of the monument on July 4, 1848, in the company of President Polk. Among the observers in the crowd that day were three future presidents, James Buchanan, Abraham Lincoln, and Andrew Johnson.[28] One former president, James Monroe, an architect of the campaign to destroy Alexander Hamilton, attempted to make amends with his widow in the 1820s by showing up at her residence unannounced and suggesting that they put aside any past differences, but he was rebuffed in no uncertain terms. Nothing short of an apology would be accepted by Eliza Hamilton, a gesture that Monroe was unwilling to make.[29]

Eliza Hamilton died on November 9, 1854, having lived long enough to witness the founding of the Republican Party, composed of heirs to the antislavery Federalists. In addition to their opposition to slavery, the Republican Party embraced Hamilton's belief in a dynamic, diversified economy supported by federal policies, including "internal improvements" that encouraged commerce and individual opportunity. The Republican Party's embrace of these Hamiltonian principles contributed to the emergence of the United States as a world power at the dawn of the new century, while the party of Jefferson persisted in clinging to the past, carrying their defense of states' rights and the onerous institutionalized racism this doctrine protected well into the twentieth century.

THE INDISPENSABLE ALLIANCE

A SHORT DISTANCE FROM where Alexander Hamilton was buried in 1804 was the site where he had first come to the attention of General George Washington. Nearby was also the site where the United States almost lost the cause of independence. For all of the romanticism that July 4, 1776, evokes in the minds of Americans, the fact is that the infant nation was almost destroyed less than two months later. On August 29, 1776, Washington's entire army was surrounded by British forces in an untenable position across the East River from New York City. The "glorious cause" would likely have been lost but for the fog and rain that rolled in the following morning to shield the American retreat back to Manhattan. In the absence of the fog and a cautious British command, George Washington would likely be a footnote in Anglo-American history texts—the man ignominiously executed for treason in the fall of 1776. Alexander Hamilton might have survived the destruction of the American army, but he would have suffered a more demeaning fate, relegated to obscurity, a sentence for him worse than death.

It was war that brought George Washington and Alexander Hamilton together. War was their formative experience; it forged the principles and practices that would animate their entire public careers.

Both men were deeply committed to the American Revolution, but they were revolutionaries who understood the virtues of prudence and moderation, which set them apart from zealots like Thomas Paine and Thomas Jefferson. Paine and Jefferson's theoretical musings veered dangerously close to the revolutionaries of modern times who profess an abstract love for humanity, frequently from the confines of a cloistered library, and who envision mankind freed from the strictures of the past and reaching new levels of perfectibility.[1] Washington and Hamilton never suffered from any illusions about the flawed nature of man, and both stood firmly for reason over passion and for stability over speculative change.

Hamilton first demonstrated his commitment to these principles when he was a twenty-year-old student at King's College, when an angry revolutionary mob stormed the house of the college's president, Myles Cooper, a Tory sympathizer. Hamilton apparently appealed for calm long enough to allow the frightened president to escape through a back door. This would be the first of many Hamiltonian appeals for reason over passion, a position to which he would adhere throughout his entire public life. In many ways, what happened on the steps of Myles Cooper's house epitomized Hamilton's conception of statesmanship—preserving order and holding the forces of passion at bay for as long as possible.

Neither Washington nor Hamilton shared the growing belief within the ranks of the Jeffersonians that the people always reasoned correctly and that the cure-all for the problems of a republic was more democracy. This also explains some of the ongoing hostility toward Hamilton and, to a lesser extent, Washington. Hamilton's candor regarding the failings of public opinion stands in contrast to the feel-good rhetoric of Thomas Jefferson, who wrote more often about the wisdom of the American people (although it should be noted that there are exceptions to Jefferson's rosy rhetoric that tend to be selectively ignored by populist historians).[2] Many of these same scholars are inclined to see Hamilton's skeptical attitude toward public opinion as evidence that he was a closet authoritarian or something worse.

As offensive as the Federalist position may seem to modern sensibilities, Hamilton believed, rightly so, that the public "sometimes err[s]" and that while the people intend to do right by the common good, they did not always "reason right about the means of promoting it." This was partly due to the ability of demagogues to flatter the people, which presented a constant threat in a republic; by appealing to public prejudices, demagogues were able to lead the people to betray their true interests. Washington and Hamilton rejected this approach, aware that the forces of populism at work in their day were prone to respond to "every sudden breeze of passion" and "temporary delusions," which was completely at odds with the permanent, long-term interests of the nation. They believed that the "deliberate sense of the community should govern," and that this was possible only through a government that allowed for "cool and sedate reflection."[3] There would be times when statesmanship would require the president to resist the wishes of the people. At its core, this is what Washington and Hamilton's Federalism was about, and it is this that was slowly but surely undone by the Jeffersonian and Jacksonian movements of the first half of the nineteenth century and whose task was completed by the Progressive movement of the early twentieth century.

The Federalist moment was a brief one, lasting from 1789 to 1796, although to some extent it carried over through the Adams years due to the influence of Washington's cabinet, which Adams retained until the last year of his presidency. This critical period allowed the new federal government to secure its footing, stabilize the nation's finances, and avoid war with the leading superpower of the day. That none of this would have happened without George Washington is almost unanimously accepted; what is far less universally accepted is that Hamilton was critical to this as well. Washington and Hamilton's biographer, Ron Chernow, captured the essence of the symbiotic relationship between the two:

Washington and Hamilton had complementary talents, values, and opinions that survived many strains over their twenty-two years together. Washington possessed the outstanding judgment, sterling character, and clear sense of purpose needed to guide his sometimes wayward protégé; he saw that the volatile Hamilton needed a steadying hand. Hamilton, in turn, contributed philosophical depth, administrative expertise, and comprehensive policy knowledge that nobody in Washington's ambit ever matched. He could transmute wispy ideas into detailed plans and turn revolutionary dreams into enduring realities. As a team, they were unbeatable and far more than the sum of their parts.[4]

Washington's intuitive judgment, or as contemporary observers might describe it, his "emotional intelligence," was superior to Hamilton's. Washington, as the modern expression goes, was comfortable enough in his own skin not to be intimidated by Hamilton, unlike some of the other Founding Fathers. He saw qualities and talents in Hamilton that were unnoticed or, more often than not, resented by other members of the founding generation. This was particularly true in the area of economics and finance, where Hamilton was constantly struggling against the forces of superstition and ignorance. But it is also true in matters of law and international relations, where Hamilton was remarkably well read and a profoundly original thinker. The great Chief Justice John Marshall was quoted by Justice Joseph Story as saying that Hamilton's "reach of thought was so far beyond [his]" that by Hamilton's side he felt like a "schoolboy."[5]

It is not too much of a stretch to proclaim Hamilton a genius at what he referred to in the *Federalist Papers* as the "science of politics." He was a horrible politician, but as a nation builder and strategic thinker, he was without parallel. Hamilton was able, as historian

Darren Staloff has noted, to transform "the federal government from an abstract constitutional frame into a concrete political reality."[6] Fortunately for the United States, Hamilton had studied politics, to borrow from John Adams, so that his children might study mathematics and philosophy, and his grandchildren painting, poetry, and music. None of this, of course, was possible without the aegis provided by George Washington.

Nowhere was the impact of the formidable alliance of Washington and Hamilton more dramatically felt than on the American presidency. Washington's ranking as one of the nation's greatest presidents will persist until the American experiment ceases to exist. As historian Gordon Wood has noted, the American presidency is "the powerful office it is in large part because of [George] Washington's initial behavior... He created an independent role for the president and made it the dominant figure in the government."[7]

The great schism between Thomas Jefferson and Alexander Hamilton stemmed from deep policy and personality differences, which drove President Washington to distraction and ultimately led to the creation of America's two-party system. The difference in temperament between the two men was profound, for Hamilton, who was twelve years younger than Jefferson, had a brash quality about him that the shy Jefferson found distasteful. The latter was averse to conflict and dealt with uncomfortable situations by indirect means, relying on surrogates to handle unpleasant matters. These surrogates were part of what Jefferson considered his extended "family," a family that avoided quarrels and operated under Jefferson's gentle, opaque guidance. (Ironically, Jefferson considered the six-hundred-plus slaves he owned during his lifetime to be part of his "family.") Hamilton seemed to relish conflict and never shied from it, much to Jefferson's disdain and the despair, on occasion, of Hamilton's own Federalist allies. His publication of a ninety-five-page document discussing an extramarital affair was but one example of his willingness to openly—and clumsily—confront awkward issues.

There were other factors that contributed to the rift. Jefferson was more theoretical, Hamilton more the pragmatic problem solver; one was the philosopher poet of the founding, the other its engineer. To compound matters, within the confines of Washington's small cabinet, Hamilton was on the scene first, while Jefferson did not arrive until almost a year after the president was inaugurated. Hamilton had served at Washington's side during much of the war, and they had come to know one another quite well. Washington did not know Jefferson well, although he attempted to keep his fellow Virginian happy and treated him with kindness and respect.

That these two Virginians were unable to see eye to eye on the great issues of the day is revealing; Washington, shedding his Virginia parochialism, envisioned a nation, the United States of America, and thus more often than not sided with the cabinet member with whom he had the least in common. Jefferson remained committed to an agrarian confederation that was slowly but surely fading away. All of this could be seen in Jefferson's fierce opposition to the administration's proposals for a national bank, a manufacturing sector of the economy, and acceptance of the idea that a publicly financed debt had its benefits. Jefferson, to give him his due, was primarily devoted to liberty, which he believed was best preserved in a simple republic in which the citizenry were truly self-sufficient, and many of Hamilton's schemes threatened to erode that self-sufficiency.

Washington and Hamilton were devoted to liberty but believed that this could be best achieved if Americans thought continentally, moving beyond the parochial and developing more of an attachment to a traditional nation-state. Nowhere did Washington more forcefully state his desire to create a nation-state than in a letter to the president of Congress in September 1787, in which he noted that "the power of making war, peace and treaties, that of levying money and regulating commerce, and the correspondent executive and judicial authorities should be fully and effectively vested in the general government."[8]

Washington and Hamilton looked at more conventional forms of national power as the surest bulwark of liberty, while Jefferson believed that the character of the citizenry, fostered in an environment of unencumbered liberty, would best protect the American experiment.

In addition to this, Hamilton was America's first foreign policy realist, while Jefferson, to an extent, was something of an idealist, although this was tempered by his appreciation for the Machiavellian nature of the international arena. Hamilton's realism led him to favor détente with Great Britain; Jefferson's hatred of all things British and his admiration for the French Revolution and for revolutionary change in general led the two even further apart. Both men had come to their positions honestly, for they were shaped by their experiences and by their reading of history. Hamilton's world was one of chaos tempered by a fragile veneer of civility; Jefferson's world was an orderly one where man's best instincts, if allowed to come to the fore, would create a new order for the ages.

Less than three years after assuming the presidency, the atmosphere in Washington's cabinet was anything but a new order—it was old world politics at its worst. Jefferson would later observe of his relationship with the treasury secretary that they were "daily pitted in the cabinet like two cocks." The administration had become a Machiavellian battleground worthy of a European court as Jefferson and Hamilton were locked in a battle that threatened to undermine the stability of the new nation. As Ron Chernow has observed, the conflict between Jefferson and Hamilton "was to take on an almost pathological intensity."[9]

Needless to say, this was at odds with Washington's conception of a healthy political order. The president despised political parties and saw himself as the head of state, a man above faction and of untarnished disinterestedness, a champion of the common good. Washington's view of the American political order was a noble one, but it proved impossible in a free society to prevent the rise of faction, something James Madison understood better than either Washington or Hamilton. As

Madison had noted in *Federalist* No. 10, "liberty is to faction what air is to fire," and despite the best efforts of Washington to form a government of national unity, the differences over the means best suited to deliver on the promises of the American Revolution almost tore the new nation apart.[10] As Ron Chernow observed, by the spring of 1792, "the period of covert skirmishing had ended. Open warfare had begun," with Hamilton on one side, and Jefferson and Madison on the other.[11]

The difference between a Federalist like Hamilton, who was a founder of New York's Society for Promoting the Manumission of Slaves, and Jefferson, one of the largest slaveholders in Virginia who began to see Northern opposition to slavery as part of a conspiracy to oppress the South, has to be factored into any honest assessment of this period in American history. And this is not an exercise in "presentism," for plenty of Jefferson's contemporaries, especially his Federalist contemporaries, and even Jefferson himself during his younger years, recognized the hypocrisy of a nation founded on the principle that all men were created equal enslaving human beings by the thousands. According to Edmund Randolph, no friend of Washington's, the latter had told him that if it came to a conflict between North and South over slavery and the fate of the Union, the general would join the Northern cause. While Washington and Hamilton were by no means abolitionists, they were more concerned than many Jeffersonians about the debilitating influence of slavery on the character of the American citizenry and feared that the issue might ultimately destroy the nation. In a sense, Jefferson correctly discerned the dangers to the South's peculiar institution presented by the Federalists, who to this day are portrayed as enemies of the common man. If that common man happened to be a black man or a Native American, then these accounts are complete distortions of the truth.

Alexander Hamilton apparently never owned slaves and had urged their recruitment as soldiers in the American Revolution in exchange for their freedom. His membership in the New York Manumission

Society stands in stark contrast to his great rival, whose efforts to restrict slavery diminished over time as he began to believe that his idealized agrarian society was under assault from "hypocritical" antislavery descendants of Hamilton and the Federalists.[12]

In contrast to Jefferson, Washington became more of a critic of slavery over time. Washington owned 318 slaves when he died in December 1799, and he had come to see the peculiar institution as a personal burden and a threat to the Union. He could be a demanding slave owner, but unlike some of his Virginia contemporaries, his position genuinely evolved to the point where he decided to set an example toward the end of his life. After some initial misgivings, Washington had endorsed the idea of allowing black soldiers to fight for the Continental army, to the point where some five thousand blacks fought for the American cause, which as Ron Chernow has observed, allowed Washington to command the most integrated American army up until the Vietnam War.[13]

After the war, Washington began to embrace the position of many of the Northern states, which had begun to abolish slavery (Vermont's constitution did so in 1777) or instituted schemes to gradually emancipate their slaves. On September 9, 1786, Washington wrote to an acquaintance, "I never mean (unless some particular circumstance should compel me to it) to possess another slave by purchase; it being among my first wishes to see some plan adopted, by which slavery in this country may be abolished by slow, sure, and imperceptible degrees."[14] The abolition of slavery, Washington told the British actor John Bernard, was an event that "no man desires more heartily than I do... Not only do I pray for it on the score of human dignity, but I can clearly foresee that nothing but the rooting out of slavery can perpetuate the existence of our union."[15]

Washington's growing appreciation for the contradictions inherent in a slaveholding republic based on the rights of man led him to an honorable act near the end of his life—he authorized the liberation of his slaves upon his wife's passing. Unlike his fellow Virginian, Washington did not support colonization schemes for freed slaves nor did he fear that an educated free slave would threaten the white community; instead, Washington wrote in his will that his freed slaves were to be "taught to read and write and to be brought up to some useful occupation."[16] In the end, the slaves that Washington owned were freed, while Martha Washington's slaves remained in a state of bondage. The Washingtons were no radical abolitionists, especially Martha Washington, but the ex-president was well ahead of most of his countrymen in seeing the destructive effects of the institution on the health and well-being of the political order he created.

George Washington and Alexander Hamilton had their flaws, to be sure, with the latter's being more pronounced. Washington's Herculean self-discipline allowed him to control his worst impulses, while Hamilton's "issues" were more readily apparent and less constrained. But Hamilton was hardly the power-mad, "un-American" bastard that Jefferson and his heirs portrayed him to be. Jefferson's hubris, which led him to revise the New Testament, also led him to define who was and was not an American, with Washington and Hamilton consigned to being agents of the Crown. Closer to our time, Jefferson's admirers, including his biographers Dumas Malone and Merrill Peterson, kept these slurs in circulation, with the former declaiming that Hamilton's "contempt for the stupidity of the lesser orders of mankind" would have led "straight to Fascism," while the latter condemned the "faintly alien…odor of [Hamilton's] character and politics." This malodorous alien had no commitment to America "but to his own glorious image of a great nation."[17]

Throughout their twenty-two-year alliance, Washington and Hamilton would be shot at, literally and figuratively, from all sides. They drew this fire partly because their wartime experience set them apart from many of their founding brethren, some of whom developed an abstract, armchair radicalism, dangerously divorced from the cold reality of revolutionary death and destruction. Washington and Hamilton saw death up close and understood that there was a thin veneer separating order from chaos, which led them to embrace the virtue of moderation and to revere stability. They were sober revolutionaries, and thankfully so, for due to them, the American Revolution did not consume itself, unlike most modern revolutions. It was a close call, but because of Washington and Hamilton, the United States escaped this fate.

Conventional wisdom holds that the epic confrontation of the founding era occurred between Hamilton and Jefferson, when in fact it occurred between Washington and Hamilton on one side and Jefferson and Madison on the other. Jefferson helped to foster this myth, celebrating his man-to-man confrontation with Hamilton by placing busts of Hamilton and himself (inadvertently revealing, once again, the titanic range of his ego) facing each other in the entrance to his plantation. When startled visitors would inquire as to why he would display a bust of Hamilton directly across from one of himself, Jefferson would dryly note, "opposed in death as in life."[18]

Over time, some Jeffersonians came to see Washington less as a victim of Hamilton's machinations and more as a coconspirator. This was an accurate assessment of the situation. Hamilton remained firmly under the president's direction throughout the over five years he served as secretary of the treasury. Jefferson himself later testified to Washington's hands-on control of his administration. The president was "always in accurate possession of all facts and proceedings in every part of the Union, and to whatsoever department they related; he formed a central point for the different branches, preserved a unity of object and action among them."[19]

Both in their time and in ours, Jefferson, Madison, and their admirers have had to choose between two unflattering options regarding the "father of his country"—he was either a puppet of the cunning "bastard" from the Caribbean or a willing accomplice to Hamilton's nefarious plots. To assuage their consciences or to minimize the political repercussions, many Jeffersonians and their ideological heirs adopted a similar position—that an elderly, doddering, intellectually challenged Washington was unaware of the plotting taking place within his executive household. As early as the summer of 1790, populist demagogues such as Senator William Maclay of Pennsylvania were claiming, in private, that Washington had "become in the hands of Hamilton the dishclo[th] of every dirty speculation, as his [Washington's] name goes to wipe away blame and silence all murmuring."[20] These slanders against Hamilton are all the more galling, since unlike Washington, Jefferson, or Madison, Hamilton "severed all outside sources of income while in office," something his illustrious contemporaries failed to do.[21]

To this day, critics of the Federalists tend to focus their fire exclusively on Hamilton so as to avoid the blowback that would accrue from attacking Washington.[22] But as Washington told Jefferson, the policies Hamilton implemented at the Treasury Department were Washington's policies, as were the administration's policies toward Great Britain and France. As early as January 1789, long before Hamilton was nominated as treasury secretary, Washington made it clear that resolving the nation's ailing credit ranking and building the allegiance of the American people to the national government were his top priorities. Writing to Marquis de Lafayette, Washington noted that his priority as president was "to extricate my country from the embarrassments in which it is entangled, through want of credit; and to establish a general system of policy, which if pursued will insure permanent felicity to the Commonwealth."[23] As the editors of The Papers of George Washington observed, "there is no doubt that the president agreed completely with the implied objectives of the secretary of the treasury's fiscal program to create economic policies designed to produce a strong centralized federal government."[24]

Remarkably, for the reasons mentioned above, these facts continue to be ignored; understandably so, for attacking Hamilton was and is a far more palatable approach than attacking the towering figure of George Washington. Regarding Hamilton's tenure as treasury secretary, it should be noted that Washington believed that Hamilton filled "one of the most important departments of Government with acknowledged abilities and integrity" and left a legacy where he had become "a conspicuous character in the United States, and even in Europe." The president went on to add that Hamilton was "enterprising, quick in his perceptions" and that his judgment was "intuitively great."[25] On the occasion of Hamilton's departure from his cabinet, the president observed that "in every relation," he found his treasury secretary's "talents, exertions, and integrity" were "well placed" and worthy of "my approbation" and "proof of your title to public regard."[26] In March 1796, a little over a year after this letter was written, Washington wrote Hamilton that he could be assured of "the warmth of my friendship and of the affectionate regard" that he felt toward Hamilton.[27] In contrast, Washington would go on to sever all contact with Jefferson, who had deceived him on multiple occasions.

As much as it pains Hamilton's critics to admit, Hamilton's vision was Washington's vision as well. Americans should put aside the caricatured account of their early history that pits the supposed "champions of the people" (Jefferson, Madison, and their party) against the "forces of privilege and authoritarianism" (Washington, Hamilton, and the Federalists). If they do so, they will discover that due to the exertions of George Washington and Alexander Hamilton, the American people began to "think continentally" and created a strong union that decades and then centuries later helped defeat fascism and communism, explored the universe, produced endless scientific and technological breakthroughs, and perhaps most importantly abolished slavery and Jim Crow, thereby securing the blessings of liberty for all of their fellow citizens.

ACKNOWLEDGMENTS

THE AUTHORS WOULD LIKE to thank the following people for their support, advice, and enthusiasm.

Tony would like to thank several people for supporting this book over the years. None perhaps was as enthusiastic as David Bobb, the former director of the Hoogland Center for Teacher Excellence at Hillsdale College, who invited Tony to deliver lectures on the topic several times at the annual George Washington Seminar. Conversations with David over the years were instrumental in shaping this book, and his friendship was good for the soul. He constantly repeated the refrain that the story was a very important one that had to be told. It is now Tony's great fortune to be working with David at the Bill of Rights Institute.

Our mutual friend and colleague, Jeff Morrison, has generously shared his deep knowledge of the American founding, and his wry sense of humor has done wonders to keep us both humble. Tony had the pleasure of discussing the vision of the book with his good friend, Bruce Khula, over many glasses of scotch through the years.

We thank the Sourcebooks team, especially our editor, Stephanie Bowen, our publicist, Liz Kelsch, and Rachel Kahn, our production editor. Tony has completed four books with Sourcebooks, and this is his first with Stephanie, who has a keen eye and excellent appreciation for narrative history and keeping the story moving. Liz has been a tireless advocate of all of Tony's books and deserves our great thanks, while Rachel demonstrated remarkable insight, and patience, during the editing process.

Tony thanks his wife, Lynne, and his children, Catherine and Paul. Lynne has supported every one of Tony's professional endeavors—teaching, writing, professional development—with great love and cheer throughout their twenty years of marriage. Paul and Catherine were toddlers when this manuscript was first written, and their father enjoyed the great discussions about the ideas in this book held at the dinner table or in the car driving to a sporting event.

Steve would like to thank his wife Maryanne and his daughter Maura for all of their love and encouragement. Additionally, Steve is truly grateful for all that he has learned from these outstanding scholars: Delane Clark, Peter McNamara, Ken Masugi, Mike Waters, Melanie Marlowe, Mackubin Owens, Hal Bidlack, David Tucker, and Karl Walling.

We dedicate this book to Brianna Doherty, who encouraged Steve to complete this work, and to J. David Gowdy, friend and colleague at the Washington, Jefferson & Madison Institute in Charlottesville, Virginia. David is a great friend, man of character, and entrepreneur. He has a profound love of the lives and writings of the Founders and has dedicated himself to advancing their study in the classroom through teacher seminars. David has been a supporter of this book since he first learned of the idea. For these reasons and many others, we have dedicated this book to him and hope it adequately expresses our appreciation.

—*Stephen Knott and Tony Williams*

NOTES

ABBREVIATIONS

AH	Alexander Hamilton
DGW	Jackson, Donald, and Dorothy Twohig, eds. *The Diaries of George Washington*. 6 vols. Charlottesville: University Press of Virginia, 1976–79.
GW	George Washington
PAH	Syrett, Harold C., and Jacob E. Cooke, eds. *The Papers of Alexander Hamilton*. 26 vols. New York: Columbia University Press, 1961–79.
PGWCol	Abbot, W. W., and Dorothy Twohig, eds. *The Papers of George Washington: Colonial Series*. 10 vols. Charlottesville: University Press of Virginia, 1983–95.
PGWCon	Abbot, W. W., and Dorothy Twohig, eds. *The Papers of George Washington: Confederation Series*. 6 vols. Charlottesville: University Press of Virginia, 1992–97.
PGWPres	Abbot, W. W., Dorothy Twohig, and Philander D. Chase, eds. *The Papers of George Washington: Presidential Series*. Charlottesville: University Press of Virginia, 1987–.
PGWRev	Abbot, W. W., Dorothy Twohig, Philander D. Chase, and Edward G. Lengel, eds. *The Papers of George Washington: Revolutionary War Series*. Charlottesville: University Press of Virginia, 1985–.

RFC   Farrand, Max, ed. *The Records of the Federal Convention of 1787*. 3
           vols. New Haven, CT: Yale University Press, 1911.

RV   Tarter, Brent, and Robert L. Scribner, eds. *Revolutionary Virginia:
           The Road to Independence*. 7 vols. Charlottesville: University Press of
           Virginia, 1973–83.

WW   Fitzpatrick, John C., ed. *The Writings of Washington from the
           Original Manuscript Sources, 1745–1799*. 39 vols. Washington,
           DC: Government Printing Office, 1931–34. Reprint, New York:
           Greenwood Press, 1970.

CHAPTER ONE

1.   The section on George Washington's family is dependent upon James
      Thomas Flexner, *George Washington: The Forge of Experience, 1732–
      1775* (Boston: Little, Brown, 1965), 9–25, and Freeman, *George
      Washington: A Biography*, 1:32–72. See also Chernow, *Washington: A
      Life*, 3–12, and Longmore, *The Invention of George Washington*, 1–6,
      which is strong on Virginia society in which Washington was born.

2.   *PGWCol*, 1:8–33; Flexner, *Forge of Experience*, 41, 45; Chase, "A
      Stake in the West," 159–87. Chase argues that Washington's survey-
      ing skills were an important part of his rise in society and shaped his
      vision of developing the West.

3.   *DGW*, 1:24–117; Chernow, *Washington: A Life*, 23–26.

4.   GW to Robert Dinwiddie, 10 June 1752, in *PGWCol*, 1:50–51.

5.   As historian Douglass Adair writes, "The love of fame encourages a
      man to make history, to leave the mark of his deeds and his ideals
      on the world; it incites a man [to become]…a being never to be
      forgotten by those later generations that will be born into a world
      his actions helped to shape… Fame can never be a gift; it cannot
      be inherited; it must be won by a person who imposes his will, his
      ideas, for good or ill, upon history in such a way that he will always
      be remembered." Adair, "Fame and the Founding Fathers," 14–15.

6.   Anderson, *Crucible of War*, 31–32; Peckham, *The Colonial Wars*,
      127–29.

7. Clary, *Washington's First War*, 51–53.

8. The instructions to Governor Dinwiddie are reprinted in Anderson, *Crucible of War*, 37–38, and Freeman, *George Washington: A Biography*, 1:275.

9. *PGWCol*, 1:58–62; *DGW*, 1:127–29.

10. *DGW*, 1:131–32; Clary, *Washington's First War*, 57.

11. *DGW*, 1:141–44.

12. Freeman, *George Washington: A Biography*, 1:309–10.

13. Ibid.

14. *DGW*, 1:151; Clary, *Washington's First War*, 64–65.

15. *DGW*, 1:158; Clary, *Washington's First War*, 66.

16. Freeman, *George Washington: A Biography*, 1:332–33.

17. Dinwiddie to GW, 15 March 1754, in *PGWCol*, 1:75.

18. GW to Dinwiddie, 18 May 1754, in *PGWCol*, 1:98–100.

19. Dinwiddie to GW, 25 May 1754, in *PGWCol*, 1:102–4.

20. GW to Dinwiddie, 27 May 1754, in *PGWCol*, 1:105; Chernow, *Washington: A Life*, 40–41.

21. The most comprehensive assessment of the different historical sources surrounding this event can be found in Anderson, *Crucible of War*, 53–60. See also Fowler, *Empires at War*, 41–43.

22. This statement is from the account in his journal, which was captured by the French and subsequently published in *DGW*, 1:166, 193–97.

23. GW to Dinwiddie, 29 May 1754, in *PGWCol*, 1:116–17.

24. GW to Dinwiddie, 3 June 1754, in *PGWCol*, 1:124.

25. Freeman, *George Washington: A Biography*, 1:378–79.

26. GW to John Augustine Washington, 31 May 1754, in *PGWCol*, 1:118.

27. Chernow, *Washington: A Life*, 44.

28. Axelrod, *Blooding at Great Meadows*, 191.

29. GW to Joshua Fry, 29 May 1754, in *PGWCol*, 1:117; Clary, *Washington's First War*, 89–90.

30. Dinwiddie to GW, 1 June 1754, in *PGWCol*, 1:119.

31. Flexner, *Forge of Experience*, 93–100.

32. "George Washington's Account of the Capitulation of Fort Necessity," 1786, in *PGWCol*, 1:172; Freeman, *George Washington: A Biography*, 1:404.

33. "George Washington's Account of the Capitulation of Fort Necessity," 1786, in *PGWCol*, 1:172; Freeman, *George Washington: A Biography*, 1:405.

34. For the relevant documents related to the "assassination" controversy, see "The Capitulation of Fort Necessity," in *PGWCol*, 1:157–73, and the summary in Chernow, *Washington: A Life*, 47–49.

35. Clary, *Washington's First War*, 116–18.

36. GW to John Augustine Washington, 14 May 1755, in *PGWCol*, 1:278; Freeman, *George Washington: A Biography*, 2:35.

37. GW to William Byrd, 20 April 1755, in *PGWCol*, 1:250; Freeman, *George Washington: A Biography*, 2:19.

38. Robert Orme to GW, 2 March 1755, in *PGWCol*, 1:241; McCardell, *Ill-Starred General*, 149.

39. McCardell, *Ill-Starred General*, 160–67, 171.

40. GW to John Augustine Washington, 28 June–2 July 1755, in *PGWCol*, 1:319.

41. McCardell, *Ill-Starred General*, 251.

42. Freeman, *George Washington: A Biography*, 2:73.

43. Clary, *Washington's First War*, 158.

44. GW to Dinwiddie, 18 July 1755, in *PGWCol*, 1:339–40.

45. Ferling, *The Ascent of George Washington*, 36.

46. On Washington and the other Virginia planters on tobacco, debt, honor, and support for resistance to British policies, see Breen, *Tobacco Culture*, and Ragsdale, *A Planter's Republic*.

47. On George and Martha's marriage, see Brady, *Martha Washington: An American Life*, and Chadwick, *The General and Mrs. Washington*.

48. Chernow, *Washington: A Life*, 99.

CHAPTER TWO

1. Chernow, *Alexander Hamilton*, 16–20.

2. Flexner, *The Young Hamilton: A Biography*, 23.

3. Dunn, *Sugar and Slaves*, 181–86.

4. Brookhiser, *Alexander Hamilton, American*, 15–17.

5. Princeton president Reverend John Witherspoon wrote a pamphlet encouraging West Indians to come to the North American colonies for an education, and British pamphleteers responded with similar defenses of the superiority of a British education. The debate underscored the idea that the islanders would study somewhere abroad because of the paucity of educational opportunities in the West Indies. O'Shaughnessy, *An Empire Divided*, 19–27.

6. Chernow, *Alexander Hamilton*, 24.

7. Mitchell, *Alexander Hamilton: Youth to Maturity*, 16–18.

8. Parker, *The Sugar Barons*, 241–42, 303–5.

9. AH to Edward Stevens, 11 November 1769, in *PAH*, 1:4–5.

10. AH to William Newton, 16 November 1771, in *PAH*, 1:14.

11. AH to Nicholas Cruger, 27 November 1771, in *PAH*, 1:16.

12. AH to Newton, 1 February 1772, in *PAH*, 1:24.

13. Nicholas Cruger to Hans Buus, 18 March 1772, in *PAH*, 1:30.

14. Flexner, *Young Hamilton: A Biography*, 46–47.

15. Mitchell, *Alexander Hamilton: Youth to Maturity*, 33.

16. Ibid., 24.

17. Schachner, *Alexander Hamilton*, 27; Schachner, "Alexander Hamilton Viewed by His Friends," 203–9.

18. See Chernow, *Alexander Hamilton*, 41–47.

19. Livingston would become the first governor of the state of New Jersey and attend the Constitutional Convention; Boudinot would serve as the president of the Continental Congress; Sterling would become a general in the Revolutionary War; Duer would serve in the Continental Congress and with Hamilton in the Treasury Department; and Burr would become Hamilton's great political rival and kill him in a duel.

For his part, Witherspoon signed the Declaration of Independence, served in the Continental Congress, and trained twelve members of the Continental Congress, five delegates to the Constitutional Convention, forty-nine members of the House of Representatives, twenty-eight senators, three Supreme Court justices, a president, and a vice president. Morrison, *John Witherspoon and the Founding of the American Republic*, 1–4.

20. Ibid., 10.

21. Ibid., 35, 91–92.

22. Ibid., 23, 28–29; Ketcham, *James Madison: A Biography*, 43–44.

23. Schachner, "Alexander Hamilton Viewed by His Friends," 209.

24. Ketcham, *James Madison: A Biography*, 51–52.

25. Schachner, "Alexander Hamilton Viewed by His Friends," 212–13.

CHAPTER THREE

1. Slaughter, *Independence*, 207, 222–23.

2. Middlekauff, *The Glorious Cause*, 70.

3. Ibid., 72.

4. "Address, Memorial, and Remonstrance of the General Assembly to King, Lords, and Commons Respectively in Opposition to a Proposed Stamp Tax," 18 December 1764, in *RV*, 1:9–14; Greene, *Landon Carter*, 50–55; Isaac, *Landon Carter's Uneasy Kingdom*, 167–75; McGaughy, *Richard Henry Lee of Virginia*, 77; Chitwood, *Richard Henry Lee*, 31–33.

5. Morgan and Morgan, *The Stamp Act Crisis*, 71.

6. May 1765, in *DGW*, 1:337–38.

7. GW to Francis Dandridge, 20 September 1765, and GW to Robert Cary & Company, 20 September 1765, in *PGWCol*, 7:395–402.

8. O'Shaughnessy, *An Empire Divided*, 90–91.

9. Capel and Osgood Hanbury to GW, 27 March 1766, in *PGWCol*, 7:431.

10. Governor Francis Fauquier, "Proclamation," 9 June 1766, in *RV*, 1:50–51.

11. GW to Robert Cary & Company, 21 July 1766, in *PGWCol*, 7:457.

12. Wood, *The American Revolution: A History*, 30–32.

13. October, November, and December 1768, in *DGW*, 2:103.

14. 2 April 1769, in *DGW*, 2:140.

15. GW to George Mason, 5 April 1769, in *PGWCol*, 8:178.

16. Ibid. Jeffry Morrison rightly states that this letter squarely places George Washington in the British liberal tradition and takes seriously Washington's imputation of the use of force. See Morrison, *The Political Philosophy of George Washington*, 36. See also Phelps, *George Washington and American Constitutionalism*, 16. Phelps argues that this is when Washington dropped his earlier accommodationist stance.

17. GW to Mason, 5 April 1769, in *PGWCol*, 8:178–80.

18. Mason to GW, 5 April 1769, in *PGWCol*, 8:182–83.

19. 17–21 April 1769, in *DGW*, 2:142–43.

20. "Resolves of the House of Burgesses Upholding the Rights to Tax and to Petition and Condemning a Resolution of Parliament," 16 May 1769, in *RV*, 1:69.

21. Ibid.

22. Ibid., 1:70–71.

23. Ibid., 1:70.

24. 17–18 May 1769, in *DGW*, 2:152; "Nonimportation Resolutions of the Former Burgesses," 18 May 1769, in *RV*, 1:72–73.

25. "Nonimportation Resolutions of the Former Burgesses," 18 May 1769, in *RV*, 1:74–77.

26. 20 May 1769, in *DGW*, 2:153.

27. GW to Robert Cary & Company, 25 July 1769, in *PGWCol*, 8:229–31.

28. "Nonimportation Association of Burgesses and Merchants," 22 June 1770, in *RV*, 1:78–79.

29. Williams, *America's Beginnings*, 79–80.

30. Zobel, *The Boston Massacre*, 113–79.

31. Archer, *As If an Enemy's Country*, 178–81.

32. Zobel, *Boston Massacre*, 180–294.

33. Carp, *Defiance of the Patriots*, 20.

34. Ibid., 122–24.

35. Williams, *America's Beginnings*, 85.

36. GW to George William Fairfax, 10 June 1774, in *PGWCol*, 10:96.

37. Ferling, *Leap in the Dark*, 107; Isaacson, *Benjamin Franklin: An American Life*, 275.

38. Carp, *Defiance of the Patriots*, 191.

39. Slaughter, *Independence*, 352–53.

40. Williams, *America's Beginnings*, 85–86.

41. "Boston Town Committee to Virginia Committee via Philadelphia," 13 May 1774, in *RV*, 2:71–72; Alexander, *Samuel Adams: America's Revolutionary Politician*, 130–31.

42. "At a Meeting of the Freeholders and Other Inhabitants of the Town of Boston," 13 May 1774, in *RV*, 2:72–73.

43. Miller, *The Revolutionary Paul Revere*, 174–77; Triber, *A True Republican: The Life of Paul Revere*, 97–99.

44. Unger, *American Tempest*, 182–83.

45. 12–25 May, in *DGW*, 3:249–50; and Virginia Committee, 12–25 May 1774, in *RV*, 2:73–82.

46. Ketchum, *Divided Loyalties*, 269–71.

47. Meacham, *Thomas Jefferson*, 71.

48. "Resolution of the House of Burgesses Designating a Day of Fasting and Prayer," 24 May 1774, in *RV*, 1:94–95.

49. 12–25 May, in *DGW*, 3:251–52.

50. "Resolution of the House of Burgesses Designating a Day of Fasting and Prayer," 24 May 1774, in *RV*, 1:94.

51. GW to George William Fairfax, 10 July 1774, in *PGWCol*, 10:94–98.

52. "Association of Former Burgesses, with a Proposal to Hold Annual General Congresses," 27 May 1774, in *RV*, 1:97–98.

53. "The Convention of 1774: The Decision," 30 May 1774, in *RV*, 1:99–100.

54. "The Convention of 1774: The Summons," 31 May 1774, in *RV*, 1:101–2.

55. "Fasting and Prayer: Psalms 103:19," 1 June 1774, in *RV*, 1:103.

56. 1 June 1774, in *DGW*, 3:254.

57. GW to Robert Cary & Company, 1 June 1774, in *PGWCol*, 10:83.

58. GW to George William Fairfax, 10 June 1774, in *PGWCol*, 10:97.

59. GW to Bryan Fairfax, 4 July 1774, in *PGWCol*, 10:109–10.

60. GW to Bryan Fairfax, 20 July 1774, in *PGWCol*, 10:129–31. Washington later told Fairfax, "An innate spirit of freedom first told me, that the measures which administration hath for sometime been, and now are, most violently pursuing, are repugnant to every principle of natural justice; whilst much abler heads than my own, hath fully convinced me that it is not only repugnant to natural right, but subversive of the laws and constitution of Great Britain itself." This letter demonstrates that Washington was thinking primarily in terms of natural rights and natural law principles of justice and secondarily in terms of the traditional rights of Englishmen. GW to Fairfax, 24 August 1774, in *PGWCol*, 10:155.

61. GW to George William Fairfax, 10 June 1774, in *PGWCol*, 10:96–97.

62. GW to Bryan Fairfax, 24 August 1774, in *PGWCol*, 10:155. Washington believed that if the Americans' right to govern themselves was stripped away, they would be just like the slaves that he and the other Virginia slave owners ruled over—arbitrarily, as he admits, and thus tyrannically. It was no metaphor. If Americans lost their natural and constitutional rights, were governed without their consent, and lost their independence, they would be slaves.

63. GW to B. Fairfax, 4 July 1774, in *PGWCol*, 10:109–10. Elsewhere, he stated unequivocally: "There has been a regular systematic plan formed, to enforce them; and that nothing but unanimity in the

colonies...and firmness can prevent it." GW to Fairfax, 24 August 1774, in *PGWCol*, 10:156.

64. Ketchum, *Divided Loyalties*, 272–73.

65. Chernow, *Alexander Hamilton*, 55–56; Mitchell, *Alexander Hamilton: Youth to Maturity*, 63–64; Flexner, *Young Hamilton: A Biography*, 65–66. The event was reconstructed by Hamilton's son and is largely accepted by the above biographers with a bit of skepticism.

66. "Remarks on the Quebec Bill, Part One," 15 June 1775, in *PAH*, 1:166.

67. For example, Washington wrote Dunmore in June 1772, "The very obliging offer your Lordship was pleased to make me the day I left Williamsburg, in behalf of the officers and soldiers who (under faith of government) lay claim to 200,000 acres of land, on the waters of Ohio (promised them by Proclamation in 1754) I did not embrace, because it is evident to me, who am in some degree acquainted with the situation of that country, and the rapid progress that is making in the settlement of it, that delay at this time in the prosecution of our plan, would amount to the loss of the land, inasmuch as emigrants are daily and hourly settling on the choice spots waiting a favorable opportunity to solicit legal titles, on the grounds of preoccupancy." GW to Lord Dunmore, 15 June 1772, in *PGWCol*, 9:55–56.

Washington raised the issue again a year later and wrote, "I say, if it be true, that your Lordship will now grant patents for these lands, I shall receive the advice of it as a particular favor." GW to Dunmore, 12 September 1773, in *PGWCol*, 9:323. Dunmore wrote to GW with the frustrating answer that "I do not mean to grant any patents on the western waters, as I do not think I am at present empowered so to do." Dunmore to GW, 24 September 1773, in *PGWCol*, 9:327.

68. 14 July 1774, in *DGW*, 3:260–61.

69. Ibid.

70. GW to B. Fairfax, 20 July 1774, in *PGWCol*, 10:128–29.

71. 18 July 1774, in *DGW*, 3:260–261.

72. "Fairfax County Resolves," 18 July 1774, in *RV*, 1:127–32. Jeffry Morrison calls the Fairfax Resolves a document reflecting British liberal thought rooted in consent, self-government, and liberty. He also accepts the idea that Washington and Mason believed that blacks as well as whites had natural rights that the slave trade violated. Morrison, *Political Philosophy of George Washington*, 115, 118. Phelps says that they had a view that the British threatened the very fabric of American constitutional liberties. Phelps, *George Washington and American Constitutionalism*, 17.

73. "The Convention of 1774: The Convocation of August 1," in *RV*, 1:223.

74. 28 July–7 August 1774, in *DGW*, 3:264–69.

75. GW to Thomas Johnson, 5 August 1774, in *PGWCol*, 10:143.

76. "The Convention of 1774: The Convocation of August 1," in *RV*, 1:223–24.

77. "The Convention of 1774: The Election of Deputies to Attend a General Congress," 5 August 1774, in *RV*, 1:227–29.

78. 31 August 1774, in Adams, *Diary and Autobiography*, 2:117.

79. *RV*, 1:227.

80. "Convention Association," 6 August 1774, in *RV*, 1:231–35.

81. "Instructions to the Deputies Elected to Attend the General Congress," 6 August 1774, in *RV*, 1:236–39.

82. 7 August 1774, in *DGW*, 3:269.

83. GW to B. Fairfax, 24 August 1774, in *PGWCol*, 10:154–56.

84. 30 August–4 September, in *DGW*, 3:271–75.

85. 2 September 1774, in Adams, *Diary and Autobiography*, 2:120.

86. Beeman, *Our Lives, Our Fortunes, and Our Sacred Honor*, 123–32.

87. GW to Robert McKenzie, 9 October 1774, in *PGWCol*, 10:171–72.

88. "Declaration and Resolves of the First Continental Congress," 14 October 1774, in Morison, *Sources and Documents*, 119.

89. Beeman, *Our Lives, Our Fortunes*, 155–62.

90. Ketchum, *Divided Loyalties*, 299.

91. Ibid.

92. "A Full Vindication of the Measures of the Congress," 15 December 1774, in *PAH*, 1:47.

93. "The Farmer Refuted," 23 February 1775, in *PAH*, 1:88.

94. Ibid.

95. Ibid., 1:122.

96. GW to John Taylor, 31 October 1774, in *PGWCol*, 10:175.

97. "Resolutions of Fairfax County Committee," 17 January 1775, in *PGWCol*, 10:237; 13 November 1774, 16–18 January 1775, in *DGW*, 3:291, 303.

98. William Milnor to GW, 29 November 1774, 27 December 1774, 3 January 1775, 21 February 1775, 7 March 1775, in *PGWCol*, 10:189–90, 216, 224, 270, 294; William Grayson to GW, 27 December 1774, 8 February 1775, 10:214–15, 259; George Mason to GW, 6 February 1775, 10:240–42; GW to Milnor, 23 January 1775, 10:254–55; James Scott Jr. to GW, 16 February 1775, 10:263; Mason to GW, 17 February 1775, 10:265–67; 30 December 1774, 4 January 1775, 8–11 February 1775, in *DGW*, 3:298, 302, 308.

99. On January 19, 1775, Moderator Peyton Randolph had issued the call for each county to hold elections to select delegates "to represent them in convention, who are desired to meet at the town of Richmond, in the county of Henrico, on Monday the 20th of March next." "Second Virginia Convention: Call for Election of Delegates," 19 January 1775, in *RV*, 2:245.

100. GW to John Connolly, 25 February 1775, in *PGWCol*, 10:273–74.

101. "The Second Virginia Convention," 20–22 March 1775, in *RV*, 2:334–61; 15–22 March 1775, in *DGW*, 3:313–15.

102. "Second Virginia Convention: March 23, 1775," in *RV*, 2:368–69. For historical background, analysis of the speech, and the debate surrounding Henry's actual words, see Kidd, *Patrick Henry: First Among Patriots*, 97–101.

103. "Second Virginia Convention: March 23, 1775," in *RV*, 2:366–67.

104. "Second Virginia Convention: March 24–March 27, 1775," in *RV*, 2:370–86; 28–31 March 1775, in *DGW*, 3:316–17.

105. Chernow, *Alexander Hamilton*, 64; McDonald, *Alexander Hamilton: A Biography*, 14.

106. AH to John Jay, 26 November 1775, in *PAH*, 1:176–77; Brookhiser, *Alexander Hamilton, American*, 25–26.

107. Ketchum, *Divided Loyalties*, 311.

CHAPTER FOUR

1. AH to Edward Stevens, 11 November 1769, in *PAH*, 1:4. "My Ambition is prevalent that I con[d]emn the grov'ling and condition of a Clerk... [I] would willingly risk my life tho' not my Character to exalt my Station...I wish there was a War." This letter is frequently cited by those who claim that Hamilton possessed a dangerous Napoleonic streak, ignoring the fact that the sentiments expressed are commonly heard from young teenaged boys.

2. Middlekauff, *Glorious Cause*, 270–73.

3. On the creation of the Continental army and the selection of Washington as commander in chief, see Ferling, *Almost a Miracle*, 39–48.

4. Ellis, *His Excellency*, 68–69, and Brookhiser, *Founding Father*, 20–22.

5. Eliphalet Dyer to Joseph Trumbull, 17 June 1775, TeachingAmericanHistory.org, http://teachingamericanhistory.org/library/index.asp?document=887.

6. Ferling, *Independence: The Struggle to Set America Free*, 149.

7. "Commission from the Continental Congress," in *PGWRev,* 1:7.

8. "Address to the Continental Congress," in *PGWRev*, 1:1.

9. *PGWRev*, 1:3.

10. Ibid., 1:2.

11. GW to Martha Washington, 18 June 1775, in *PGWRev*, 1:3–4; Middlekauff, *Glorious Cause*, 293–96.

12. GW to Burwell Bassett, 19 June 1775, in *PGWRev*, 1:12–13. On

the belief in a providential God, see Gragg, *By the Hand of Providence*, Kidd, *God of Liberty*, and Williams, *Hurricane of Independence.*

13. Ellis, *His Excellency*, 76.

14. "Address to the New York Provincial Congress," 26 June 1775, in *PGWRev*, 1:40–41.

15. GW to Thomas Gage, 19 August 1775, in *PGWRev*, 1:326–28.

16. GW to John Hancock, 21 July 1775, in *PGWRev*, 1:138.

17. "General Orders," 4 July 1775, in *PGWRev*, 1:55.

18. GW to Hancock, 10 July 1775, in *PGWRev*, 1:88.

19. "General Orders," 18 November 1775, in *PGWRev*, 1:393.

20. "General Orders," 5 August 1775, in *PGWRev*, 1:245.

21. GW to Lund Washington, 20 August 1775, in *PGWRev*, 1:335–36.

22. GW to Joseph Reed, 28 November 1775, in *PGWRev*, 2:449.

23. Quoted in Chernow, *Alexander Hamilton*, 67.

24. Quoted in Chernow, *Alexander Hamilton*, 71.

25. Middlekauff, *Glorious Cause*, 308–11.

26. Chernow, *Alexander Hamilton*, 72–74.

27. GW to John Augustine Washington, 31 May 1776, in *PGWRev*, 4:13.

28. "General Orders," 2 July 1776, in *PGWRev*, 5:180.

29. Quoted in Williams, *America's Beginnings*, 112.

30. Recent books on the Declaration of Independence include Arnn, *The Founders' Key*, Beeman, *Our Lives, Our Fortunes*, Ellis, *Revolutionary Summer*, Ferling, *Independence*, and Maier, *American Scripture.*

31. "General Orders," 9 July 1776, in *PGWRev*, 5:246.

32. "General Orders," 1 August 2776, in *PGWRev*, 5:534.

33. GW to Adam Stephen, 20 July 1776, in *PGWRev*, 5:408.

34. "General Orders," 23 August 1776, in *PGWRev*, 6:109–10.

35. McCullough, *1776*, 191. Other books on the Battle of New York include Ellis, *Revolutionary Summer*, Ferling, *Almost a Miracle*, 120–55, Higginbotham, *War of American Independence*, 148–71, and Schecter, *Battle for New York.*

36. Brookhiser, *Founding Father*, 19–20.

37. GW to Lund Washington, 30 September 1776, in *PGWRev*, 6:441.

38. GW to Lund Washington, 22 September 1776, in *PGWRev*, 6:371–74.

39. McCullough, *1776*, 230.

40. Chernow, *Washington: A Life*, 259–60.

41. McCullough, *1776*, 243.

42. Chernow, *Washington: A Life*, 263.

43. GW to Charles Lee, in *PGWRev*, 7:193.

44. GW to Lee, in *PGWRev*, 7:224.

45. Mitchell, *Alexander Hamilton: Youth to Maturity*, 96.

46. Chernow, *Alexander Hamilton*, 83.

47. Fruchtman, *Thomas Paine*, 91.

48. Ferling, *Almost a Miracle*, 156–86; Fischer, *Washington's Crossing*; Higginbotham, *War of American Independence*, 162–71; Ketchum, *The Winter Soldiers*; McCullough, *1776*.

49. GW to Robert Morris, 25 December 1776, in *PGWRev*, 7:439.

50. McCullough, *1776*, 285–86.

51. GW to Executive Committee of the Continental Congress, 1 January 1777, in *PGWRev*, 7:500.

52. Chernow, *Washington: A Life*, 280.

53. McCullough, *1776*, 289.

54. Chernow, *Alexander Hamilton*, 84.

55. Chadwick, *George Washington's War*, 31.

56. AH to GW, 29 July–1 August 1798, in Abbot and Twohig, *The Papers of George Washington: Retirement Series*, 2:466.

57. Brookhiser, *Alexander Hamilton, American*, 29.

58. Brookhiser, *Founding Father*, 29.

59. Schachner, *Alexander Hamilton*, 62.

60. Flexner, *Young Man Hamilton*, 143, 147; Chernow, *Alexander Hamilton*, 87.

61. Chadwick, *George Washington's War*, 79–89.

62. Flexner, *Young Man Hamilton*, 140–41.

63. Chernow, *Alexander Hamilton*, 92.

64. On the battles of Brandywine Creek and Germantown, see Ferling, *Almost a Miracle*, 242–58; and Higginbotham, *War of American Independence*, 175–88.

65. Chernow, *Alexander Hamilton*, 98–99.

66. Ibid., 99–100.

67. GW to AH, 30 October 1777, in *PAH*, 1:347.

68. Chernow, *Alexander Hamilton*, 101–3.

69. AH to Horatio Gates, 5 November 1777, in *PAH*,1:352.

70. GW to AH, 15 November 1777, in *PAH*,1:365.

71. Quoted in Williams, *America's Beginnings*, 127. See also Bodle, *The Valley Forge Winter*, and Fleming, *Washington's Secret War*.

72. Lockhart, *The Drillmaster of Valley Forge*.

73. *PGWRev*, 11:529–30.

74. *PAH*, 1:428.

75. Gates to GW, 8 December 1777, in *PGWRev*, 12:576–77.

76. GW to Thomas Conway, 5 November 1777, in *PGWRev*, 12:129.

77. GW to Gates, 4 January 1778, in *PGWRev*, 13:139.

78. Brookhiser, *Founding Father*, 32.

79. *PAH*, 1:512.

80. Lefkowitz, *George Washington's Indispensable Men*, 174–82.

81. *PAH*, 1:510.

82. Quoted in Quarles, *The Negro in the American Revolution*, 11–12.

83. Quoted in Egerton, *Death or Liberty*, 74–75.

84. Quoted in Chernow, *Washington: A Life*, 212–13.

85. Quoted in Chernow, *Alexander Hamilton*, 121.

86. Quoted in Wiencek, *An Imperfect God*, 227. Wiencek calls Washington's letter puzzling and untruthful. In *Washington: A Life*, Chernow argues that Washington was self-interested and lacked courage. While Washington did not live up to his principles in the case, he was burdened by many considerations and had to exercise prudential judgment at the time.

87. GW to Benedict Arnold, 3 August 1780, in *WW*, 19:309.

88. GW to Arnold, 2 April 1777, in *PGWRev*, 9:45.

89. Brookhiser, *Alexander Hamilton, American*, 37.

90. AH to Elizabeth Schuyler, 25 September 1780, in *PAH*, 2:441.

91. Ibid., 2:442.

92. Flexner, *Young Man Hamilton*, 308.

93. AH to Greene, 25 September 1780, in *PAH*, 2:440–41.

94. *PAH*, 2:467.

95. Ibid.

96. AH to Philip Schuyler, 18 February 1781, in *PAH*, 2:563–68.

97. Ibid.

98. Ibid.

99. Ibid.

100. AH to Major James McHenry, 18 February 1781, in *PAH*, 2:569.

101. AH to Schuyler, 18 February 1781, in *PAH*, 2:563–68.

102. Ibid.

103. AH to GW, 22 November 1780, in *PAH*, 2:509.

104. Schuyler to AH, 25 February 1781, in *PAH*, 2:575–77.

105. AH to GW, 27 April 1781, in *PAH*, 2:600–601.

106. GW to AH, 27 April 1781, in *PAH*, 2:601–2.

107. McDonald, *Alexander Hamilton: A Biography*, 25.

108. AH to GW, 7 August 1781, in *PAH*, 2:659–60; GW to AH, 9 August 1781, in *PAH*, 2:665.

109. Ferling, *Almost a Miracle*, 523–39; Higginbotham, *War of American Independence*, 376–83; Ketchum, *Victory at Yorktown*; Nelson, *George Washington's Great Gamble*.

110. Quoted in Williams, *America's Beginnings*, 133.

111. AH to Elizabeth Hamilton, 6 September 1781, in *PAH*, 2:675.

112. McDonald, *Alexander Hamilton: A Biography*, 25.

113. Chernow, *Alexander Hamilton*, 163–64.

114. Middlekauff, *Glorious Cause*, 559–71.

CHAPTER FIVE

1. For more on the national outlook of the each man, see Brookhiser, *Alexander Hamilton, American*; and Higginbotham, *Uniting a Nation*.

2. AH to John Laurens, 15 August 1782, in *PAH*, 3:145.

3. GW to Benjamin Harrison, 18 December 1778, in *WW*, 13:464.

4. GW to George Clinton, 16 February 1778, in *WW*, 10:470.

5. GW to Mason, 27 March 1779, in *WW*, 14:300–301.

6. GW to Fielding Lewis, 6 July 1780, in *WW*, 19:132.

7. AH to Clinton, 13 February 1778, in *PAH*, 1:427.

8. AH to James Duane, 3 September 1780, in *PAH*, 2:406.

9. AH to Laurens, 30 June 1780, in *PAH*, 2:347–48.

10. GW to Harrison, 18 December 1778, in *WW*, 13:466.

11. AH to Clinton, 13 February 1778, in *PAH*, 1:426.

12. GW to Harrison, 21 March 1781, in *WW*, 21:342.

13. GW to Greene, 6 February 1783, in *WW*, 26:104.

14. AH to Clinton, 13 February 1778, in *PAH*, 1:426.

15. AH to Duane, 3 September 1780, in *PAH*, 2:402.

16. "Circular to State Governments," 27 August 1780, in *WW*, 19:450.

17. GW to Laurens, 15 January 1781, in *WW*, 21:107.

18. "General Orders," 30 January 1781, in *WW*, 21:158–59.

19. AH to Duane, 3 September 1780, in *PAH*, 2:402.

20. GW to Joseph Jones, 31 May 1780, in *WW*, 18:453.

21. GW to Harrison, 18 December 1778, in *WW*, 13:464.

22. GW to John Banister, 21 April 1778, in *WW*, 11:291.

23. GW to Lewis, 6 July 1780, in *WW*, 19:132.

24. GW to John Parke Custis, 28 February 1781, in *WW*, 21:320–21.

25. AH to Clinton, 13 February 1778, in *PAH*, 1:426.

26. GW to Harrison, 4 March 1783, in *WW*, 26:184–85.

27. AH to Duane, 3 September 1780, in *PAH*, 2:407.

28. GW to Joseph Reed, 28 May 1780, in *WW*, 18:436.

29. AH to Duane, 3 September 1780, in *PAH*, 2:404–5.

30. AH to Laurens, 12 September 1780, in *PAH*, 2:427–28.

31. "Continentalist No. III," 9 August 1781, in *PAH*, 2:661.

32. "Continentalist No. IV," 30 August 1781, in *PAH*, 2:670.

33. Ellis, *His Excellency*, 126–27.

34. McDonald, *Alexander Hamilton: A Biography*, 50–57.

35. AH to GW, 1 March 1782, in *PAH*, 3:4–5.

36. McDonald, *Alexander Hamilton: A Biography*, 43.

37. Lewis Nicola to GW, 22 May 1782, in *WW*, 24:273.

38. GW to Nicola, 22 May 1782, in *WW*, 24:273.

39. Books that deal primarily with the period after the Battle of Yorktown include Ferling, *A Leap in the Dark*, 227–55, Fleming, *The Perils of Peace*, Fowler, *American Crisis*.

40. GW to Jones, 14 December 1782, in *WW*, 25:430.

41. GW to Benjamin Lincoln, 2 October 1782, in *WW*, 25:228.

42. GW to James McHenry, 17 October 1782, in *WW*, 25:269–70.

43. Kohn, *Eagle and Sword*, 18–20.

44. Cerami, *Young Patriots*, 23, 32.

45. Kohn, *Eagle and Sword*, 21. For the role of each Morris in the affair, see Adams, *Gouverneur Morris: An Independent Life*, 123–40; and Rappleye, *Robert Morris: Financier of the American Revolution*, 331–57.

46. Quoted in Williams, *America's Beginnings*, 136.

47. AH to GW, 13 February 1783, in *PAH*, 3:253–55.

48. GW to AH, 4 March 1783, in *PAH*, 3:278.

49. "Newburgh Addresses," in *Journals of the Continental Congress 1774–1789*, ed. Worthington C. Ford et al. (Washington, DC, 1922), 24:295–97.

50. GW to AH, 12 March 1783, in *PAH*, 3:287.

51. "To the Officers of the Army," in *WW*, 26:222–27.

52. AH to GW, 17 March 1783, in *PAH*, 3:290–93.

53. AH to GW, 24 March 1783, in *PAH*, 3:304.

54. AH to GW, 8 April 1783, in *PAH*, 3:317–21.

55. GW to AH, 31 March 1783, 4, 16, and 22 April 1783, in *PAH*, 3:309–10, 315–16, 329–31, 334–36.

56. McDonald, *E Pluribus Unum*, 67–68.

57. Walling, *Republican Empire*, 63–65.

58. Kohn, *Eagle and Sword*, 39.

59. "Circular to the States," 8 June 1783, in *WW*, 26:483–96.

60. AH to GW, 30 September 1783, in *PAH*, 3:461–63.

61. Weintraub, *General Washington's Christmas Farewell*, 83–84.

62. GW to John Augustine Washington, 15 June 1783, in *WW*, 27:11–13.

63. "Farewell Address to the Armies of the United States," 2 November 1783, in *WW*, 27:224–27.

64. Weintraub, *Washington's Farewell*, 55–56.

65. Ibid., 58–59.

66. Ibid., 85–86.

67. "Address to Congress on Resigning His Commission," 23 December 1783, in *WW*, 27:284–86.

68. Wills, *Cincinnatus: George Washington and the Enlightenment*, 13.

CHAPTER SIX

1. AH to Robert R. Livingston, 13 August 1783, in *PAH*, 3:431; Brookhiser, *Alexander Hamilton, American*, 57.

2. AH to Clinton, 1 June 1783, in *PAH*, 3:371.

3. AH to Gouverneur Morris, 21 February 1784, in *PAH*, 3:513; Mitchell, *Alexander Hamilton: Youth to Maturity*, 335.

4. "A Letter from Phocion to the Considerate Citizens of New York on the Politics of the Day," January 1784, in *PAH*, 3:483–96; Freeman, *Alexander Hamilton: Writings*, 127–40. Stourzh calls the Phocion letters the "most forceful defense of a government of laws" and not men and claimed that they "remain to this day among the most notable documents of American constitutionalism." Stourzh, *Alexander Hamilton and the Idea of Republican Government*, 57.

5. AH to Morris, 21 February 1784, in *PAH*, 3:512; Brookhiser, *Alexander Hamilton, American*, 58.

6. Michael Federici argues that Hamilton's defense of Tories was "one of the several instances when he sacrificed popularity for what he perceived as a greater good, a habit of conduct that contributed, as much as any factor, to the perception that he was unrepublican." Federici, *The Political Philosophy of Alexander Hamilton*, 73.

7. Chernow, *Alexander Hamilton*, 198.

8. Walling, *Republican Empire*, 78–82.

9. Chernow, *Alexander Hamilton*, 199. Chernow calls the decision a "smashing triumph" for Hamilton.

10. GW to James Duane, 19 April 1785, in *PGWCon*, 2:485–86; Brookhiser, *Alexander Hamilton, American*, 59.

11. GW to Richard Varick, 26 September 1785, in *PGWCon*, 3:283–84.

12. GW to Jonathan Trumbull Jr., 5 January 1784, in *PGWCon*, 1:12–13.

13. GW to Benjamin Harrison, 18 January 1784, in *PGWCon*, 1:56–57.

14. Mitchell, *Alexander Hamilton: Youth to Maturity*, 357.

15. Wood, "The Greatness of George Washington," in Higginbotham, *George Washington Reconsidered*, 318.

16. Meyerson, *Liberty's Blueprint*, 45–46.

17. GW to Duane, 10 April 1785, in *PGWCon*, 2:485–86.

18. AH to John Jay, 25 July 1783, in *PAH*, 3:416–17.

19. "Unsubmitted Resolution Calling for A Convention to Amend the Articles of Confederation," July 1783, in *PAH*, 3:420–26.

20. Meyerson, *Liberty's Blueprint*, 47–48.

21. "Appointment as Commissioner to the Annapolis Convention," 5 May 1786, in *PAH*, 3:665–66.

22. Meyerson, *Liberty's Blueprint*, 48.

23. Banning, *The Sacred Fire of Liberty*, 69.

24. Miller, *The Business of May Next*, 14–20; Morris, *Witnesses at the Creation*, 164–65; Ketcham, *James Madison: A Biography*, 183–85; Garrett Ward Sheldon, *The Political Philosophy of James Madison* (Baltimore: Johns Hopkins University Press, 2001), 49; Jack N.

Rakove, *James Madison and the Creation of the American Republic* (New York: Harper Collins, 1990), 46–47.

25. Meyerson, *Liberty's Blueprint*, 55.

26. "Annapolis Convention: Address of the Annapolis Convention," 14 September 1786, in *PAH*, 3:686.

27. Williams, *America's Beginnings*, 151.

28. "Annapolis Convention: Address of the Annapolis Convention," 14 September 1786, in *PAH*, 3:686–90; see reprint in Morris, *Witnesses at the Creation*, 167–68.

29. GW to Lafayette, 10 May 1786, in *PGWCon*, 4:42.

30. GW to Jay, 18 May 1786, in *PGWCon*, 4:55.

31. Szatmary, *Shays' Rebellion*, 1–36.

32. Ibid., 47.

33. Richards, *Shays' Rebellion*, 15–19.

34. David Humphreys to GW, 2 and 9 November 1786, in *PGWCon*, 4:299–302, 325; Henry Knox to GW, 23 October 1786, 17 December 1786, in *PGWCon*, 4:351, 418–21; Benjamin Lincoln to GW, 4 December 1786, in *PGWCon*, 4:460–62, are representative samples of letters Washington received regarding Shays's Rebellion.

35. GW to Lincoln, 7 November 1786, in *PGWCon*, 4:339.

36. GW to Humphreys, 26 December 1786, in *PGWCon*, 4:478–80.

37. Ibid.

38. Szatmary, *Shays' Rebellion*; McDonald, *E Pluribus Unum*, 254.

39. Richards, *Shays' Rebellion*, 27–42.

40. Williams, *America's Beginnings*, 155–56.

41. GW to Jabez Bowen, 9 January 1787, in *PGWCon*, 4:504–5.

42. Ellis, *His Excellency*, 159.

43. GW to AH, 11 December 1785, in *PAH*, 3:639.

44. "Report of a Committee of the New York State Society of the Society of the Cincinnati," 6 July 1785, in *PAH*, 3:675–78.

45. Chernow, *Washington: A Life*, 497–500.

46. GW to Humphreys, 26 December 1786, in *PGWCon*, 4:478–80.

47. GW to Henry Knox, 2 April 1787, in *PGWCon*, 5:119.

48. GW to Humphreys, 3 March 1787, in *PGWCon*, 5:72–73.

49. Edmund Randolph to GW, 11 March 1787, in *PGWCon*, 5:83–84.

50. GW to Randolph, 9 April 1787, in *PGWCon*, 5:135.

51. James Madison to GW, 18 March 1787, in *PGWCon*, 5:92; Mitchell, *Alexander Hamilton: Youth to Maturity*, 358–59, 371–72.

52. Knox to GW, 19 March 1787, in *PGWCon*, 5:95–98.

53. Madison to GW, 16 April 1787, in *PGWCon*, 5:144–50.

54. GW to Robert Morris, 5 May 1787, in *PGWCon*, 5:171.

55. Chernow, *Washington: A Life*, 526.

56. GW to George Augustine Washington, in *PGWCon*, 5:189.

57. George Mason to George Mason Jr., 20 May 1787, in *RFC*, 3:23.

58. 18 May 1787, in *DGW*, 5:158.

59. GW to Arthur Lee, 20 May 1787, in *PGWCon*, 5:191; 19–24 May 1787, in *DGW*, 5:159–62.

60. Rufus King to Jeremiah Wadsworth, 24 May 1787, in *RFC*, 3:26.

61. Joseph Ellis calls Washington "simultaneously the most important person at the Constitutional Convention and the least involved in the debate that shaped the document that emerged. His importance was a function of his presence, which lent an air of legitimacy to the proceedings that otherwise might have been criticized as extralegal." Ellis, *His Excellency*, 177. Biographer Ron Chernow asserts, "He embodied the public excluded from the secret proceedings, and his mere presence reassured Americans that the delegates were striving for the public good instead of hatching a secret cabal behind closed doors." Chernow, *Washington: A Life*, 530.

62. Proceedings, 25 May 1787, in *RFC*, 1:3–4.

63. Ibid., 1:2.

64. 25 May 1787, in *DGW*, 5:162.

65. "Anecdote," in *RFC*, 3:85.

66. Chernow, *Alexander Hamilton*, 228.

67. "Amicus," *National Gazette*, 11 September 1792, in *PAH*, 12:355.

Madison also later defended the secrecy rule and averred, "No Constitution would ever have been adopted by the convention if the debates had been public." Even the Anti-Federalist George Mason concurred that the rule of secrecy was "a necessary precaution to prevent misrepresentations or mistakes; there being a material difference between the appearance of a subject in its first crude and undigested shape, and after it shall have been properly matured and arranged."

When James Madison told Thomas Jefferson that "it was thought expedient in order to secure unbiased discussion within doors, and to prevent misconceptions and misconstructions without, to establish some rules of caution which will for no short time restrain even a confidential communication of our proceedings," Jefferson, somewhat naïvely from Paris, complained that the delegates "began their deliberations by so abominable a precedent as that of tying up the tongues of their members. Nothing can justify this example but the innocence of their intentions, and ignorance in the value of public discussions." Madison, Mason, and Jefferson are quoted in Beeman, *Plain, Honest Men*, 83–84; George Mason to George Mason Jr., 1 June 1787, in *RFC*, 3:32–33; Madison to Jefferson, 6 June 1787, in *RFC*, 3:36.

68. "William Pierce: Anecdote," in *RFC*, 3:86. Washington even followed the secrecy rule scrupulously in his own diary: "Attending in Convention and nothing being suffered to transpire no minutes of the proceedings has been, or will be inserted in this diary." 1 June 1787, in *DGW*, 5:164.

Washington was generally as scrupulous about the secrecy of the convention with his correspondents, not sharing details of the debate, though he would give a general sense of the sentiments in favor of achieving the objective of a new government. He wrote his brother: "As the proceedings of the Convention are not intended to be made known till the business is finished I can give you no information on this score except that the sentiments of the different members seem to accord more than I expected they would, as far as we have yet gone. There are now eleven states represented and not much hope of another as Rhode Island refused to send and New Hampshire seems unable by some means or another to come on." GW to George Augustine Washington, 3 June 1787, in *PGWCon*, 5:219.

69. "William Pierce: Character Sketches of Delegates to the Federal Convention," in *RFC*, 3:89.

70. Ibid., 3:94.

71. Madison to Jefferson, 6 June 1787, in *RFC*, 3:35–36. Virginian Edward Carrington also wrote to Jefferson, guessing that Washington's attendance was proof that he thought that a revision to the Articles of Confederation was necessary. "The latitude thus given, together with the generality of the commission from the states, have doubtless operated to bring General Washington forward, contrary to his more early determination—his conduct in both instances indicate a deep impression upon his mind, of the necessity of some material change." Carrington to Jefferson, 9 June 1787, in *RFC*, 3:37–38.

72. Madison to Edmund Pendleton, 27 May 1787, in *RFC*, 3:27; Beeman, *Plain, Honest Men*, 58.

73. Miller, *Business of Next May*, 67–69; Stewart, *The Summer of 1787*, 52–57.

74. Proceedings, 29 May 1787, in *RFC*, 1:23.

75. Ibid., 1:27.

76. Ibid., 1:35.

77. Proceedings, 1 June 1787, in *RFC*, 1:65.

78. Ibid., 1:66.

79. Proceedings, 2 June 1787, in *RFC*, 1:84–85.

80. Ibid., 1:85.

81. Proceedings, 4 June 1787, in *RFC*, 1:98.

82. 4 June 1787, in *DGW*, 5:165.

83. "Extracts from the Diary of Jacob Hiltzheimer," 4 June 1787, in *PGWCon*, 5:219.

84. 5–9 June 1787, in *DGW*, 5:165–66.

85. Berkin, *A Brilliant Solution*, 100–103.

86. 18 June 1787, in *DGW*, 5:170.

87. Proceedings, 18 June 1787, in *RFC*, 1:282–83.

88. Ibid., 1:283–88.

89. Ibid., 1:288–90.

90. Ibid., 1:289–90.

91. Ibid., 1:290–91.

92. Hamilton's son related that Gouverneur Morris was supposed to have judged the speech "the most able and impressive he had ever heard." William Samuel Johnson of Connecticut said it had "been praised by everybody…supported by none." Proceedings, 18 June 1787, in *RFC*, 1:293, 323.

93. There is a large historical debate over Hamilton's speech. Ron Chernow calls it a "brilliant, courageous, and in retrospect completely daft" speech. He correctly notes that the speech "acquired diabolical status in the rumor mills of the early republic, providing gloating opponents with damning proof of his supposed political apostasy." Chernow admits that if "no consensus was reached" on the other plans, "his speech would be dusted off and its merits belatedly better appreciated" from a strategic point of view and that "in fact, Madison's Virginia Plan may have profited from Hamilton's speech because it now seemed moderate by comparison. (Some scholars have argued that this was the true intent of Hamilton's speech.)" Yet he calls the speech "hare-brained" and says that the speech was "to prove one of three flagrant errors in his career…each time, he was spectacularly wrongheaded and indiscreet, yet convinced he was right." Chernow, *Alexander Hamilton*, 231–35.

David Stewart is similarly divided over the speech, and after examining the debate, he stated that Hamilton "made poor use" of the opportunity and that the "theory does not meet the facts." Stewart, *Summer of 1787*, 92–96. Jack Rakove says that the "heart of this speech was an analysis of the 'great and essential principles necessary for the support of government," and that the "speech had at least one of its intended effects." Rakove, *Original Meanings*, 63–64. Richard Beeman argues that Hamilton was "indulging in an extraordinary exegesis of his political philosophy" and that "at best, Hamilton's speech amounted to a diversion from the main issues." He concludes that Hamilton's plan "would have little influence on the subsequent proceedings of the Convention." Beeman, *Plain, Honest Men*, 164–70.

Several scholars have argued that Hamilton's speech was a strategic move. Carol Berkin agrees that Hamilton may very well have had a strategic purpose in mind: "Perhaps he thought his plan would put the more reasonable and measured Virginia Plan in a better light. He was certainly capable of such a tactic." Berkin, *A Brilliant Solution*, 118–19. See also Knott, *Alexander Hamilton and the Persistence of Myth*, 4; Walling, *Republican Empire*, 98–101; McDonald, *Alexander Hamilton: A Biography*, 105.

94. Proceedings, 19 June 1787, in *RFC*, 1:322.

95. Ibid., 1:323.

96. Ibid., 1:324–25.

97. Proceedings, 21 June 1787, in *RFC*, 1:358–59.

98. Proceedings, 22 June 1787, in *RFC*, 1:373.

99. Proceedings, 21 June 1787, in *RFC*, 1:362.

100. Wood, *The Americanization of Benjamin Franklin*, 219.

101. Proceedings, 28 June 1787, in *RFC*, 1:451.

102. Ibid., 1:450–52.

103. Ibid., 1:452.

104. AH to GW, 3 July 1787, in *PAH*, 4:223–25.

105. July 4–10, in *DGW*, 5:175.

106. GW to AH, 10 July 1787, in *PGWCon*, 5:257.

107. Berkin, *A Brilliant Solution*, 118.

108. Chernow, *Alexander Hamilton*, 236–37.

109. 21 July 1787, *New York Daily Advertiser*, in *PAH*, 4:229–32.

110. Berkin, *A Brilliant Solution*, 112.

111. Collier and Collier, *Decision in Philadelphia*, 289–300.

112. 27 July 1787, in *DGW*, 5:178.

113. 6 August 1787, in *DGW*, 5:180.

114. Chernow, *Washington: A Life*, 537.

115. Proceedings, 13 August 1787, in *RFC*, 2:268.

116. Chernow, *Alexander Hamilton*, 239.

117. GW to Henry Knox, 19 August 1787, in *PGWCon*, 5:297.

118. 19 August 1787, in *DGW*, 5:181.

119. Proceedings, 29 August 1787, in *RFC*, 2:445.

120. Proceedings, 31 August 1787, in *RFC*, 2:478.

121. Proceedings, 6 September 1787, in *RFC*, 2:524–25.

122. Proceedings, 8 September 1787, in *RFC*, 2:553.

123. Ibid., 2:553–54.

124. Proceedings, 17 September 1787, in *RFC*, 2:644.

125. GW to George Augustine Washington, 9 September 1787, in *PGWCon*, 5:321.

126. "Report of Committee of Style," in *RFC*, 2:590–603.

127. Proceedings, 13 September 1787, in *RFC*, 2:604.

128. Proceedings, 17 September 1787, in *RFC*, 2:641–42.

129. Ibid., 2:645–46.

130. Washington noted in his diary that Hamilton's vote did not count: "Met in convention, when the Constitution received the unanimous consent of 11 states, and Col. Hamilton's from New York (the only delegate from thence in Convention) and was subscribed to by every member present except Governor Randolph and Col. Mason from Virginia and Mr. Gerry from Massachusetts." 17 September 1787, in *DGW*, 5:185.

131. Proceedings, 17 September 1787, in *RFC*, 2:643.

132. "Anecdote," in *RFC*, 3:85.

133. 17 September 1787, in *DGW*, 5:185.

134. GW to Lafayette, 18 September 1787, in *PGWCon*, 5:334.

135. 18–22 September 1787, in *DGW*, 5:186–87.

136. "Conjectures about the New Constitution," 17–30 September 1787, in *PAH*, 4:275–76.

CHAPTER SEVEN

1. Rakove, *Original Meanings*, 108.

2. Mason to GW, 7 October 1787, in *PGWCon*, 5:355–57.

3. *New-York Journal*, 6 September 1787, in *PAH*, 4:249.

4. Chernow, *Alexander Hamilton*, 245.

5. *New-York Journal*, 20 September 1787, in *PAH*, 4:281.

6. GW to AH, 18 October 1787, in *PGWCon*, 5:380–81.

7. AH to GW, 30 October 1787, in *PAH*, 4:306.

8. Maier, *Ratification*, 76.

9. Madison to GW, 18 October 1787, in *PGWCon*, 5:383.

10. Hamilton, "Federalist No.1," in Rossiter, *Federalist Papers*, 27.

11. AH to GW, 30 October 1787, in *PAH*, 4:306.

12. GW to David Humphreys, 10 October 1787, in *PGWCon*, 5:365; Williams, *America's Beginnings*, 166–68.

13. Madison to GW, 18 November 1787, in *PGWCon*, 5:444.

14. GW to David Stuart, 30 November 1787, in *PGWCon*, 5:466–67.

15. GW to AH, 10 November 1787, in *PGWCon*, 5:426–27.

16. The above quotes are from GW to AH, 10 November 1787, in *PGWCon*, 5:426–27.

17. GW to AH, 18 October 1787, in *PGWCon*, 5:380–81.

18. Maier, *Ratification*, 89.

19. GW to AH, 10 November 1787, in *PGWCon*, 5:426–27.

20. GW to Madison, 7 December 1787, in *PGWCon*, 5:480.

21. AH to GW, 11 October 1787, in *PAH*, 4:281.

22. AH to GW, 30 October 1787, in *PAH*, 4:306.

23. AH to Benjamin Rush, 21 November 1787, in *PAH*, 4:332–33.

24. Maier, *Ratification*, 100–23.

25. GW to Henry Knox, 30 March 1788, in *PGWCon*, 6:182–83.

26. Burstein and Isenberg, *Madison and Jefferson*, 172.

27. Hamilton complied with Madison's request to send copies to Virginia: "I executed your commands respecting the first volume of the *Federalist*. I sent 40 of the common copies and twelve of the finer ones addressed to the care of Governor Randolph. The printer announces the second volume in a day or two, when an equal number of the two kinds shall also be forwarded. He informs that the judicial department, trial by jury, bill of rights, etc., is discussed in some additional papers which have not yet appeared in the Gazettes." AH to Madison, 19 May 1788, in *PAH*, 4:649–50. See also AH to Madison, 11 May 1788, in *PAH*, 4:647–48.

28. Washington, who would support the Bill of Rights in his first inaugural address, also questioned the need for a Bill of Rights privately during the ratification debate: "There was not a member of the convention, I believe, who had the least objection to what is contended for by the advocates for a bill of rights and trial by jury. The first, where the people evidently retained everything which they did not in express terms give up, was considered nugatory as you will find to have been more fully explained by Mr. Wilson and others. And as to the second, it was only the difficulty of establishing a mode which should not interfere with the fixed modes of any of the states that induced the Convention to leave it as a matter of future adjustment." GW to Lafayette, 28 April 1788, in *PGWCon*, 6:243–45.

29. AH to James Madison, 3 April 1788, in *PAH*, 4:644–45.

30. GW to AH, 28 August 1788, in *PGWCon*, 6:480–81. Elsewhere, he offered similar praise: "Upon the whole I doubt whether the opposition to the Constitution will not ultimately be productive of more good than evil. It has called forth, in its defense, abilities (which would not perhaps have been otherwise exerted) that [have] thrown new lights upon the science

of government, they have given the rights of man a full and fair discussion, and have explained them in so clear and forcible a manner as cannot fail to make a lasting impression upon those who read the best publications on the subject, and particularly the pieces under the signature of Publius." GW to John Armstrong, 25 April 1788, in *PGWCon*, 6:225–26.

31. AH to Madison, 3 April 1788, in *PAH*, 4:644–45.

32. For the above quotes, see AH to Madison, 19 May 1788, and AH to Gouverneur Morris, 19 May 1788, in *PAH*, 4:649–52.

33. AH to Madison, 19 May 1788, in *PAH*, 4:649–50.

34. Hamilton, "Federalist No. 85," in Rossiter, *Federalist Papers*, 527.

35. GW to Lafayette, 28 May 1788, in *PGWCon*, 6:298–99.

36. Banning, *The Sacred Fire of Liberty*, 234–64.

37. Maier, *Ratification*, 361, 370.

38. "New York Ratifying Convention: First Speech of June 21," 21 June 1788, in *PAH*, 5:43.

39. "New York Ratifying Convention: Second Speech, July 17," 17 July 1788, in *PAH*, 5:176.

40. Madison to GW, 24 August 1788, in *PGWCon*, 6:468.

41. Madison to GW, 11 August 1788, in *PGWCon*, 6:438.

42. GW to James Madison, 17 August 1788, in *PGWCon*, 6:454.

43. Maier, *Ratification*, 380–98.

44. Chernow, *Alexander Hamilton*, 269.

45. AH to GW, 13 August 1788, in *PAH*, 5:201–2.

46. Maier, *Ratification*, 318.

47. Brookhiser, *Founding Father*, 71.

CHAPTER EIGHT

1. Hamilton, "Federalist No. 1," in Rossiter, *Federalist Papers*, 27.

2. Quoted in Mark J. Rozell, "Washington and the Origins of Presidential Power," in Gregg and Spalding, *Patriot Sage*, 124.

3. McDonald, "Presidential Character," 136.

4. GW to AH, 28 August 1788, in *PGWPres*, 1:481.

5. AH to GW, September 1788, in *PGWPres*, 1:23–24.

6. Washington's election was not official until the president of the Senate read the ballots in front of members of the House and Senate. This was supposed to occur on March 4, 1789, but the House did not reach a quorum until April 1 and the Senate until April 6. Washington delayed his arrival until this formality was completed. See Milkis and Nelson, *American Presidency*, 71.

7. Elkins and McKitrick, *Age of Federalism*, 46–48.

8. AH to GW, 5 May 1789, in *PGWPres*, 2:211–14.

9. Morrison, *Political Philosophy of George Washington*, 87.

10. Wood, *Empire of Liberty*, 64.

11. GW to John Armstrong, 25 April 1788, in *PGWCon*, 6:224–27.

12. Hamilton, "Federalist No. 74," in Rossiter, *Federalist Papers*, 446.

13. Hamilton, "Federalist No. 70," in Rossiter, *Federalist Papers*, 423.

14. Quoted in Bernstein, *The Founding Fathers Reconsidered*, 110.

15. Ibid., 286–87.

16. Chernow, *Washington: A Life*, 506–7.

17. Milkis and Nelson, *American Presidency*, 75–77; Elkins and McKitrick, *Age of Federalism*, 53–54.

18. AH to GW, 8 April 1783, in *PAH*, 3:317–21.

19. Wood, *Empire of Liberty*, 85; "Thanksgiving Proclamation," 3 October 1789, in *PGWPres*, 4:131–32.

20. Tillman, "The Puzzle of Hamilton's *Federalist* No. 77," 149–85.

21. Wood, *Empire of Liberty*, 86–88.

22. Ibid.

23. Ibid.

24. Spitzer, "The President's Veto Power," in Cronin, *Inventing the American Presidency*, 172–74.

25. *PGWPres*, 4:200–201; "A Chilly Reception: President George Washington's Trip to Boston, October, 1789," *The Dial*, Old South Meeting House Newsletter, Spring/Summer 2004.

26. Elkins and McKitrick, *Age of Federalism*, 74–75.

27. Chernow, *Alexander Hamilton*, 330.

28. Ibid., 354.

29. McCulloch v. Maryland, 17 U.S. 316 (1819).

30. Chernow, *Alexander Hamilton*, 354.

31. Ibid., 352.

32. Hamilton, "Federalist No. 79," in Rossiter, *Federalist Papers*, 471.

33. Elkins and McKitrick, *Age of Federalism*, 258, 270.

34. Ellis, *His Excellency*, 206.

35. Chernow, *Alexander Hamilton*, 402.

36. Scigliano, "The War Powers Resolution and the War Powers," 128.

37. Grant and Grant, "The Madisonian Presidency," in Bessette and Tulis, *The Presidency in the Constitutional Order*, 48–50.

38. Wood, *Empire of Liberty*, 177–81; Elkins and McKitrick, *Age of Federalism*, 357.

39. Wood, *Empire of Liberty*, 177.

40. "Memorandum on the French Revolution," 1794, in Freeman, *Alexander Hamilton: Writings*, 835.

41. Chernow, *Washington: A Life*, 658–61.

42. Wood, *Empire of Liberty*, 180.

43. Chernow, *Alexander Hamilton*, 408.

44. Ibid.

45. Some scholars contend that Washington was actually more of a reader than many of his contemporaries assumed and that historians continue to underestimate his interest in reading and its impact on his life. In 1771, he wrote, "I conceive a knowledge of books is the basis upon which other knowledge is to be built." See Rothstein, "Washington as Reader, Not Soldier."

46. AH to GW, 30 July–3 August 1792, in *PAH*, 12:137–39.

47. Chernow, *Washington: A Life*, 684.

CHAPTER NINE

1. Staloff, *Hamilton, Adams, Jefferson*, 121–22.

2. Ibid., 122.

3. Washington, Sixth Annual Message, 19 November 1794, in *PGWPres*, 17:181–88.

4. McDonald, *Alexander Hamilton: A Biography*, 307.

5. Wood, *Empire of Liberty*, 197.

6. Elkins and McKitrick, *Age of Federalism*, 415–16.

7. Herring, *From Colony to Superpower*, 76–81.

8. Ibid., 79.

9. GW to AH, 3 July 1795, in Allen, *George Washington: A Collection*, 609.

10. Elkins and McKitrick, *Age of Federalism*, 420.

11. McDonald, *Alexander Hamilton: A Biography*, 315–16; GW to AH, 29 July 1795, in Allen, *George Washington: A Collection*, 611.

12. Chernow, *Alexander Hamilton*, 489–90.

13. Elkins and McKitrick, *Age of Federalism*, 442.

14. Wood, *Empire of Liberty*, 235.

15. For an account of Governor Jefferson's hasty departure from Monticello, see Kranish, *Flight from Monticello*.

16. Ellis, *His Excellency*, 231–32.

17. McDonald, *Alexander Hamilton: A Biography*, 318–19; GW to AH, 31 August 1795, in *PAH*, 19:204–6; Chernow, *Alexander Hamilton*, 503–4.

18. GW to AH, 29 October 1795, in *PAH*, accessed February 27, 2015, http://founders.archives.gov/documents/Hamilton/01-19-02-0067.

19. McDonald, *Alexander Hamilton: A Biography*, 319.

20. AH to GW, 7 March 1796, in *PAH*, 20:64–69.

21. Elkins and McKitrick, *Age of Federalism*, 444–49; Herring, *From Colony to Superpower*, 78–80.

22. Introductory Note to Washington, and AH to GW, 7 March 1796, in *PAH*, 20:64–68.

23. GW to AH, 31 March 1796, in *PAH*, 20:103–5.

24. AH to GW, 2 April 1796, in *PAH*, 20:106–7.

25. AH to GW, 5 May 1796, in *PAH*, 20:161.

26. AH to GW, 16 June 1796, in *PAH*, 20:225–26.

27. GW to AH, 26 June 1796, in *PAH*, 20:237–40.

28. AH to GW, 5 July 1796, in *PAH*, 20:246–47.

29. Ammon, *James Monroe*, 155.

30. Herring, *From Colony to Superpower*, 82.

31. Furstenberg, *In the Name of the Father*, 6.

32. Chernow, *Alexander Hamilton*, 505.

33. Ellis, *His Excellency*, 230–31.

34. Elkins and McKitrick, *Age of Federalism*, 497.

35. Chernow, *Alexander Hamilton*, 505; AH to GW, 10 May 1796, in *PAH*, 20:169–74.

36. The full quote from Hamilton, in reference to Jefferson and Madison, was "in respect to our foreign politics, the views of these gentlemen are, in my judgment, equally unsound, and dangerous. They have a womanish attachment to France, and a womanish resentment against Great Britain." AH to Edward Carrington, 26 May 1792, in *PAH*, 11:439.

37. Ellis, *His Excellency*, 235–36; Chernow, *Alexander Hamilton*, 506–7; Washington's Farewell Address, 19 September 1796, in *WW*, 35:214–38.

38. Elkins and McKitrick, *Age of Federalism*, 497.

39. Chernow, *Alexander Hamilton*, 507; Ellis, *His Excellency*, 245.

40. John Langhorne [Peter Carr] to GW, 25 September 1797, in Abbot and Twohig, *The Papers of George Washington: Retirement Series*, 1:373–74; GW to John Nicholas, 8 March 1798, 2:127–29.

41. Ellis, *His Excellency*, 246–247.

42. Comments on Monroe's *A View of the Conduct of the Executive of the United States*, March 1798, http://founders.archives.gov/documents/Washington/06-02-02-0146.

43. Chernow, *Alexander Hamilton*, 364–70, 409–18.

44. Ibid., 529–37.

45. Ibid., 542. The Reynolds affair damaged Hamilton's reputation, deservedly so, and opened him up to the widely circulated allegation that he was a serial adulterer. As with many of the myths surrounding Hamilton, this accusation was initially disseminated by his opponents including James Monroe and John Adams. Historians who should know better continue to spread unfounded rumors regarding Hamilton's alleged insatiable appetite for women, including the myth that Martha Washington named her amorous tomcat "Hamilton" in honor of his wild ways. John Ferling, Michael Beschloss, Arnold Rogow, Thomas J. Fleming, Cokie Roberts, among many others, have all repeated this claim. To assume that Martha Washington, of all people, would do such a thing reveals a complete lack of understanding of her character. The tomcat tale is categorically false, but lives on, along with the canard that Hamilton considered the people to be a "great beast." For an account of the origins of the mythical tomcat, see "Letting the Cat Out of the Bag," *Alexander Hamilton Patriot* (blog), August 12, 2008, accessed February 7, 2015, http://ahpatriot.blogspot.com/2008/08/letting-cat-out-of-bag.html.

46. GW to AH, 21 August 1791, in *PAH*, accessed February 27, 2015, http://founders.archives.gov/documents/Hamilton/01-21-02-0137.

47. Ibid., 522; Elkins and McKitrick, *Age of Federalism*, 292; McCullough, *John Adams*, 538; John Adams to Benjamin Rush, 25 January 1806, 11 November 1807, www.facstaff.bucknell.edu/mdrexler/Eng305/JOHN%20ADAMS%20to%20BENJAMIN%20RUSH.htm.

48. Burns and Dunn, *George Washington*, 12.

49. Thomas Jefferson to James Madison, 14 February 1783, Madison Papers, http://founders.archives.gov/documents/Madison/01-06-02-0071.

50. Chernow, *Alexander Hamilton*, 550–51; Herring, *From Colony to Superpower*, 86; McCullough, *John Adams*, 501.

51. Ellis, *His Excellency*, 249.

52. Wood, *Empire of Liberty*, 262.

53. Knott, *Persistence of Myth*, 219; Chernow, *Alexander Hamilton*, 573–74.

54. AH to GW, 19 May 1798, in Abbot and Twohig, *The Papers of George Washington: Retirement Series*, 2:279–81.

55. Walling, *Republican Empire*, 231; Knott, *Persistence of Myth*, 219.

56. GW to AH, 27 May 1798, in Abbot and Twohig, *The Papers of George Washington: Retirement Series*, 2:297–99.

57. GW to AH, October 27, 1799, http://founders.archives.gov /documents/Hamilton/01-23-02-0516.

58. McDonald, *Alexander Hamilton: A Biography*, 347–48.

59. Chernow, *Alexander Hamilton*, 535; Walling, *Republican Empire*, 228;   http://lehrmaninstitute.org/history/foundingeconomists.asp; McCullough, *John Adams*, 518.

60. McCullough, *John Adams*, 540.

61. Kohn, *Eagle and Sword*, 286.

62. Knott, *Persistence of Myth*, 3, 166; McDonald, *Alexander Hamilton: A Biography*, 443n21.

63. Trees, *Founding Fathers and the Politics of Character*, 70–71.

64. Ibid.

65. Harper, *American Machiavelli*, 257.

66. Steele, *Thomas Jefferson and American Nationhood*, 235.

67. Chernow, *Alexander Hamilton*, 658.

68. GW to AH, 12 December 1799, in *PAH*, 24:99; Ellis, *His Excellency*, 268–70.

69. Tobias Lear to AH, 15 December 1799, in *PAH*, 24:100–101; AH to Charles Cotesworth Pinckney, 22 December 1799, in *PAH*, 24:116.

70. Chernow, *Alexander Hamilton*, 601.

71. AH to Lear, 2 January 1800, in *PAH*, 24:155.

72. Chernow, *Alexander Hamilton*, 601.

73. Mary Stockwell, "Thomas Jefferson," www.mountvernon.org /educational-resources/encyclopedia/thomas-jefferson#note2.

74. AH to William Macpherson, 22 December 1799, in *PAH*, 24:115.

75. AH to Pinckney, 22 December 1799, in *PAH*, 24:116.

76. Royster, *Light-Horse Harry Lee*, 202.

CHAPTER TEN

1. Hamilton, *Reminiscences of James A. Hamilton*, 22–23.

2. Thomas Jefferson, First Inaugural Address, 4 March 1801, http:// avalon.law.yale.edu/19th_century/jefinau1.asp.

3. Elkins and McKitrick, *Age of Federalism*, 753–54.

4. Thomas Jefferson to Levi Lincoln, 25 October 1802, in *The Writings of Thomas Jefferson*, ed. Andrew A. Lipscomb and Albert E. Bergh (Washington, DC: The Thomas Jefferson Memorial Association, 1904), 10:338–40.

5. Hamilton, "Federalist No. 68," in Rossiter, *Federalist Papers*, 412.

6. For a description of the repeated use of the "monarchist" epithet, see Donald Stewart, *The Opposition Press of the Federalist Period* (Albany: State University Press of New York, 1969), 606.

7. Knott, *Persistence of Myth*, 217.

8. AH to James Bayard, 16–21 April 1802, http://founders.archives .gov/documents/Hamilton/01-25-02-0321.

9. Anastaplo, *Abraham Lincoln: A Constitutional Biography*, 231.

10. Even sympathetic biographers such as Ron Chernow express serious reservations about Hamilton's proposed Christian Constitutional Society. Chernow claims that the proposal was part of Hamilton's drift into "more retrograde modes of thought" and an "execrable idea that would have grossly breached the separation of church and state." Chernow, *Alexander Hamilton*, 659.

11. Troup quoted in John Church Hamilton, *The Life of Alexander Hamilton* (New York: Halsted & Voorhies, 1834), 1:10.

12. Chernow, *Alexander Hamilton*, 651–56.

13. AH to Benjamin Rush, 29 March 1802, in *PAH*, 25:583–84.

14. Levy, *Jefferson and Civil Liberties*, 58–59.

15. Chernow, *Alexander Hamilton*, 667–70.

16. "The Duel Between Aaron Burr and Alexander Hamilton: Introductory Note," in *PAH*, 26:238–39.

17. Freeman, *Affairs of Honor*, xviii.

18. Ibid., 172–73.

19. "William P. Van Ness's Regulations for the Duel," 9 July 1804, and "Nathaniel Pendleton's Second Statement of the Regulations for the Duel," 10 July 1804, in *PAH*, 26:306–9.

20. AH to Elizabeth Hamilton, 4 and 10 July 1804, in *PAH*, 26:293, 307–8.

21. AH to Theodore Sedgwick, 10 July 1804, in *PAH*, 26:309–10.

22. Knott, *Persistence of Myth*, 9, 13.

23. Ibid., 18–19.

24. "Trinity Church," http://allthingshamilton.com/index.php/2012 -04-21-00-31-09/final-years/trinity-church; Knott, *Persistence of Myth*, 1–2, 234n4.

25. Elizabeth Hamilton to James Madison, 20 May 1809, http:// founders.archives.gov/documents/Madison/03-01-02-0222.

26. Chernow, *Alexander Hamilton*, 724–27.

27. Knott, *Persistence of Myth*, 21–23; Chernow, *Alexander Hamilton*, 727–31; Desmond, *Alexander Hamilton's Wife*, 259, 262.

28. "Washington Monument," National Park Service, www.nps.gov /wamo/historyculture/index.htm.

29. Ron Chernow, *Alexander Hamilton*, 727–28.

POSTSCRIPT

1. "I believe also, with Condorcet, as mentioned in your letter, that his [man's] mind is perfectible to a degree of which we cannot as yet form any conception." Thomas Jefferson to William Green Munford, 18 June 1799, in *The Papers of Thomas Jefferson*, ed. Barbara B. Oberg (Princeton, NJ: Princeton University Press, 2004), 31:126–30.

2. See, for instance, Jefferson's reference to the people at the time of the French Revolution as a "blind" "machine" and also his proposal for an educational system in Virginia that would allow the best students to emerge while the "residue" would be "dismissed." Under this system, geniuses would be "raked from the rubbish annually." Knott, *Persistence of Myth*, 74–75.

3. Ibid., 230–31.

4. Chernow, *Alexander Hamilton*, 88.

5. McClellan, *Joseph Story and the American Constitution*, 79n67.

6. Staloff, *Hamilton, Adams, Jefferson*, 90.

7. Wood, *Empire of Liberty*, 85–86.

8. Edling, epigraph to *A Revolution in Favor of Government*.

9. Chernow, *Alexander Hamilton*, 390.

10. James Madison, "Federalist No. 10," in Rossiter, *Federalist Papers*, 73.

11. Chernow, *Alexander Hamilton*, 402.

12. Staloff, *Hamilton, Adams, Jefferson*, 353.

13. Chernow, *Washington: A Life*, 213.

14. GW to John Mercer, 9 September 1786, http://memory.loc.gov /cgi-bin/query/r?ammem/mgw:@field(DOCID+@lit(gw290013)).

15. Quoted in James P. Pfiffner, "George Washington's Character and Slavery," *White House Studies* 1, no. 4, 456.

16. Chernow, *Washington: A Life*, 802.

17. Knott, *Persistence of Myth*, 134, 163, 229.

18. Ibid., 212, 286n46.

19. Wood, *Empire of Liberty*, 86.

20. *PGWPres*, 6:72n1.

21. Chernow, *Alexander Hamilton*, 287.

22. A recent example of this, which reiterates many of the hackneyed, populist canards regarding Hamilton and the Federalists (but not Washington), can be found in Ferling, *Jefferson and Hamilton*.

23. Wood, *Empire of Liberty*, 86.

24. *PGWPres*, 5:240n1.

25. GW to John Adams, 25 September 1798, in *WW*, 36:460–61.

26. GW to AH, 2 February 1795, in *PAH*, 18:248.

27. Chernow, *Alexander Hamilton*, 500.

BIBLIOGRAPHY

PRIMARY SOURCE COLLECTIONS

Abbot, W. W., and Dorothy Twohig, eds. *The Papers of George Washington: Colonial Series*. 10 vols. Charlottesville: University Press of Virginia, 1983–95.

———. *The Papers of George Washington: Confederation Series*. 6 vols. Charlottesville: University Press of Virginia, 1992–97.

———. *The Papers of George Washington: Retirement Series*. 4 vols. Charlottesville: University Press of Virginia, 1997–99.

Abbot, W. W., Dorothy Twohig, and Philander D. Chase, eds. *The Papers of George Washington: Presidential Series*. Charlottesville: University Press of Virginia, 1987–.

Abbot, W. W., Dorothy Twohig, Philander D. Chase, and Edward G. Lengel, eds. *The Papers of George Washington: Revolutionary War Series*. Charlottesville: University Press of Virginia, 1985–.

Adams, John. *Diary and Autobiography of John Adams*. Edited by L. H. Butterfield, Leonard C. Faber, and Wendell D. Garrett. Cambridge, MA: Harvard University Press, 1961.

Allen, William B., ed. *George Washington: A Collection*. Indianapolis: Liberty Fund, 1988.

Boyd, Julian P., Charles T. Cullen, John Catanzariti, and Barbara B. Oberg, eds. *The Papers of Thomas Jefferson*. Princeton, NJ: Princeton University Press, 1950–.

Commager, Henry Steele, and Richard B. Morris, eds. *The Spirit of 'Seventy-Six: The Story of the American Revolution as Told by Participants*. New York: Da Capo, 1995.

Farrand, Max, ed. *The Records of the Federal Convention of 1787*. 3 vols. New Haven, CT: Yale University Press, 1911.

Fitzpatrick, John C., ed. *The Writings of Washington from the Original Manuscript Sources, 1745–1799*. 39 vols. Washington, DC: Government Printing Office, 1931–34. Reprint, New York: Greenwood Press, 1970.

Franklin, Benjamin. *Benjamin Franklin's Autobiography: An Authoritative Text, Backgrounds, Criticism*. Edited by J. A. Leo Lemay and P. M. Zall. New York: Norton, 1986.

Freeman, Joanne B., ed. *Alexander Hamilton: Writings*. New York: Library of America, 2001.

Hutchinson, William T., Robert A. Rutland, and John C. Stagg, eds. *The Papers of James Madison*. Chicago and Charlottesville: University of Chicago Press and University of Virginia Press, 1962–.

Jackson, Donald, and Dorothy Twohig, eds. *The Diaries of George Washington*. 6 vols. Charlottesville: University Press of Virginia, 1976–79.

McDonald, Forrest, ed. *Empire and Nation: Letters from a Pennsylvania Farmer, John Dickinson, and Letters from the Federal Farmer, Richard Henry Lee*. Indianapolis: Liberty Fund, 1999.

Morison, Samuel Eliot, ed. *Sources and Documents Illustrating the American Revolution, 1764–1788 and the Formation of the Federal Constitution*. 2nd ed. Oxford: Oxford University Press, 1965.

Rhodehamel, John, ed. *The American Revolution: Writings from the War of Independence*. New York: Library of America, 2001.

———. *George Washington: Writings.* New York: Library of America, 1997.

Rossiter, Clinton, ed. *The Federalist Papers.* By Alexander Hamilton, James Madison, and John Jay. New York: Signet Classics, 2003.

Syrett, Harold C., and Jacob E. Cooke, eds. *The Papers of Alexander Hamilton.* 26 vols. New York: Columbia University Press, 1961–79.

Tarter, Brent, and Robert L. Scribner, eds. *Revolutionary Virginia: The Road to Independence.* 7 vols. Charlottesville: University Press of Virginia, 1973–83.

Twohig, Dorothy, ed. *George Washington's Diaries: An Abridgement.* Charlottesville: University Press of Virginia, 1999.

BOOKS

Achenbach, Joel. *George Washington's Potomac and the Race to the West.* New York: Simon and Schuster, 2004.

Adair, Douglass. "Fame and the Founding Fathers." In *Fame and the Founding Fathers: Essays by Douglass Adair,* edited by Trevor Colbourn, 3–36. Indianapolis: Liberty Fund, 1998.

Adams, William Howard. *Gouverneur Morris: An Independent Life.* New Haven, CT: Yale University Press, 2003.

Alden, John R. *George Washington: A Biography.* Baton Rouge: Louisiana State University Press, 1984.

Alexander, John K. *Samuel Adams: America's Revolutionary Politician.* Lanham, MD: Rowman & Littlefield, 2002.

Allen, William B. *George Washington: America's First Progressive.* New York: Peter Lang, 2008.

Ammon, Harry. *The Genet Mission.* New York: Norton, 1973.

———. *James Monroe: The Quest for National Identity.* Charlottesville: University Press of Virginia, 1990.

Anastaplo, George. *Abraham Lincoln: A Constitutional Biography.* Lanham, MD: Rowman & Littlefield, 1999.

Anderson, Fred. *Crucible of War: The Seven Years' War and the Fate of Empire in British North America, 1754–1766*. New York: Vintage, 2000.

Archer, Richard. *As If an Enemy's Country: The British Occupation of Boston and the Origins of Revolution*. Oxford: Oxford University Press, 2010.

Arnn, Larry P. *The Founders' Key: The Divine and Natural Connection Between the Declaration and the Constitution and What We Risk by Losing It*. Nashville, TN: Thomas Nelson, 2012.

Axelrod, Alan. *Blooding at Great Meadows: Young George Washington and the Battle that Shaped the Man*. Philadelphia: Running Press, 2007.

Babits, Lawrence E., and Joshua B. Howard. *Long, Obstinate, and Bloody: The Battle of Guilford Courthouse*. Chapel Hill: University of North Carolina Press, 2009.

Bailyn, Bernard. *Faces of Revolution: Personalities and Themes in the Struggle for American Independence*. New York: Vintage, 1990.

———. *The Ideological Origins of the American Revolution*. Cambridge, MA: Harvard University Press, 1967.

———. *The Ordeal of Thomas Hutchinson*. Cambridge, MA: Harvard University Press, 1974.

Banning, Lance. *The Sacred Fire of Liberty: James Madison and the Founding of the Federal Republic*. Ithaca, NY: Cornell University Press, 1995.

Becker, Carl. *The Declaration of Independence: A Study in the History of Political Ideas*. New York: Vintage, 1922.

Beeman, Richard. *Our Lives, Our Fortunes, and Our Sacred Honor: The Forging of American Independence, 1775–1776*. New York: Basic Books, 2013.

———. *Patrick Henry: A Biography*. New York: McGraw-Hill, 1974.

———. *Plain, Honest Men: The Making of the American Constitution*. New York: Random House, 2009.

Beirne, Logan. *Blood of Tyrants: George Washington and the Forging of the Presidency.* New York: Encounter Books, 2013.

Bemis, Samuel Flagg. *The Diplomacy of the American Revolution.* Bloomington: Indiana University Press, 1935.

Berkin, Carol. *A Brilliant Solution: Inventing the American Constitution.* New York: Harcourt, 2002.

Bernstein, R. B. *The Founding Fathers Reconsidered.* New York: Oxford University Press, 2009.

Billias, George Athan. *George Washington's Generals and Opponents: Their Exploits and Leadership.* New York: Da Capo, 1994.

Bobb, David J. *Humility: An Unlikely Biography of America's Greatest Virtue.* Nashville, TN: Thomas Nelson, 2013.

Bodle, Wayne. *The Valley Forge Winter: Civilians and Soldiers in War.* University Park: Pennsylvania State University Press, 2002.

Borneman, Walter R. *American Spring: Lexington, Concord, and the Road to Revolution.* New York: Little, Brown, 2014.

———. *The French and Indian War: Deciding the Fate of North America.* New York: Harper, 2006.

Bowen, Catherine Drinker. *Miracle at Philadelphia: The Story of the Constitutional Convention, May to September 1787.* Boston: Little, Brown, 1966.

Brady, Patricia. *Martha Washington: An American Life.* New York: Penguin, 2005.

Brands, H. W. *The First American: The Life and Times of Benjamin Franklin.* New York: Anchor, 2000.

———. *The Heartbreak of Aaron Burr.* New York: Anchor, 2012.

Breen, T. H. *Tobacco Culture: The Mentality of the Great Tidewater Planters on the Eve of Revolution.* Princeton, NJ: Princeton University Press, 1985.

Broadwater, Jeff. *George Mason: Forgotten Founder.* Chapel Hill: University of North Carolina Press, 2006.

Brookhiser, Richard. *Alexander Hamilton, American.* New York: Simon and Schuster, 1999.

————. *Founding Father: Rediscovering George Washington*. New York: Free Press, 1996.

————. *Gentleman Revolutionary: Gouverneur Morris—The Rake Who Wrote the Constitution*. New York: Free Press, 2003.

Brumwell, Stephen. *George Washington: Gentleman Warrior*. London: Quercus, 2012.

————. *Redcoats: The British Soldier and War in the Americas, 1755–1763*. Cambridge, MA: Cambridge University Press, 2002.

Burns, James MacGregor, and Susan Dunn. *George Washington*. New York: Times Books, 2004.

Burstein, Andrew, and Nancy Isenberg. *Madison and Jefferson*. New York: Random House, 2010.

Carbone, Gerald M. *Nathanael Greene: A Biography of the American Revolution*. New York: Palgrave Macmillan, 2008.

————. *Washington: Lessons in Leadership*. New York: Palgrave Macmillian, 2010.

Carp, Benjamin. *Defiance of the Patriots: The Boston Tea Party and the Making of America*. New Haven, CT: Yale University Press, 2010.

Carp, E. Wayne. *To Starve the Army at Pleasure: Continental Army Administration and American Political Character, 1775–1783*. Chapel Hill: University of North Carolina Press, 1984.

Cerami, Charles. *Young Patriots: The Remarkable Story of Two Men, Their Impossible Plan, and the Revolution that Created the Constitution*. Naperville, IL: Sourcebooks, 2005.

Chadwick, Bruce. *The General & Mrs. Washington: The Untold Story of a Marriage and Revolution*. Naperville, IL: Sourcebooks, 2007.

————. *George Washington's War: The Forging of a Revolutionary Leader and the American Presidency*. Naperville, IL: Sourcebooks, 2005.

————. *Triumvirate: The Story of the Unlikely Alliance that Saved the Constitution and United the Nation*. Naperville, IL: Sourcebooks, 2009.

Chase, Philander D. "A Stake in the West: George Washington as Backcountry Surveyor and Landholder." In *George Washington and the Virginia Backcountry*, edited by Warren R. Hofstra. Madison, WI: Madison House, 1998.

Chernow, Ron. *Alexander Hamilton*. New York: Penguin, 2004.

———. *Washington: A Life*. New York: Penguin, 2010.

Clary, David A. *George Washington's First War: His Early Military Adventures*. New York: Simon and Schuster, 2011.

Chitwood, Oliver Perry. *Richard Henry Lee: Statesman of the Revolution*. Morgantown: University of West Virginia Foundation, 1967.

Colbourn, Trevor, ed. *Fame and the Founding Fathers: Essays by Douglass Adair*. Indianapolis: Liberty Fund, 1998.

Collier, Christopher, and James Lincoln Collier. *Decision in Philadelphia: The Constitutional Convention of 1787*. New York: Ballantine, 1986.

Cooke, Jacob E. *Alexander Hamilton*. New York: Scribner's, 1982.

Cornell, Saul. *The Other Founders: Anti-Federalism and the Dissenting Tradition in America, 1788–1828*. Chapel Hill: University of North Carolina Press, 1999.

Countryman, Edward. *A People in Revolution: The American Revolution and Political Society in New York, 1760–1790*. New York: Norton, 1989.

Crocker, Thomas E. *Braddock's March: How the Man Sent to Seize a Continent Changed American History*. Yardley, PA: Westholme, 2009.

Cunliffe, Marcus. *George Washington: Man and Monument*. Boston: Little, Brown, 1958.

Davis, Burke. *A Williamsburg Galaxy*. Williamsburg, VA: Colonial Williamsburg Foundation, 1968.

Desmond, Alice Curtis. *Alexander Hamilton's Wife: A Romance of the Hudson*. New York: Dodd, Meade & Company, 1952.

Dreisbach, Daniel L., Mark D. Hall, and Jeffry H. Morrison. *The

Founders on God and Government. Lanham, MD: Rowman & Littlefield, 2004.

Dull, Jonathan R. *A Diplomatic History of the American Revolution*. New Haven, CT: Yale University Press, 1985.

Dunn, Richard S. *Sugar and Slaves: The Rise of the Planter Class in the English West Indies, 1624–1713*. Chapel Hill: University of North Carolina Press, 1972.

Dunn, Susan. *Jefferson's Second Revolution: The Election Crisis of 1800 and the Triumph of Republicanism*. Boston: Houghton Mifflin, 2004.

Edling, Max M. *A Revolution in Favor of Government: Origins of the U.S. Constitution and the Making of the American State*. New York: Oxford University Press, 2003.

Egerton, Douglas R. *Death or Liberty: African Americans and Revolutionary America*. Oxford: Oxford University Press, 2009.

Elkins, Stanley, and Eric McKitrick. *The Age of Federalism: The Early American Republic, 1788–1800*. New York: Oxford University Press, 1993.

Ellis, Joseph J. *American Creation: Triumphs and Tragedies at the Founding of the Republic*. New York: Knopf, 2007.

———. *American Sphinx: The Character of Thomas Jefferson*. New York: Knopf, 1998.

———. *Founding Brothers: The Revolutionary Generation*. New York: Knopf, 2000.

———. *His Excellency: George Washington*. New York: Knopf, 2004.

———. *Revolutionary Summer: The Birth of American Independence*. New York: Knopf, 2013.

Farrand, Max. *The Framing of the Constitution of the United States*. New Haven, CT: Yale University Press, 1913.

Federici, Michael P. *The Political Philosophy of Alexander Hamilton*. Baltimore: Johns Hopkins University Press, 2012.

Ferling, John. *Adams v. Jefferson: The Tumultuous Election of 1800*. Oxford: Oxford University Press, 2004.

———. *Almost a Miracle: The American Victory in the War of Independence.* New York: Oxford University Press, 2007.

———. *The Ascent of George Washington: The Hidden Political Genius of an American Icon.* New York: Bloomsbury, 2009.

———. *The First of Men: A Life of George Washington.* Knoxville: University of Tennessee Press, 1988.

———. *Independence: The Struggle to Set America Free.* New York: Oxford University Press, 2011.

———. *Jefferson and Hamilton: The Rivalry That Forged a Nation.* New York: Bloomsbury Press, 2013.

———. *John Adams: A Life.* New York: Henry Holt, 1992.

———. *A Leap in the Dark: The Struggle to Create the American Republic.* Oxford: Oxford University Press, 2003.

———. *Setting the World Ablaze: Washington, Adams, Jefferson, and the American Revolution.* New York: Oxford University Press, 2000.

Fischer, David Hackett. *Paul Revere's Ride.* New York: Oxford University Press, 1994.

———. *Washington's Crossing.* New York: Oxford University Press, 2004.

Fleming, Thomas. *The Intimate Lives of the Founding Fathers.* New York: Harper, 2009.

———. *The Perils of Peace: America's Struggle for Survival after Yorktown.* New York: Harper, 2007.

———. *Washington's Secret War: The Hidden History of Valley Forge.* New York: Harper Collins, 2005.

Flexner, James Thomas. *George Washington.* 4 vols. Boston: Little Brown, 1965–72.

———. *The Young Hamilton: A Biography.* New York: Fordham University Press, 1997.

Foner, Eric. *Tom Paine and Revolutionary America.* London: Oxford University Press, 1976.

Fowler, William M. Jr. *American Crisis: George Washington and the*

Dangerous Two Years after Yorktown, 1781–1783. New York: Walker, 2011.

———. *Empires at War: The French and Indian War and the Struggle for North America, 1754–1763*. New York: Walker, 2005.

Freeman, Douglas Southall. *George Washington: A Biography*. 7 vols. New York: Charles Scribner's Sons, 1948–57.

Freeman, Joanne B. *Affairs of Honor: National Politics in the New Republic*. New Haven, CT: Yale University Press, 2001.

Fruchtman, Jack. *Thomas Paine: Apostle of Freedom*. New York: Four Walls Eight Windows, 1994.

Furstenberg, Francois. *In the Name of the Father: Washington's Legacy, Slavery, and the Making of a Nation*. New York: Penguin, 2006.

Gilbert, Felix. *To the Farewell Address: Ideas of Early American Foreign Policy*. Princeton, NJ: Princeton University Press, 1961.

Golway, Terry. *Washington's General: Nathaniel Greene and the Triumph of the American Revolution*. New York: Henry Holt, 2006.

Gragg, Rod. *By the Hand of Providence: How Faith Shaped the American Revolution*. New York: Simon and Schuster, 2011.

Grant, James. *John Adams: Party of One*. New York: Farrar, Straus, and Giroux, 2005.

Grant, Ruth Weisbourd, and Stephen Grant. "The Madisonian Presidency." In *The Presidency in the Constitutional Order*, edited by Joseph M. Bessette and Jeffrey Tulis. Baton Rouge: Louisiana State University Press, 1981.

Greene, Jack P. *Landon Carter: An Inquiry into the Personal Values and Social Imperatives of the Eighteenth-Century Virginia Gentry*. Charlottesville: University Press of Virginia, 1965.

Gregg, Gary L., and Matthew Spalding, eds. *Patriot Sage: George Washington and the American Political Tradition*. Wilmington, DE: ISI Books, 1999.

Gross, Robert A. *The Minutemen and Their World*. New York: Hill and Wang, 1976.

Hamilton, James A. *Reminiscences of James A. Hamilton, or, Men and Events, at Home and Abroad, During Three Quarters of a Century.* New York: Charles Scribner & Co., 1869.

Harper, John Lamberton. *American Machiavelli: Alexander Hamilton and the Origins of U.S. Foreign Policy.* Cambridge: Cambridge University Press, 2004.

Henriques, Peter R. *Realistic Visionary: A Portrait of George Washington.* Charlottesville: University Press of Virginia, 2006.

Herring, George C. *From Colony to Superpower; U.S. Foreign Relations Since 1776.* New York: Oxford University Press, 2008.

Hibbert, Christopher. *Redcoats and Rebels: The American Revolution through British Eyes.* New York: Norton, 1990.

Higginbotham, Don. *George Washington and the American Military Tradition.* Athens: University of Georgia Press, 1985.

———, ed. *George Washington Reconsidered.* Charlottesville: University Press of Virginia, 2001.

———. *George Washington: Uniting a Nation.* Lanham, MD: Rowman & Littlefield, 2002.

———. *The War of American Independence: Military Attitudes, Policies, and Practice, 1763–1789.* Boston: Northeastern University Press, 1971.

Hofstra, Warren R., ed. *George Washington and the Virginia Backcountry.* Madison, WI: Madison House, 1998.

Hogeland, William. *Declaration: The Nine Tumultuous Weeks When America Became Independent, May 1–July 4, 1776.* New York: Simon and Schuster, 2010.

———. *The Whiskey Rebellion: George Washington, Alexander Hamilton, and the Frontier Rebels Who Challenged America's Newfound Sovereignty.* New York: Scribner, 2006.

Isaac, Rhys. *Landon Carter's Uneasy Kingdom: Revolution and Rebellion on a Virginia Plantation.* Oxford: Oxford University Press, 2004.

Isaacson, Walter. *Benjamin Franklin: An American Life.* New York: Simon and Schuster, 2003.

Isenberg, Nancy. *Fallen Founder: The Life of Aaron Burr.* New York: Viking, 2007.

Johnson, Paul. *George Washington: The Founding Father.* New York: Harper Collins, 2005.

Kaufman, Burton I., ed. *Washington's Farewell Address: The View from the 20th Century.* Chicago: Quadrangle Books, 1969.

Ketcham, Ralph. *Framed for Posterity: The Enduring Philosophy of the Constitution.* Lawrence: University Press of Kansas, 1993.

————. *James Madison: A Biography.* Charlottesville: University Press of Virginia, 1971.

————. *Presidents Above Party: The First American Presidency, 1789–1829.* Chapel Hill: University of North Carolina Press, 1984.

Ketchum, Richard M. *Decisive Day: The Battle for Bunker Hill.* New York: Henry Holt, 1962.

————. *Divided Loyalties: How the American Revolution Came to New York.* New York: Henry Holt, 2002.

————. *Saratoga: Turning Point of America's Revolutionary War.* New York: Henry Holt, 1997.

————. *Victory at Yorktown: The Campaign That Won the Revolution.* New York: Henry Holt, 2004.

————. *The Winter Soldiers: The Battles for Trenton and Princeton.* New York: Henry Holt, 1973.

Kidd, Thomas S. *God of Liberty: A Religious History of the American Revolution.* New York: Basic, 2010.

————. *Patrick Henry: First Among Patriots.* New York: Basic Books, 2011.

Knollenberg, Bernard. *George Washington: The Virginia Period, 1732–1775.* Durham, NC: Duke University Press, 1964.

Knott, Stephen F. *Alexander Hamilton and the Persistence of Myth.* Lawrence: University Press of Kansas, 2002.

Kohn, Richard H. *Eagle and Sword: The Beginnings of the Military Establishment in America.* New York: Free Press, 1975.

Kranish, Michael. *Flight from Monticello: Thomas Jefferson at War*. New York: Oxford University Press, 2010.

Labaree, Benjamin Woods. *The Boston Tea Party*. Boston: Northeastern University Press, 1979.

Labunski, Richard. *James Madison and the Struggle for the Bill of Rights*. Oxford: Oxford University Press, 2006.

Larson, Edward J. *A Magnificent Catastrophe: The Tumultuous Election of 1800, America's First Presidential Campaign*. New York: Free Press, 2007.

———. *The Return of George Washington, 1783–1789*. New York: William Morrow, 2014.

Lefkowitz, Arthur S. *George Washington's Indispensable Men: The 32 Aides-de-Camp Who Helped Win American Independence*. Mechanicsburg, PA: Stackpole Books, 2003.

Leibiger, Stuart. *Founding Friendship: George Washington, James Madison, and the Creation of the American Republic*. Charlottesville: University Press of Virginia, 1999.

Lengel, Edward G. *General George Washington: A Military Life*. New York: Random House, 2005.

———. *Inventing George Washington: America's Founder, in Myth & Memory*. New York: Harper, 2011.

Levy, Leonard W. *Jefferson and Civil Liberties: The Darker Side*. Chicago: Ivan R. Dee, 1989.

Lewis, Thomas A. *For King and Country: George Washington, The Early Years*. New York: Wiley, 1993.

Liell, Scott. *46 Pages: Thomas Paine, Common Sense, and the Turning Point to Independence*. Philadelphia: Running Press, 2003.

Lillback, Peter A. *George Washington's Sacred Fire*. Bryn Mawr, PA: Providence Forum Press, 2006.

Lockhart, Paul. *The Drillmaster of Valley Forge: The Baron de Steuben and the Making of the American Army*. New York: Harper, 2008.

———. *The Whites of Their Eyes: Bunker Hill, the First American Army, and the Emergence of George Washington.* New York: Harper Collins, 2011.

Longmore, Paul. *The Invention of George Washington.* Charlottesville: University Press of Virginia, 1999.

Maier, Pauline. *American Scripture: Making the Declaration of Independence.* New York: Vintage, 1997.

———. *From Resistance to Revolution: Colonial Radicals and the Development of American Opposition to Britain, 1765–1772.* New York: Norton, 1972.

———. *Ratification: The People Debate the Constitution, 1787–1788.* New York: Simon and Schuster, 2010.

Main, Jackson Turner. *The Anti-Federalists: Critics of the Constitution, 1781–1788.* Chapel Hill: University of North Carolina Press, 1961.

McBurney, Christian M. *The Rhode Island Campaign: The First French and American Operation in the Revolutionary War.* Yardley, PA: Westholme, 2011.

McCardell, Lee. *Ill-Starred General: Braddock of the Coldstream Guards.* Pittsburgh: University of Pittsburgh Press, 1958.

McClellan, James. *Joseph Story and the American Constitution: A Study in Political and Legal Thought.* Norman: University of Oklahoma Press, 1971.

McCraw, Thomas K. *The Founders and Finance: How Hamilton, Gallatin, and Other Immigrants Forged a New Economy.* Cambridge, MA: Harvard University Press, 2012.

McCullough, David. *1776.* New York: Simon and Schuster, 2005.

———. *John Adams.* New York: Simon and Schuster, 2001.

McDonald, Forrest. *Alexander Hamilton: A Biography.* New York: Norton, 1979.

———. *E Pluribus Unum: The Formation of the American Republic, 1776–1790.* New York: Liberty Fund, 1979.

———. *Novus Ordo Seclorum: The Intellectual Origins of the Constitution.* Lawrence: University Press of Kansas, 1985.

————. *The Presidency of George Washington.* Lawrence: University Press of Kansas, 1974.

————. "Presidential Character: The Example of George Washington." *Perspectives on Political Science* 26, no. 3 (Summer 1997): 134–39.

McDonald, Robert M. S., ed. *Sons of the Father: George Washington and His Proteges.* Charlottesville: University Press of Virginia, 2013.

McGaughy, J. Kent. *Richard Henry Lee of Virginia: A Portrait of an American Revolutionary.* Lanham, MD: Rowman & Littlefield, 2004.

Meacham, Jon. *Thomas Jefferson: The Art of Power.* New York: Random House, 2012.

Meade, Robert Douthat. *Patrick Henry: Patriot in the Making.* Philadelphia: J. B. Lippincott, 1957.

Meyerson, Michael I. *Liberty's Blueprint: How Madison and Hamilton Wrote the Federalist Papers, Defined the Constitution, and Made Democracy Safe for the World.* New York: Basic Books, 2008.

Middlekauff, Robert. *The Glorious Cause: The American Revolution, 1763–1789.* Oxford: Oxford University Press, 1982.

————. *Washington's Revolution: The Making of America's First Leader.* New York: Knopf, 2015.

Milkis, Sidney M., and Michael Nelson. *The American Presidency: Origins and Development, 1776–2011.* Washington, DC: CQ Press, 2012.

Miller, Joel J. *The Revolutionary Paul Revere.* Nashville, TN: Thomas Nelson, 2010.

Miller, John C. *Alexander Hamilton: Portrait in Paradox.* New York: Harper Collins, 1959.

————. *The Federalist Era, 1789–1801.* New York: Harper, 1960.

Miller, William Lee. *The Business of May Next: James Madison and the Founding.* Charlottesville: University Press of Virginia, 1992.

Mintz, Max M. *The Generals of Saratoga: John Burgoyne and Horatio Gates.* New Haven, CT: Yale University Press, 1990.

Mitchell, Broadus. *Alexander Hamilton: The National Adventure, 1788–1804*. New York: Macmillan, 1962.

———. *Alexander Hamilton: Youth to Maturity, 1755–1788*. New York: Macmillan, 1957.

Morgan, Edmund S. *The Birth of the Republic, 1763–1789*. Chicago: University of Chicago Press, 1956.

———. *The Meaning of Independence: John Adams, George Washington, and Thomas Jefferson*. New York: Norton, 1976.

Morgan, Edmund S., and Helen M. Morgan. *The Stamp Act Crisis: Prologue to Revolution*. 3rd ed. Chapel Hill: University of North Carolina Press, 1995.

Morris, Richard B. *The Peacemakers: The Great Powers and American Independence*. New York: Harper and Row, 1965.

———. *Witnesses at the Creation: Hamilton, Madison, Jay, and the Constitution*. New York: Holt, Rinehart, and Winston, 1985.

Morrison, Jeffry H. *John Witherspoon and the Founding of the American Republic*. South Bend, IN: University of Notre Dame Press, 2005.

———. *The Political Philosophy of George Washington*. Baltimore: Johns Hopkins University Press, 2009.

Munoz, Vincent Phillip. *God and the Founders: Madison, Washington, and Jefferson*. Cambridge: Cambridge University Press, 2009.

Murchison, William. *The Cost of Liberty: The Life of John Dickinson*. Wilmington, DE: ISI Books, 2013.

Nelson, James L. *George Washington's Great Gamble and the Sea Battle that Won the American Revolution*. New York: McGraw-Hill, 2010.

———. *With Fire and Sword: The Battle of Bunker Hill and the Beginning of the American Revolution*. New York: St. Martin's, 2011.

Novak, Michael, and Jana Novak. *Washington's God: Religion, Liberty, and the Father of Our Country*. New York: Basic Books, 2006.

O'Brien, Conor Cruise. *First in Peace: How George Washington Set the Course for America*. New York: Da Capo, 2009.

———. *The Long Affair: Thomas Jefferson and the French Revolution, 1785–1800.* Chicago: University of Chicago Press, 1996.

O'Shaughnessy, Andrew Jackson. *An Empire Divided: The American Revolution and the British Caribbean.* Philadelphia: University of Pennsylvania Press, 2000.

———. *The Men Who Lost America: British Leadership, the American Revolution, and the Fate of the Empire.* New Haven, CT: Yale University Press, 2013.

Palmer, Dave R. *George Washington and Benedict Arnold: A Tale of Two Patriots.* Washington, DC: Regnery, 2006.

———. *George Washington's Military Genius.* Washington, DC: Regnery, 2012.

Parker, Matthew. *The Sugar Barons: Family, Corruption, Empire, and War in the West Indies.* New York: Walker, 2011.

Pasley, Jeffrey L. *The First Presidential Contest: 1796 and the Founding of American Democracy.* Lawrence: University Press of Kansas, 2013.

Paul, Joel Richard. *Unlikely Allies: How a Merchant, a Playwright, and a Spy Saved the American Revolution.* New York: Riverhead Books, 2009.

Peckham, Howard H. *The Colonial Wars, 1689–1762.* Chicago: University of Chicago Press, 1964.

Peterson, Merrill D. *Thomas Jefferson and the New Nation: A Biography.* London: Oxford University Press, 1970.

Phelps, Glenn A. *George Washington and American Constitutionalism.* Lawrence: University Press of Kansas, 1993.

Phillips, Kevin. *1775: A Good Year for Revolution.* New York: Viking, 2012.

Puls, Mark. *Henry Knox: Visionary General of the American Revolution.* New York: Palgrave Macmillan, 2008.

Quarles, Benjamin. *The Negro in the American Revolution.* New York: Norton, 1961.

Ragsdale, Bruce A. *A Planters' Republic: The Search for Economic Independence in Revolutionary Virginia.* Madison, WI: Madison House, 1996.

Rakove, Jack. *The Beginnings of American Politics: An Interpretive History of the Continental Congress.* New York: Knopf, 1979.

———. *Original Meanings: Politics and Ideas in the Making of the Constitution.* New York: Vintage, 1996.

———. *Revolutionaries: A New History of the Invention of America.* Boston: Houghton Mifflin Harcourt, 2010.

Randall, Willard Sterne. *George Washington: A Life.* New York: Owl Books, 1997.

Rappleye, Charles. *Robert Morris: Financier of the American Revolution.* New York: Simon and Schuster, 2010.

Reardon, John J. *Edmund Randolph: A Biography.* New York: Macmillan, 1974.

Richards, Leonard L. *Shays' Rebellion: The American Revolution's Final Battle.* Philadelphia: University of Pennsylvania Press, 2002.

Robertson, David Brian. *The Original Compromise: What the Constitution's Framers Were Really Thinking.* Oxford: Oxford University Press, 2013.

Rogow, Arnold A. *A Fatal Friendship: Alexander Hamilton and Aaron Burr.* New York: Hill and Wang, 1998.

Rossiter, Clinton. *Alexander Hamilton and the Constitution.* New York: Harcourt, Brace and World, 1964.

Rothstein, Edward. "Washington as Reader, Not Soldier." *New York Times,* September 27, 2013.

Royster, Charles. *A Revolutionary People at War: The Continental Army and American Character, 1775–1783.* Chapel Hill: University of North Carolina Press, 1979.

———. *Light-Horse Harry Lee and the Legacy of the American Revolution.* Baton Rouge: Louisiana State University Press, 1981.

Rutland, Robert. *The Birth of the Bill of Rights, 1776–1791*. Rev. ed. Boston: Northeastern University Press, 1983.

————. *George Mason: Reluctant Statesman*. Charlottesville: University Press of Virginia, 1961.

Schachner, Nathan. *Alexander Hamilton*. New York: A. S. Barnes, 1947.

————. "Alexander Hamilton Viewed by His Friends: The Narratives of Robert Troup and Hercules Mulligan." *William and Mary Quarterly* 4, no. 2 (April 1947): 203–9.

Schecter, Barnet. *The Battle for New York: The City at the Heart of the American Revolution*. New York: Walker, 2002.

Scigliano, Robert. "The War Powers Resolution and the War Powers." In *The Presidency in the Constitutional Order*, edited by Joseph M. Bessette and Jeffrey Tulis. Baton Rouge: Lousiana State University Press, 1981.

Sharp, James Roger. *American Politics in the Early Republic: The New Nation in Crisis*. New Haven, CT: Yale University Press, 1993.

————. *The Deadlocked Election of 1800: Jefferson, Burr, and the Union in the Balance*. Lawrence: University Press of Kansas, 2010.

Shelby, John E. *The Revolution in Virginia*. Williamsburg, VA: Colonial Williamsburg Foundation, 1988.

Slaughter, Thomas P. *Independence: The Tangled Roots of the American Revolution*. New York: Hill and Wang, 2014.

————. *The Whiskey Rebellion: Frontier Epilogue to the American Revolution*. Oxford: Oxford University Press, 1986.

Smith, Richard Norton. *Patriarch: George Washington and the New American Nation*. New York: Houghton Mifflin, 1993.

Spalding, Matthew, and Patrick J. Garrity. *A Sacred Union of Citizens: George Washington's Farewell Address and the American Character*. Lanham, MD: Rowman & Littlefield, 1996.

Spitzer, Robert J. "The President's Veto Power." In *Inventing the American Presidency*, edited by Thomas E. Cronin, 154–79. Lawrence: University Press of Kansas, 1989.

Stahr, Walter. *John Jay*. New York: Hambledon and London, 2005.

Staloff, Darren. *Hamilton, Adams, Jefferson: The Politics of Enlightenment and the American Founding*. New York: Hill and Wang, 2005.

Steele, Brian. *Thomas Jefferson and American Nationhood*. New York: Columbia University Press, 2012.

Stewart, David O. *American Emperor: Aaron Burr's Challenge to Jefferson's America*. New York: Simon and Schuster, 2011.

————. *Madison's Gift: Five Partnerships that Built America*. New York: Simon and Schuster, 2015.

————. *The Summer of 1787: The Men Who Invented the Constitution*. New York: Simon and Schuster, 2007.

Stinchcombe, William C. *The American Revolution and the French Alliance*. Syracuse: Syracuse University Press, 1969.

Stoll, Ira. *Samuel Adams: A Life*. New York: Free Press, 2008.

Storing, Herbert. *What the Anti-Federalists Were For: The Political Thought of the Opponents of the Constitution*. Chicago: University of Chicago Press, 1981.

Stourzh, Gerald. *Alexander Hamilton and the Idea of Republican Government*. Stanford, CA: Stanford University Press, 1970.

Szatmary, David P. *Shays' Rebellion: The Making of an Agrarian Insurrection*. Amherst: University of Massachusetts Press, 1980.

Thompson, C. Bradley. *John Adams and the Spirit of Liberty*. Lawrence: University Press of Kansas, 1998.

Thompson, Mary V. *"In the Hands of a Good Providence": Religion in the Life of George Washington*. Charlottesville: University Press of Virginia, 2008.

Tillman, Seth Barrett. "The Puzzle of Hamilton's *Federalist* No. 77." *Harvard Journal of Law and Public Policy* 33, no. 1 (Winter 2010): 149–85.

Trees, Andrew S. *The Founding Fathers and the Politics of Character*. Princeton, NJ: Princeton University Press, 2004.

Triber, Jayne E. *A True Republican: The Life of Paul Revere.* Amherst: University of Massachusetts Press, 1998.

Tucker, Philip Thomas. *George Washington's Surprise Attack: A New Look at the Battle that Decided the Fate of America.* New York: Skyhorse Publishing, 2014.

Unger, Harlow Giles. *American Tempest: How the Boston Tea Party Sparked a Revolution.* New York: Da Capo, 2011.

———. *Lion of Liberty: Patrick Henry and the Call to a New Nation.* New York: Da Capo, 2010.

———. *"Mr. President": George Washington and the Making of the Nation's Highest Office.* New York: Da Capo, 2013.

Van Doren, Carl. *The Great Rehearsal: The Story of the Making and Ratifying of the Constitution of the United States.* New York: Time, 1965.

Van Steeg, Clarence L. *Robert Morris: Revolutionary Financier.* Philadelphia: University of Pennsylvania Press, 1954.

Walling, Karl-Friedrich. *Republican Empire: Alexander Hamilton on War on Free Government.* Lawrence: University Press of Kansas, 1999.

Walmsley, Andrew Stephen. *Thomas Hutchinson and the Origins of the American Revolution.* New York: New York University Press, 1999.

Weintraub, Stanley. *General Washington's Christmas Farewell: A Mount Vernon Homecoming, 1783.* New York: Free Press, 2003.

Weisberger, Bernard A. *America Afire: Jefferson, Adams, and the Revolutionary Election of 1800.* New York: William Morrow, 2000.

Wiencek, Henry. *An Imperfect God: George Washington, His Slaves, and the Creation of America.* New York: Farrar, Straus, and Giroux, 2003.

Williams, Tony. *America's Beginnings: The Dramatic Events that Shaped a Nation's Character.* Lanham, MD: Rowman & Littlefield, 2010.

———. *Hurricane of Independence: The Deadly Storm at the Deciding Moment of the American Revolution.* Naperville, IL: Sourcebooks, 2008.

Wills, Garry. *Cincinnatus: George Washington and the Enlightenment; Images of Power in Early America.* New York: Doubleday, 1984.

———. *Explaining America: The Federalist.* Garden City, NY: Doubleday, 1981.

———. *Inventing America: Jefferson's Declaration of Independence.* Garden City, NY: Doubleday, 1978.

Wood, Gordon. *The American Revolution: A History.* New York: Modern Library, 2002.

———. *The Americanization of Benjamin Franklin.* New York: Penguin, 2004.

———. *The Creation of the American Republic, 1776–1787.* New York: Norton, 1969.

———. *Empire of Liberty: A History of the Early Republic, 1789–1815.* Oxford: Oxford University Press, 2009.

———. *The Radicalism of the American Revolution.* New York: Vintage, 1991.

———. *Revolutionary Characters: What Made the Founders Different.* New York: Penguin, 2006.

Young, Alfred F. *The Shoemaker and the Tea Party.* Boston: Beacon Press, 1999.

Zobel, Hiller B. *The Boston Massacre.* New York: Norton, 1970.

INDEX

ABOUT THE AUTHORS

Stephen F. Knott is a professor of national security affairs at the United States Naval War College in Newport, Rhode Island. He earned a BA in political science from Assumption College and a PhD in political science from Boston College. He is the author of *Alexander Hamilton and the Persistence of Myth* and *Secret and Sanctioned: Covert Operations and the American Presidency*. He and his wife live in Canton, Massachusetts.

PHOTO BY YOUN JUNG HO

Tony Williams is the professional development director at the Bill of Rights Institute and program director of the Washington, Jefferson & Madison Institute in Charlottesville, Virginia. He earned a BA in history from Syracuse University and a MA in U.S. history from Ohio State University. He taught history for fifteen years in Ohio and Virginia. He is the author of five books on early America and lives in Williamsburg, Virginia, with his wife and children.

PHOTO BY MATTHEW ESPENSHADE, COURTESY OF BILL OF RIGHTS INSTITUTE